LEARN

TO DRIVE

LEARN TO DRIVE

in 10 Easy Stages!

5TH EDITION

JOHN WELLS AND
MARGARET STACEY

KoganPage

LONDON PHILADELPHIA NEW DELHI

Publisher's note

Every possible effort has been made to ensure that the information contained in this book is accurate at the time of going to press, and the publisher and authors cannot accept responsibility for any errors or omissions, however caused. No responsibility for loss or damage occasioned to any person acting, or refraining from action, as a result of the material in this publication can be accepted by the editor, the publisher or either of the authors.

First published in Great Britain in 1987
Revised edition 1990
Second edition published in 1993
Revised edition 1998
Third edition published in 1999
Fourth edition 2009
Fifth edition 2013

Kogan Page Limited
120 Pentonville Road
London N1 9JN
United Kingdom
www.koganpage.com

© Margaret Stacey and Andrew Rice, 1987, 1990, 1993, 1998, 1999
© John Wells and Margaret Stacey 2009, 2013

Illustrated by John Wells

The *Official Highway Code* by the Department for Transport is published by the Stationery Office. Further information can also be accessed at www.highwaycode.gov.uk.

British Library Cataloguing in Publication Data

A CIP record for this book is available from the British Library.

ISBN   978 0 7494 6599 5
E-ISBN   978 0 7494 6763 0

Typeset by Graphicraft Limited, Hong Kong
Printed and bound in India by Replika Press Pvt Ltd

Contents

PART 3 The Highway Code rules

Highway Code rules for car drivers

Appendix 1
Show me, tell me questions for car drivers

Appendix 2
Checkpoint answers and progress record

Learn to drive

from only

£10.50*

- The AA is the ONLY national driving school to exclusively use fully qualified instructors

- All levels of ability catered for, nervous drivers welcome

- Discounts for family of AA Members / block booking

Call
0800 980 1822
or
visit theAA.com/driving-school

With over 42 years of publishing, more than 80 million people have succeeded in business with thanks to **Kogan Page**

www.koganpage.com

KoganPage

About the authors

Dr John Wells is well known in the driver training profession as a specialist author of training materials for driving instructors. Used nationwide by independent instructors and training establishments, John's materials are recommended by the leading trade body in the industry, the Driving Instructors Association (DIA). John has also provided a consultancy service, advising on training and quality for those wishing to register with ORDIT (The Official Register of Driving Instructor Trainers whose members provide training and professional development courses for other driving instructors). He is a member of the DIA Education Committee and adviser to BUSK, the school transport safety consultancy.

Margaret Stacey was the co-author of *The Driving Instructor's Handbook* and *Practical Teaching Skills for Driving Instructors*, both of which are published by Kogan Page. These books are recommended by the Driving Standards Agency to those preparing for the Approved Driving Instructors' exam and also to experienced instructors. Margaret also supplied establishments throughout the UK with other training materials including *The Advanced Driver's Handbook* and the *Autodriva Instructor Home Study Programme*. Margaret represented the Approved Driving Instructors' National Joint Council on various national committees and served on the management committees of ADITE, ORDIT and the NVQ Steering Group.

Acknowledgements

The authors thank all those who gave feedback on previous editions of this book and Theory First Publishing for permission to include diagrams from *Colourfile Professional*, *Colour Lesson Recaps* and *The Motor Car: Mechanical principles*.

Introduction

This book has been written by leaders in the driver training profession. It is a comprehensive course designed to help provisional licence holders prepare for both the theory and the practical parts of the driving test and is linked to the Driving Standards Agency (DSA) recommended syllabus for learner drivers.

This book has been written to:

- help with your studies for the theory and hazard perception test;
- supplement your practical driving lessons;
- provide guidance for you and your supervisor when you are practising.

It shows you:

- what to expect on your lessons;
- how to develop driving as a life skill;
- what you need to know to pass the theory and practical driving tests.

Your provisional licence

Before you can start driving for the first time you need to have received your provisional driving licence. The minimum age for driving a car is normally 17. However, if you receive higher-rate disability living allowance, you can obtain a pro- visional car licence at 16. A provisional licence allows you to drive only whilst supervised by a suitably qualified driver or professional driving instructor.

The Driver and Vehicle Licensing Agency (DVLA), or Driver and Vehicle Agency in Northern Ireland, issues driving licences. You can get an application form (D1) from any post office. All new licences issued are of the photocard type shown here. You will need to include a passport-style photo with your application. When you receive the licence, check that the details on the photocard and paper counterpart are correct. If not, you will need to contact the issuing agency.

Your eyesight

HK55 WES

W123 ABC

You must be able to read a number plate at the prescribed distance with glasses if worn

When you apply for your provisional driving licence, you sign to the effect that you can read a new-style number plate in the format XX50 XXX from 20 metres (66 feet). Alternatively, for older-style number plates in the format X123 XXX you need to be able to read them from 20.5 metres (about 67 feet). Make sure that you can. In today's busy conditions you need to be looking well ahead. If you need glasses to read the number plate, you must also wear them for driving. If you are in doubt, get your eyes tested professionally. Your driving instructor should also check your eyesight on your first lesson!

Essential reading

The best way of preparing for both parts of your driving test and to become a safe and competent driver is to combine theory with practice. To help you prepare for both the theory and the practical tests you need to study the following books:

- *The Highway Code* – rules of the road for all. The *Highway Code* rules referred to in *Learn to Drive* can be found in Part 3.

- *The Official DSA Guide to Learning to Drive* – tells you how to apply for your provisional licence, details the key skills required and explains what a driving examiner is looking for.

- *The Official DSA Guide to Driving: The essential skills* – advice for all drivers, skilled or novice, on how to make driving 'safe for life'.

These books will help you to understand the rules so that you can apply them during your practical lessons. If your driving instructor doesn't keep a stock you should be able to buy them at any good bookshop or online. The books are a worthwhile investment. The more you can read and understand, the less time your instructor needs to spend explaining, and the more time you have for practice! There are numerous interactive CDs and DVDs covering some of the material you need to learn. Ask your instructor to recommend the products that best suit your learning needs.

Reducing the risk of accidents

A high percentage of newly qualified drivers are involved in accidents. Under the New Driver Act, if you accumulate more than six penalty points within two years of passing your test you will have to:

- go back to using a provisional licence;
- display L plates; and
- take another driving test.

This book explains how to develop your control skills so that you will be able to handle your car safely and efficiently. This will make learning to drive an enjoyable experience.

Your instructor will explain how to apply the rules you are learning and teach you to plan ahead and anticipate what could happen. This will help you to learn how to avoid problems of conflict with other road users, which in turn will help you keep your full licence and enjoy 'safe driving for life'.

How to use this programme

Organizing your course of training

This training programme has now been in use for many years. By following this programme, and combining learning the theory with your practical lessons, you will soon learn how to apply the rules to different road situations more easily. This book includes common-sense advice, starting with how to choose your instructor and progressing to the driving test itself and further training. The task of learning to drive is broken down into easy stages that will enable you to plan and pace yourself according to your own natural aptitude and driving ability.

Charting your progress

The systematic step-by-step programme of learning in this book is designed to take the panic and confusion out of your practice and therefore make more effective use of your time. You can map your progress through the course by completing the assessment sections and entering your scores at the end of each stage of learning.

Key points

Each stage identifies key learning points. Before your lesson, study these points carefully along with any relevant Highway Code rules. If your next session is private practice get your supervisor to study the key points and the rules as well. Read the introduction to each stage and follow the instructions carefully.

The DSA syllabus for learners

The book *The Official DSA Guide to Learning to Drive* has been compiled by the Driving Standards Agency. Their motto is 'Safe Driving for Life'. This book is essentially the syllabus for learner drivers. Read the pages listed at the beginning of each stage of *Learn to Drive* and make sure you get lots of practice at all of the skills involved.

Completing the checkpoint

At the end of each stage there are some multiple-choice and multiple-response questions similar to those you will take in your theory test. The questions are designed to help you judge how well you have learned from this book, your lessons and the rules of driving from *The Highway Code*. Choose the most appropriate answers and check with the answer list in Appendix 2. Record your scores and try again if you need to.

Using illustrations to help you understand

Most of the key learning points are illustrated with diagrams. This will help you to:

- understand more easily;
- recognize risks earlier;
- predict danger; and
- avoid conflict with other road users.

Many of the illustrations in this book are adapted from *Colourfile Professional*, the driver training aid by John Wells, which is approved by the lead body in the driver training profession, the Driving Instructors Association (DIA). These tried-and-tested diagrams are clear, easily understood and used by thousands of professional instructors.

Learning in stages

Try to follow the sequence of the stages, making sure you have learned and practised all of the points before going on to the next. Sometimes the area you live in may mean that some topics will need to be covered in a different sequence. For example, if you live near roundabouts and dual carriageways you will have to be taught how to drive on them fairly early on in your course of lessons. The manoeuvre exercises can be introduced at any point. However, it is advisable that your clutch control skills are fairly well developed before you start learning how to reverse, as you will be more confident and achieve success more easily.

Using this guide as your personal logbook

When learning something new, your instructor/supervisor should begin by giving you a full explanation and 'talk-through' practice. As your skill improves, you should progress and carry out the various tasks with less assistance. Finally, you should be able to complete the exercises without any help at all.

Use this book to chart your progress when you have studied and then practised each exercise. You can get your instructor/supervisor to help by adding their constructive comments as well. Keep practising each skill until you and your instructor are happy with your progress and then proceed to the next topic. You should be ready for a practical test when you are confident that you can complete all the exercises in this book without any help from your instructor.

Notes:
I've studied it

Notes:
I can do it with help from my instructor

Notes:
I can do it without help

Use this book as your personal progress logbook

In-car lessons and practice

You must feel confident in yourself. Be prepared to take your instructor's advice and have enough lessons and practice on all of the subjects covered.

If you are unsure of anything or don't understand the reasons for it, ask your instructor to go over it again. Remember, you must feel confident that you can carry out the skills reasonably well if you want to become safe and efficient and also enjoy your driving.

Concentration

It is important that you maintain your concentration all of the time. When learning a new skill, don't try to practise for too long. Take short breaks to discuss your performance and then practise again. Following this system will help you to keep your concentration and therefore make your learning more effective.

Recapping at the start of each lesson

At the beginning of each lesson or practice session, your instructor or supervisor should spend a few minutes going over what you learned previously. Not only will this confirm whether or not you know and understand the rules and procedures, but it will also help in your preparation for the theory test.

Keeping a check on appointments and progress

Your instructor will probably use a record system to keep a note of your lesson appointments and progress, but you can keep your own record by filling in the 'Can do' statements in Appendix 2 (page 423).

The driving test

There are two parts to the driving test: the theory and hazard perception test and the practical test.

The theory and hazard perception test

You can apply for the theory and hazard perception test as soon as you have received your provisional driving licence. However, the test requires more than just theoretical knowledge of the rules of driving. You will need some driving experience to understand the scenarios in some of the questions. Your instructor will then be able to teach you how to apply the rules and respond to the different situations that will arise during your lessons. This will help you to understand the rules more easily and enable you to develop 'defensive' driving techniques. Take advice from your instructor on when you will be ready to take your test.

The theory and hazard perception test is computer-based, and you have to pass each element in one sitting. All of the subjects tested are dealt with in this book. The theory test comprises 50 multiple-choice questions that are displayed on-screen one at a time. You touch the screen to select your choice, and some of the questions have more than one correct answer. At the time of writing, to pass this element, you must score at least 43 correct answers within 57 minutes. A theory test section with sample questions is included in Part 2 of this book. The checkpoint questions at the end of each stage are also in the same style as the theory test, so by studying *Learn to Drive* you will have had plenty of practice by the time you take your theory test for real.

When you have completed the theory section of the test, there will be a short break before you move on to the hazard perception test. Fourteen film clips will be shown featuring various types of hazard as seen from the driver's seat of a moving car. These film clips are actual scenes taken from a moving vehicle but may, in future, comprise very lifelike computer generated scenes. Each clip lasts for about a minute, and you will need to 'click' when you see a potential hazard *developing* into a moving hazard, that is a situation which you would have to change speed or course to deal with. At the time of writing, up to five marks can be scored for each hazard, and the more quickly you respond to the developing hazard the more you will score. However, you must be careful not to go 'click-crazy', because the programme is designed to disqualify your score if you do so. To pass this part of the test, you must score 44 out of the possible 75 marks. Your instructor will advise you of any changes in the criteria for passing this part of the test.

For further reference and for a small charge, there is a DVD *The Complete Theory Test*, available to readers. This comprehensive product features actual DSA revision questions and hazard perception clips with other learning support material, It can be obtained from Grade Six Supplies Ltd; tel 01353 749807; www.g6s.co.uk.

A theory test pass certificate is valid for two years. You must pass the practical driving test within the two-year period; otherwise you will have to take the theory part again.

The practical test

When you have passed the theory test, take your instructor's advice and only apply for the practical test when you are told you will be ready. It could also shorten the length of time between the theory and practical tests if you start having your driving lessons whilst studying for the theory test.

Be prepared to have enough professional driving tuition. It is far better to be properly prepared and pass first time than be disappointed! Remember, a failed test means extra cost in terms of:

- another test fee;
- more driving lessons;
- time – there may be a long waiting list for a test at your local centre.

At the start of the test your examiner will check your eyesight by asking you to read a number plate. Once at your vehicle, you will be asked to explain or demonstrate how you would carry out certain safety checks. Referred to as 'show me, tell me', this part of the test will ensure that you are familiar with the vehicle you are driving and are aware of safety checks you must be able to make. Whilst dependent on the car you take for your driving test, most of the information you need to answer these questions is contained in this book, and you will learn it as you proceed with your course of tuition.

The practical part of the test lasts about 40 minutes, and the route will cover as many road and traffic conditions as possible. You will have to perform some 'set manoeuvres' to show that you can control the vehicle correctly and safely. You will also need to demonstrate that you can drive 'independently' without directions from the examiner for part of your practical test. The examiner will try to put you at ease and give you directions and instructions clearly and in good time. More detailed information on the practical part of the test is given in Stage 10. By following the structured approach to learning in this book and applying for your test only when you are thoroughly prepared, you should have no difficulty in passing first time!

Take advice from your instructor on when and how to apply for your theory and practical tests.

Changes to the driving test

From time to time, and in line with government consultation, the Driving Standards Agency may introduce changes to the content of the theory and practical parts of the driving test. Your instructor should be able to give you up-to-date information but you can also check at www.dft.gov.uk/dsa.

PART ONE
DRIVING SKILLS

Stage 1
Before you drive

*W*hat do I need before I can start learning? How do I choose a good driving instructor? How can I practise what I'm learning? What do I need to study? How much is it all going to cost? These are some of the questions that you will have asked yourself when you decided to learn to drive. So, before you drive, read through Stage 1 and start preparing yourself for a lifetime of safe driving!

Before driving you should read:

- *The Official DSA Guide to Driving: The essential skills*, Part 1 – The driver, and Part 2 – The driver and the law.

- *The Official DSA Guide to Learning to Drive*, Section 1 and Section 2, Legal responsibilities.

These emphasize the importance of a structured approach to learning and outline the qualities of the 'good driver'.

Remember that you must be in possession of your provisional driving licence before you can begin driving!

The Highway Code

Learning the rules by heart will not necessarily make you a good driver! Your instructor should teach you how the rules apply in different situations, so that you can put them into practice safely.

Make sure that you have an up-to-date edition of *The Highway Code* and read up on the rules in the following sections:

- Rules about animals:
  - animals in your vehicle.
- Rules for drivers and motorcyclists:
  - vehicle condition;
  - fitness to drive;

- – alcohol and drugs;
- – seat belts and child restraints;
- – children in cars.
- General rules:
  - – lighting requirements.
- Annes 3:
  - – documents;
  - – learner drivers.
- Annex 5:
  - – penalties.

When you have studied the rules in *The Highway Code*, work through this chapter and complete the checkpoint at the end of it. Your instructor should be able to help if you have any problems or don't understand some of the rules.

Who should I get to teach me?

The best way to learn to drive safely and with confidence is to combine professional tuition with private practice. In law, the only people who can accept payment in money or money's worth for giving driving instruction are those on the DSA register of approved instructors. They have the qualification 'Driving Standards Agency Approved Driving Instructor (car)' and are usually known as 'ADIs'. It is unlikely that anyone other than an ADI

If you are paying for driving instruction make sure that the person teaching you is on the DSA register of instructors

would have the skills, knowledge and experience to teach you to the standard required for the driving test.

ADIs must pass challenging theory and practical tests to join the DSA register. They must maintain a satisfactory standard to remain on the ADI register. Their tuition is regularly checked by a DSA supervising examiner. Your instructor should display his or her green ADI certificate in the left-hand side of the windscreen. It shows:

- the instructor's photograph;
- his or her ADI number;
- the date of issue and date of expiry.

Your instructor may display a red triangular certificate. This means that the instructor is a 'licensed trainee driving instructor', who is part-qualified. He or she can use the trainee badge to gain teaching experience before taking the final part of the register qualifying examinations.

Ask around for recommendations and go to a school with a good reputation and a high pass rate. It is a good idea to speak with the instructor who will be teaching you before committing yourself to paying for a course of lessons. You need to be sure that you will feel comfortable with your instructor and be able to communicate easily.

Driving schools and instructors vary in the way they give tuition and the order in which subjects are taught, but all should cover the syllabus outlined in *The Official DSA Guide to Learning to Drive*.

Safe driving for life

Gaining a full driving licence can seem expensive. Passing the 'L' test means you have reached a basic minimum standard to be able drive by yourself. Remember that inexperienced drivers are at the highest risk of accident involving serious or fatal injury. It is worth investing in quality tuition that will keep you safe on the road for the rest of your life. You should avoid falling into the trap of wanting to have as few lessons as possible and at the cheapest possible price!

Older drivers are often aghast at the number of lessons it could take to pass the modern-day driving test, particularly if they are parents or guardians paying the bill! DSA research has shown that on average a newly qualified driver will have had about 70 hours of driving experience, including some 45 hours' professional tuition. Driving is a skill that improves with practice and experience, but not everyone will master these skills at the same rate. Providing that you are getting good instruction, you should not be worried if you take longer to learn than others. Younger learners often feel under pressure from their friends or relatives to get through the test as quickly as possible. You shouldn't feel pressurized into applying for a test before you are ready. You will be wasting your time and money!

Pass Plus

After passing your test your instructor may offer you extra training under the Pass Plus scheme. Designed by the DSA with the help of the motor insurance industry and driver training profession, the course comprises a minimum six hours' additional tuition. You will be able to gain experience in a wider variety of situations, for example driving on more rural roads and on motorways. Your instructor will assess your progress and issue a certificate on satisfactory completion. Participating insurance companies can offer a reduction in your insurance premium if you have completed the Pass Plus course.

How often should I have driving lessons?

This will depend largely on your budget and time commitments and the availability of your instructor. However, one of the most effective ways of learning is to have two or three lessons each week, with practice in between. As you have to pass the theory test before you can apply for the practical driving test, combining your lessons with your studies helps you prepare for both elements at the same time. Some people do need to learn more quickly, for example if a job depends on having a driving licence. In these cases an intensive course leading up to a pre-booked practical test can seem an attractive option. Before committing yourself, however, it would be sensible to arrange for an assessment so that your instructor can establish whether or not you are likely to be up to the required standard in time. Even then, you need to bear in mind that learning to drive over a relatively short period can be stressful and tiring. Remember that you will still have to pass the theory test first!

How much will it cost?

Whilst the cost will vary with where you live, a quick scan of your local newspaper will show you that driving lessons can be had at remarkably low prices. Driving schools can sometimes seem desperate to get your business, with offers of cheap tuition and 'free lesson' deals. Whilst some offers will be genuine promotions from successful ADIs (their students have passed!), consistently low prices may just reflect the quality of the tuition you will get.

Think about how much it costs to run a driving school – typically between £9 and £10 per lesson to cover fuel, insurance, servicing and depreciation. That's just for the vehicle. If you are booking lessons at, say, 10 for £120, how motivated is your instructor going to be earning less than £30 for 10 hours' work? That's less than the legal minimum wage!

The lead body in the profession, the Driving Instructors Association, suggests that, to earn an average wage, an instructor should be charging around £33 per hour. The reality is that you will pay less than this. Budget for between £18 and £26 per hour according to region.

Choosing the wrong school, because lessons are cheap, may cost you more in the long run. So if you must ring round to compare schools, don't just ask 'How much are your lessons?' Ask how long the lessons are, what vehicle is used and what the instructor's pass rate is. Does the instructor have qualifications over and above the ADI certificate?

Go for quality, not quantity.

Are you learning already?

If you are already learning to drive but are not quite sure about the quality of training you are getting, ask yourself whether your instructor:

- gives an outline of the course;
- arrives on time for your lessons;
- behaves professionally;
- helps you with your studies for the theory test;
- recaps on your previous lesson;
- explains what you're going to do at the start of lessons;
- explains things in simple and understandable terms;
- demonstrates when you don't understand;
- assesses your progress and gives you feedback;
- praises you when you get things right;
- helps you to understand when you get things wrong;
- fills in your progress card or logbook for each lesson;

- allows you to ask questions without feeling awkward;
- tells you what to study before the next lesson;
- shows a real interest in your progress.

If you have a good instructor, you should have been able to answer yes to most of these questions. If you can't, then you should try to discuss the problems. If you are offered no remedy, you should perhaps consider looking for another driving instructor. Remember – it's your money and your choice.

If you feel you have a justifiable complaint, write to The Registrar – ADI, The Driving Standards Agency, The Axis Building, 112 Upper Parliament Street, Nottingham NG1 6LP.

Sometimes it happens that you just can't get on well with an instructor. You can always change to another school or an instructor with a different teaching style.

Ready for your lesson?

Learning to drive takes a great deal of concentration, especially in the early stages. To maintain your concentration you must be comfortable when driving. Visit the toilet before your lessons. Get ready in plenty of time so that you can spend a few minutes relaxing. This will help you collect your thoughts and prepare yourself mentally for driving.

Being worried or stressed will not help your concentration. Try to avoid any arguments before going out – they will put you in the wrong mood for learning. Even just feeling 'under the weather' will affect your mood and ability to concentrate. If you are ill it probably isn't worth having a lesson – but do try to give your instructor adequate notice if you need to cancel.

You must concentrate all the time. You should not drive if you're not feeling well. You'd be surprised how even a common cold can affect your concentration.

Modern cars have very effective heating and ventilation systems that allow you to keep a comfortable temperature in the car whatever the weather, so there's no need to wear heavy coats or sweaters. Wear light, comfortable clothes. Avoid anything that is heavy or tight-fitting when driving, as this could either distract you or restrict your body movements. You might find yourself getting 'hot and bothered' in the early stages no matter what you've chosen to wear. If this happens, open a window to get some fresh air and keep you alert.

Flat shoes are normally the best for driving. Heavy boots or fashion shoes may make controlling the pedals difficult. The ridged soles of some trainers can catch on the pedals and make driving difficult.

Are you fit to drive?

Driving whilst impaired through alcohol or drugs is against the law. Apart from the dangers you could cause on the road, the penalties are heavy and can cost you your licence. Alcohol is a drug. It can make you feel overconfident and less aware of danger. It makes people think they can achieve the impossible and adversely affects judgement of speed and distance. Even small amounts of alcohol will slow down your reactions. If you drink the night before a lesson, the amount of alcohol in your body may still exceed the legal limit in the morning!

Drinking and driving don't mix!

If you are taking medicines or drugs, ask your doctor if they are likely to affect your driving. Even some common cough and cold remedies can cause drowsiness – read the directions carefully. If unsure, ask the pharmacist for advice. Even if a medicine is not supposed to affect your ability to drive, remember that some people do respond differently. If in doubt, don't drive!

Even over-the-counter medicines can affect your ability to drive!

Practising with friends and relatives

The DSA recommend that you get plenty of practice to supplement your lessons. However, you should take advice from your instructor on when you are safe and confident enough to practise in another car. Starting private practice too soon could ruin your confidence or result in a serious loss of control.

Full photocard licence

In law, anyone supervising a learner driver must be over 21 and have held a full EC/EEA driving licence (European standard licence) for at least three years for the group of vehicle you will be driving.

Recommended driving techniques have changed over the years and it can be that there is conflict between what your driving instructor has taught you and what the person supervising your private practice tells you. Furthermore, your supervisor may well have developed some bad habits that could be passed on to you. To avoid these conflicts, both you and your supervisor should follow the guidance in this book. You will both then be using up-to-date methods and following the latest rules.

Involve your driving instructor: he or she should have no objection to allowing your friend or relative to sit in on a driving lesson to find out what to expect. Ask your instructor to help you plan and advise what skills you are ready to practise.

Very often, close relatives and friends are too personally involved and may find it unnerving and frustrating to accompany you in private practice. Try to avoid conflict by staying calm. Friction between learner and supervisor will only lead to loss of concentration that will impede your progress.

The vehicle you use for private practice may be different from the car you are taking professional lessons in. This shouldn't present a problem providing you've mastered the basic control skills. However, do take the time to familiarize yourself with the practice vehicle and make sure you know where all the controls are and how they operate. Remember:

- The practice vehicle must display L plates (or D plates in Wales) clearly visible at the front and rear of the vehicle. Do not attach them to the car windows, as they will obscure your view. L plates must be removed or covered up when a learner is not driving the car.

- Your accompanying driver will need an additional rear-view mirror to keep track of what's happening behind. These are available from car accessory shops.

- It is illegal to give payment of any kind, either in money or in goods, to anyone supervising your driving unless they are on the Register of Approved Driving Instructors.

Documents

Make sure that the vehicle can be legally driven by you before commencing practice. Check the insurance certificate. If it is not clear whether you are covered, the policyholder needs to check with the insurance company.

Make sure the vehicle you are driving is taxed. The tax disc should be displayed in the front nearside of the windscreen.

If the vehicle is more than three years old, make sure it has a current MOT certificate. If it does not, your insurance could be invalid!

Is your tax disc valid?

Is your vehicle roadworthy?

It is your responsibility as the driver to make sure your vehicle is in a roadworthy condition before driving. Get into the habit of making regular checks for obvious faults:

- Tyres (including spare). It is a good idea to walk round the car and check that the tyres appear to be properly inflated and undamaged and that there is nothing wedged in the tyre treads. You should also check that the tread depth is legal and that tyre pressures are correct at least once a week.

- Windscreen, windows and mirrors should be clean and free from defects. Scratched or dirty windows are a hazard, adding to glare in bright sunlight and dazzle from the headlights of other vehicles at night. Condensation can restrict your vision, particularly in damp or cold weather. Do not drive away if any of the windows are steamed up. Clear the windows before driving with a cloth or with the demister and rear screen heater. A slightly open window can help prevent condensation from reforming once you are on the move.

- Check windscreen wiper blades and that the wipers operate correctly. The wash bottle should also be topped up.

- Lights (including indicators). Check that the lenses are clean and free from defects and that the bulbs are working. Get someone to help you if necessary. Replace any dead bulbs immediately. It is a good idea to carry spares in the car.

- Check that the horn is working.

- Brakes. Check that the brakes are working at the first safe opportunity. Stop driving if you think the brakes may be faulty.

Practising safely

Your instructor should advise you on the parts of this book to study with your supervisor before going out to practise. Remember that the car in which you practise is unlikely to have dual controls – don't be tempted to try too much too soon.

To help you during the early stages of learning, you and your supervisor need to give some thought to the time and the place. Choose a level road in a quiet area where there won't be too much traffic and where you won't irritate other road users or local residents. Although your practice sessions may have to be timed with your supervisor's availability, try to avoid peak traffic times – rush hour and the school run! Be aware of any traffic problems that might be caused by road works or local events and plan accordingly. When you first start practising, it's best to avoid driving in bad weather conditions.

Avoid problems by asking your supervisor to select routes that you will be able to cope with. Your supervisor should also help by planning well ahead and giving you instructions and directions in plenty of time for you to be able to carry them out without rushing. If things get too complicated your supervisor should be prepared to compensate, for example with steering corrections or by applying the parking brake.

Being a learner is no excuse for breaking the law – careless driving could result in disqualification for you and your supervisor. Make sure that you are able to stop under control before you drive in traffic. If you feel you can't cope ask your supervisor to take over. If you find something is too difficult, ask for a further explanation or a demonstration. If you still have difficulty in understanding or carrying out a routine, ask your instructor to work on it with you on your next lesson.

As your driving skills improve, your supervisor should be able to widen the range of road and traffic conditions you experience. Providing you have mastered control of the vehicle and weather conditions aren't dangerous, there is nothing to stop you gaining experience in heavier traffic, on faster roads and in windy or wet conditions.

Don't get distracted

De-clutter your vehicle. You don't want any unnecessary window stickers, dangling mascots or other loose articles in the car. Loose articles may move about whilst you are driving, causing you distraction. Make sure there is nothing on the floor likely to roll around, such as a child's toy or an aerosol can. Apart from being a distraction, it could roll under the pedals and prevent you from applying the brakes properly.

It is not normally a good idea to carry extra passengers during the early stages of learning. It could affect your concentration. If this is unavoidable, make sure they get in safely and sit where they will not restrict your view in the mirrors. Children can get bored travelling in cars. This will make it difficult for you to concentrate on your driving. If they must go with you, make sure they are properly restrained and kept under control. This also applies if you take your pets in the car.

Checkpoint 1

Before going out to practise, answer the following questions. Just as with the theory test, some of them will have more than one correct answer. If you can't answer a question, or you don't understand what it means, refer back to the books or *Highway Code* rules listed at the beginning of this stage. If you still don't understand, ask your instructor for help.

1   You want to pay someone to give you driving tuition.
    You must be certain that the person:
    Choose one answer

    a. is old enough and has the correct driving licence
    b. is an approved driving instructor (ADI) or holds a trainee licence
    c. has dual controls in his or her car
    d. has held a driving licence for at least two years

2 Anyone supervising a learner driver must be:
Choose one answer

    a.   18 and have passed the L test
    b.   18 and have held a full licence for six months
    c.   21 and have held a full licence for two years
    d.   21 and have held a full licence for three years

3 Before applying for your theory test you must:
Choose one answer

    a.   apply for your driving licence
    b.   apply for your practical driving test
    c.   have had at least 10 driving lessons
    d.   have received your provisional licence

4 A relative offers the use of his or her car for private practice. Before driving it you must make sure that:
Choose one answer

    a.   the vehicle has insurance cover
    b.   your use of the car is insured
    c.   your relative has third-party insurance
    d.   you have the insurance documents for the car

5 Before driving a car for the first time you must: *Choose two answers*

    a.   have applied for your photocard licence
    b.   make sure your eyesight is up to the required standard
    c.   have received your provisional licence
    d.   pass the theory test

6 To meet the legal eyesight requirements, you should be able to read a car number plate in this format from:

HK55 WES

Choose one answer

    a.   10 metres
    b.   15 metres
    c.   18 metres
    d.   20 metres

7 If you need to wear glasses or contact lenses to read a car number plate at the distance required for driving, you:
Choose one answer

a. must keep them in the car
b. needn't wear them when driving
c. might need to use them in poor weather or when driving at night
d. must wear them at all times when driving

8 Cars used for driving lessons must be:
Choose one answer

a. fitted with dual controls
b. roadworthy
c. less than three years old
d. saloon models

9 You are using your own car for private practice. The L plates displayed on the car:
Choose two answers

a. can be made up to a size of your choice
b. must be clearly visible to the front and from behind
c. are best placed in the front and rear windows
d. must conform to legal specifications

10 Cars being driven on the road must display:
Choose one answer

a. a valid tax disc
b. a current MOT certificate
c. a vehicle registration document
d. an insurance certificate

11 You have been to a party the night before a driving lesson and had a few alcoholic drinks. In the morning you:
Choose one answer

a. should be all right to drive
b. could still be over the legal limit
c. should have more confidence
d. should ask your ADI to test your breath

12 You should apply for your practical test:
Choose two answers

   a. when your instructor says you are ready
   b. when you've had a minimum of 10 lessons
   c. after you've passed the theory and hazard perception tests
   d. as soon as you've read *The Highway Code* and driving manual

13 The driver is legally responsible for the wearing of seat belts by:
Choose one answer

   a. all passengers, regardless of age
   b. children over 14 but under 16
   c. all children under 14
   d. any adult with a disability

14 The most effective ways to counter sleepiness when driving are to:
Choose three answers

   a. avoid driving at night
   b. avoid driving for too long without a break
   c. keep fresh air circulating in the car
   d. take regular breaks
   e. play loud music on the car audio system

15 Driving after drinking alcohol will:
Choose three answers

   a. reduce your sense of confidence
   b. speed up your reaction time
   c. make you more likely to take risks
   d. slow down your reactions
   e. affect your judgements

16 If carrying children in a vehicle the driver should ensure that they:
Choose two answers

   a. enter by the door nearest their seat
   b. enter by the door nearest the kerb
   c. all wear an adult seat belt
   d. use a child restraint appropriate for their height and weight

17 Which of these do you need before you can legally drive a car?
Choose three answers

a. fully comprehensive insurance
b. a valid driving licence
c. the car registration certificate (logbook)
d. a current MOT certificate if the car is over three years old
e. a valid tax disc displayed on the car

18 Who has responsibility for seeing that a vehicle isn't overloaded?
Choose one answer

a. the owner of the vehicle
b. the driver of the vehicle
c. the person who loaded the vehicle
d. the registered keeper of the vehicle

19 You have arranged a practice session with your supervisor but find yourself very tired after a hard day at work. You should:
Choose one answer

a. take some 'pep pills' to stay awake
b. not drive
c. drive faster to lessen the danger of falling asleep at the wheel
d. take a flask of hot coffee with you

20 A full driving licence is valid until your:
Choose one answer

a. 60th birthday
b. 65th birthday
c. 70th birthday
d. retirement

You will find the answers on page 423.

You will find the answers on page 423.

Scores: First try   Second try   Third try

Record your scores in Appendix 2 (page 426).

Record your scores in Appendix 2 (page 426).

Stage 2
Get to know your car

In this stage you will learn about the 'cockpit drill' – the routine to go through each time you get into the driving seat. You will find out what the main car controls do and how they operate. You will also learn about the driving mirrors and other driving aids. Your instructor will refer to this stage as the 'controls lesson', and although you'll be anxious actually to get moving it is essential for safe driving that you understand the function and use of the main car controls before moving off for the first time.

To help you prepare for this stage, you can also read:

- *The Official DSA Guide to Driving: The essential skills, Part 3 –* The controls, and Part 4 – Mirrors.
- *The Official DSA Guide to Learning to Drive, Section 2 –* Cockpit checks, and Section 2 – Controls and instruments.

The cockpit drill

Before you drive any vehicle you need to carry out the cockpit drill. This is a simple routine to ensure the safety of yourself, your passengers and other road users and is easily remembered as **DSMS**, which stands for Doors, Seat, Mirrors and Seat belt.

Take care getting into the driving seat!

Doors

The first thing to do is get in the driver's seat! Your instructor will probably have parked facing the traffic flow and put the seat back to make it easy for you to get in promptly. Open the driver's door from behind so you don't have to walk round it to get in. Beware of other traffic – you don't want to cause another road user to swerve when you open the door!

You should close the door as soon as you are seated and then check that the parking brake is applied – your instructor will show you how to do this.

Pull the door to make sure there's no movement. Check in the outside mirrors that the doors are flush with the bodyline of the car. Listen to make sure that passengers (including your instructor!) have closed their doors properly. Remember – you are responsible for the safety of your passengers. A door not closed properly will rattle. It could fly open as you drive along or go around a bend.

Make sure all the doors are closed

Seat

The next thing to do is adjust the driving seat so that you can see all round and reach the hand and foot controls comfortably and easily. To do so, hold the steering wheel with one hand and pull the lever at the side/beneath the seat with your other hand so that you can move the seat to the correct position. You need to be able to push the left foot pedal down fully with your left foot without stretching.

Release the lever when you are happy with the seat position and push yourself back in the seat to make sure it is locked in place. You can then adjust the angle of the back of the seat by the lever/knob on the side of the seat so that you are comfortable, can see clearly over the steering wheel and can move your arms freely.

Can you reach all around the steering wheel? If not, you may need to adjust the back of the seat or move the steering wheel if the car you are in has that option. Your instructor will guide you.

The next thing to do is adjust the head restraint so that it will protect your head and neck. Reach behind you and raise or lower the restraint so that the rigid part is at least as high as the top of your ears and as close as is comfortable to the back

Make sure you can reach and use all the controls comfortably and easily

of your head (note that in some vehicles the position of the head restraint is fixed).

Mirrors

The mirrors are your most important visual driving aid, which must be checked at regular intervals as you drive along. It's as important to know what's happening behind as it is to see what's happening ahead. There will be more about using the mirrors later. For now you need to know how to adjust them.

Adjust the interior mirror to give the best possible rear view

Only adjust the mirrors when the car is stationary and you are seated in your normal driving position. Start with the interior mirror. Hold the mirror by the edges to avoid finger marks. Adjust the mirror so that you get the best possible view through the back window without having to move your head. You should be able to frame the whole of the rear window in the interior mirror, but, if you can't, make sure you can see the top and right-hand side of the rear window.

Adjust the exterior mirrors so that you can get the best rear view with minimal head movements. You should be able to see a small strip of the

side of the car, and the horizon should appear about in the middle of the mirror.

Anti-dazzle

Most interior mirrors have an anti-dazzle lever. This is for use at night so that you are not blinded by the glare of headlights from vehicles behind.

Seat belt

Having adjusted the mirrors, you should now put on the seat belt. You must use the seat belt whenever you drive, no matter how short your journey. Use your left hand to reach for the buckle and stretch it across. Ensure that the belt is not twisted and that it lies flat across your chest and stomach. Secure the belt in the buckle at the side of your seat. To remove it again you need simply press the button on top/at the side of the buckle. When putting the belt on and taking it off, hold the buckle so that it doesn't fly up and hit you in the face or bang into the window. Your instructor will demonstrate how to do this if needed.

Seat belts save lives and reduce the risk of serious injury. The law requires that all drivers and passengers (unless they have an exemption certificate) must wear a seat belt. As the driver, you should encourage all of your passengers to wear their seat belts. If you are carrying passengers under 14 years of age, it is your responsibility to make sure they wear seat belts.

Fuel

On your first lesson your instructor will have made sure that there is enough fuel in the car, but you should get into the habit of checking the fuel gauge before setting off.

Parking brake and neutral

After you have completed the DSMS routine, it is good practice to check once more that the parking brake (sometimes referred to as the handbrake) is applied and that the gear lever is in the neutral position. You'll learn how to do this a little later in this stage as you go through the main controls.

It is very important that you complete the cockpit drill *before* starting the engine and moving off. It would be very dangerous to adjust the seat, steering column or mirrors whilst the vehicle was moving.

Notes: Notes: Notes:

Assessment – the cockpit drill

The main controls

Now that you're seated correctly and the vehicle is secure, it's time to learn about the main controls and driving aids.

Foot controls

Cars with manual transmission have three foot pedals. From right to left these are the accelerator, the footbrake and the clutch pedal.

Accelerator or 'gas' pedal

The pedal on the right is the accelerator or 'gas' pedal and controls the rate at which fuel and air are supplied to the engine. The accelerator should only be used with the right foot.

The harder the pedal is pressed, the faster the engine will run and the more power is generated. You should press the pedal lightly, using gentle changes of pressure in normal driving. It takes practice and experience to know how much to press the pedal to make the car speed up. Easing the pressure on the pedal will make the car slow down.

The footbrake

The middle pedal is the footbrake and is used to slow down and stop the car by applying pressure to the front and rear brakes. The footbrake should normally only be used with the right foot, as you would not have to use both the accelerator and brake at the same time.

Using the accelerator and footbrake

Position your right foot so that it will pivot comfortably between the accelerator and brake pedals. To do this, cover the brake pedal with your right foot. Without looking down or moving your heel, practise pivoting between these pedals. When you have found a comfortable position for your foot, get a feel for the brake pedal by pressing it lightly.

You should be able to pivot your foot between the accelerator and footbrake

The first pressure puts the brake lights on at the back of the car. When driving along, this will let anyone behind know you are slowing down. The harder you press the pedal, the more the car will slow down. You should brake progressively, using the ball of your foot to press the pedal lightly, increasing pressure gradually as the car slows, and easing the pressure just before stopping so that the vehicle halts smoothly.

Brake light signals come on when you press the footbrake

The left foot pedal operates the clutch. The main purpose of the clutch is to connect and disconnect the power from the engine to the road wheels. It is needed so that changes can be made smoothly from one gear into another. The clutch pedal should only be pressed with the left foot.

How the clutch works

In its simplest form, the clutch is made up of two circular friction plates, held firmly together by spring pressure. One of these plates is attached to the engine and rotates all the time that the engine is running. The other plate is attached, through the gearbox, to the drive wheels. Pressing the clutch pedal down forces the plates apart, breaking the link between the engine and the wheels. Controlling the clutch pedal correctly is a vital part of safe and skilled driving and takes practice and experience.

The clutch pedal

Controlling the clutch is an important driving skill that takes practice to learn

Using the clutch

To move off, change gear and stop, you should be able to use the clutch smoothly and without looking at your feet. To begin with, cover the clutch with your left foot and then press it down. This will disconnect the engine from the gearbox. You will have to do this when changing gear and just before stopping. Next let the pedal up smoothly. You will feel a powerful spring pushing your foot up.

Only a small part of the total pedal travel, known as the biting range, has any noticeable effect on the car. To move off and control very low speeds, you must be able to find the **biting point** (sometimes called the holding point) at the bottom of this range. The biting point is where the two clutch plates are just in contact so that they slip against one another. Lifting the clutch pedal up beyond this point brings the plates into full contact, causing the engine to drive the road wheels.

Hand controls

Parking brake

The parking brake is used to secure the car when you park it or are stationary for more than a few moments. A lever positioned beside the driver's seat usually operates the parking brake. You must make sure the car has stopped before applying the parking brake, and you must be able to apply and release it promptly, without looking down.

Only use the parking brake when the vehicle is stationary

To practise, first press the footbrake with your left foot and keep it pressed down so that the car won't move. To release the parking brake, put your hand on to it with your thumb on the button. Pull the lever up slightly and press the button in. Keep the button pressed in whilst you lower the lever.

To apply the parking brake, press in the button, pull the lever firmly upwards and release the button. The button will lock against a ratchet. You should try not to forget to push in the button, as this would cause unnecessary wear.

In some vehicles the lever operating the parking brake can be an additional foot pedal or even electrically operated. Your instructor will show you how these work if fitted in your tuition vehicle.

Gear lever

The purpose of the gears is to allow the car to be driven with minimum strain on the engine, just the same as the gears on a pushbike! The gear lever enables you to change from one gear to another.

Modern cars usually have five forward and one reverse gear, although older vehicles may have only four forward gears. Newer vehicles may have a sixth forward gear, which gives greater economy when driving at higher speeds over longer distances.

The speed ranges overlap, so there is no fixed speed at which to change gear. With experience you will know from the sound of the engine when a gear change is needed. First gear is the lowest and most powerful gear, which is used to move the

The gear level is usually marked with the gear positions

The speed ranges for the gears overlap

GEAR LEVER
IN NEUTRAL

ENGINE

NEUTRAL

CLUTCH
ENGAGED

ENGINE

1ST GEAR

GEAR
SELECTED

In 'neutral' the link between engine and road wheels is broken in the gearbox

car from rest. The highest gear is the least powerful and is used for cruising at higher speeds. Low gears are used at low speeds and when the engine has extra work to do, for example climbing a steep hill. Higher gears are selected at higher speeds when the engine has less work to do.

The gear lever also has a **neutral** position where no gear is selected. With the gear lever in the neutral position the link between the engine and the driven wheels is broken in the gearbox. This allows the engine to run without turning the road wheels even if the clutch pedal is up. To check that the gear lever is in the neutral position, move it from side to side.

How to select a gear

You need to be able to select each gear without looking down at the lever.

The gear lever in most modern cars is 'spring-loaded' and, when in neutral, rests between third and fourth gears. To select a gear, use the palm of your hand on the lever. This will allow you to push the lever forwards, backwards and sideways as needed. Your instructor will demonstrate the gear positions for your car and let you practise with the car stationary and the parking brake applied.

To find first gear, push the lever across and forwards. From first gear push the lever straight back to second gear. To find third gear, palm the lever out of second and forward into the correct position, and so on for each gear. It will take practice to make smooth and unhurried gear changes. You usually change through the gears in order as you increase in speed. When you slow down, however, you usually select the appropriate gear for the new speed, and it is safe to miss one or more gears in between.

Practise changing up and down the gears until you are confident you can do so without looking at the lever. You will need to coordinate this skill with foot pedal movements when you start to drive.

Steering wheel

The steering wheel is used to control the direction of the car by turning the front wheels. Imagine the wheel as a clock face. You should hold the steering wheel lightly but firmly with your hands in the 'ten-to-two' or 'quarter-to-three' position. You should keep both hands on the wheel all the time the car is moving unless operating another hand control or giving a signal. You should never take both hands from the wheel whilst the vehicle is moving.

Hold the steering wheel at the 'ten-to-two' or 'quarter-to-three' positions as you drive ahead

To steer a straight course, look well ahead – you will always tend to 'go where you are looking'! You must be able to operate the main controls without looking at them. Looking down will result in your car wandering from side to side.

To turn the car you should use the 'pull–push' technique. This means feeding the rim of the steering wheel through your hands so that one hand is always gripping the wheel. For example, to turn right, move your right hand to the top of the wheel but not beyond the 12 o'clock position. Pull the wheel downwards with your right hand and at the

Use the 'push–pull' technique to steer

same time slide your left hand down the rim so that both hands end up at the same height on the wheel. Then change the grip to your left hand and push the wheel further round, at the same time allowing your right hand to slide up the rim of the wheel. You may need to repeat these steps according to the angle through which the front wheels need to turn. You can vary your hand movements according to the amount you need to turn.

To turn the wheel back again, or to turn left, use the same procedure, but the left hand goes to the top of the wheel first. You should not let the wheel slip back through your hands after a turn, as this lessens your control of the car.

Try not to cross your hands on the wheel, as this lessens control. You should also avoid steering when the car is stationary, as this can damage your tyres.

Operating switches

The most frequently used switches, such as the direction indicators, lights and windscreen wipers, are usually on the column just behind the steering wheel. Other important switches include the horn, windscreen washer and demisters. Your instructor will show you how the switches operate. Practise using these and other ancillary controls when safe. It is important that you are familiar with their position and method of use. You will learn when to use each of the controls as your driving experience increases.

The importance of mirrors

The driving mirrors are extremely important aids, and their use is vital for safe driving.

The purpose of the driving mirrors is to let you know what is happening behind. It is just as important to know what is behind you as what is in front of you. You must use the mirrors frequently when driving and act safely and sensibly on what you see.

Compare the view in the interior and exterior mirrors

The interior mirror is made of flat glass and gives a true picture of the following traffic. Most exterior mirrors are made with convex (curved) glass and make following traffic appear smaller and further away than it really is. You can see this effect from the driving seat when parked at the roadside. Choose an object or parked car behind you that you can see in the interior mirror. Compare this view with the view in the exterior mirrors. In practice this means that it can be difficult at first to judge the speed and position of vehicles behind.

Always remember that in a convex mirror the vehicle behind appears to be smaller and therefore will be closer than you think. With practice you will overcome this difficulty, particularly if you get into the habit of using the interior and exterior mirrors together.

You should always use the mirrors *well before* any manoeuvre, that is a change of speed or direction. This leads on to the golden rule of **mirrors–signal–manoeuvre**, referred to as **MSM**.

MSM means checking your mirrors well before signalling and doing both in good time before making your move. You need to check mirrors before:

- signalling;
- moving off;
- changing direction to overtake, turn left or right or change lane;
- slowing down or stopping;
- opening your car door.

It isn't possible to get a complete rear view with the driving mirrors. There are always areas that the mirrors don't cover. These areas are known as blind spots and can be caused by the body of the car, door pillars, etc. Here you can see that an overtaking car will momentarily disappear in your blind spot until you catch sight of it again with your peripheral vision. It is for this reason that you sometimes need to look round. This is especially important before moving off.

Be aware of blind spots not covered by your mirrors

As today's roads are getting busier and busier, looking round to check blind spots on the move can be dangerous, especially at speed. Every time you look behind, you are averting your eyes from what is happening in front of you. A quick sideways glance is necessary in certain circumstances. However, looking round on the move should be the exception rather than the rule.

You should normally check your interior mirror first and then, if changing direction, the exterior mirror on the side to which you will be moving or turning.

When you have looked in your mirrors you should assess the situation and decide whether it is safe to make your intended move. This means either making your move or waiting for a safe opportunity to do so. It is essential that you should never signal without first checking your mirrors and that you should never take it for granted that you can carry out these manoeuvres safely just because you've signalled.

When using your mirrors you should be asking yourself what's behind you, how near they are to you, what speed they are travelling at and what their intentions are. You must have enough time to decide, which makes early use of the mirrors essential.

Notes:

Notes:

Notes:

Assessment – the main controls and driving aids

Driving an 'automatic'

Vehicles fitted with automatic transmission do not have a clutch pedal. This makes the physical task of driving easier, especially in heavy traffic. Automatic vehicles are increasing in popularity and are also particularly suitable for those with physical disabilities. Learning to start, steer and stop is much easier in a car with automatic transmission because the driver can concentrate more on planning ahead and steering.

Instead of a gear lever there is a **selector lever** that allows the driver to choose between Drive, Reverse and Neutral. In most automatic cars, the driver may engage a fixed low gear for carrying out low-speed manoeuvres and for better control on hills and in slow traffic. In an automatic you will normally only use your right foot to control the accelerator and footbrake. Gear changes are carried out automatically. They are regulated by the car's speed, the load on the engine and the pressure applied on the accelerator by the driver.

When driving an automatic car, the parking brake has to be used more often because the vehicle will have a tendency to creep forwards. If you are learning in an automatic, your instructor should explain about the extra use of the parking brake and the different techniques used to control the car at low speeds.

If you pass your test in an automatic car, you will only be entitled to drive this type of vehicle.

Checkpoint 2

1   Head restraints provide protection against:
    Choose two answers

    a. neck and spinal injuries
    b. the effects of whiplash
    c. severe headaches
    d. fatigue on long journeys

2   You should check your seat position:
    Choose two answers

    a. as soon as you drive away
    b. if someone else has been driving
    c. before you switch on the engine
    d. when you have been driving for about five minutes

3   When driving, you should:
    Choose two answers

    a. never take a hand off the wheel
    b. never take both hands off the wheel if the car is moving
    c. look where you want the car to go
    d. let the wheel spin back after turning

4   You should avoid:
    Choose two answers

    a. applying the parking brake before the car has stopped
    b. applying the parking brake after the car has stopped
    c. releasing the parking brake until the car is moving
    d. releasing the parking brake until sure it is safe to move

5 In an automatic vehicle, you:
   Choose one answer

   a. only need to use the parking brake when parking
   b. will not need to apply the footbrake to stop
   c. will need to use the parking brake more frequently
   d. need to use the parking brake less frequently

6 You can check that the seat is correctly positioned by:
   Choose one answer

   a. driving a little way to ensure you have full control
   b. reaching all round the steering wheel
   c. asking your instructor
   d. asking a passenger

7 You should understand the function of those controls that have
   a bearing on road safety. These include the:
   Choose three answers

   a. indicators
   b. mobile phone
   c. radio
   d. lights
   e. demisters

8 Most interior mirrors are made of flat glass. This:
   Choose two answers

   a. gives a distorted picture
   b. gives a true picture
   c. makes it easier to judge the speed and distance of following traffic
   d. makes it difficult to judge the speed and distance of following
      traffic

9 Most exterior mirrors have convex glass. This:
   Choose three answers

   a. gives a wider field of vision
   b. makes things behind seem larger
   c. makes things behind seem smaller
   d. makes things behind seem to be nearer
   e. makes things behind seem to be further away

10 Blind spots:
Choose three answers

   a. are caused by convex mirrors
   b. can be fully overcome by mirrors
   c. may be partially overcome by mirrors
   d. may be caused by door pillars
   e. are areas ahead, behind and to the side of the car that you can't see from your normal driving position

11 The first thing to do when you've got into the driver's seat is:
Choose one answer

   a. adjust the seat
   b. apply the parking brake
   c. switch on the ignition
   d. close the door

12 When the gear lever is in neutral, the engine:

Choose one answer

   a. is disconnected from the road wheels
   b. is connected to the road wheels
   c. is disconnected from the gearbox
   d. will slow the car down

13 To adjust the interior mirror correctly you should:
Choose three answers

   a. first make sure your seat is properly adjusted
   b. operate the anti-dazzle device
   c. hold the mirror by its edges
   d. get the best possible rear view
   e. lean forward slightly in your seat

14 In a manual car, the left foot manually operates the:
Choose one answer

a.   brake and clutch pedals
b.   brake pedal only
c.   clutch pedal only
d.   accelerator pedal only

15 In a manual car, the right foot operates the:
Choose one answer

a.   clutch and brake pedals
b.   accelerator pedal only
c.   accelerator and brake pedals
d.   brake pedal only

16 To operate the parking brake lever you should:
Choose one answer

a.   always listen for the ratchet
b.   avoid wearing the ratchet
c.   always press the footbrake
d.   always press the clutch pedal down fully

17 The best position to hold the steering wheel for driving straight ahead is: *Choose one answer*

a.

b.

c.

d.

18 Looking down at the gear lever or foot pedals when driving will:
Choose two answers

a.   cause you to wander off course
b.   distract you from the traffic situation ahead
c.   help you avoid selecting the wrong gear
d.   help you select the correct gear

19 The main purpose of the clutch is to:
Choose one answer

    a. judge where your seat should be positioned
    b. disconnect power from the engine to the road wheels
    c. control the speed of the engine
    d. slow the car down

20 First gear is the:
Choose one answer

    a. least powerful gear
    b. most powerful gear
    c. most economical gear
    d. best for driving at high speeds

You will find the answers on page 423.

Scores:	First try	Second try	Third try

Record your scores in Appendix 2 (page 426).

Stage 3
Starting to drive

During this stage you will be learning how to start the engine, move off, change gear, and stop the car. You will also get the feel of the steering and learn to use some of the ancillary controls. Make sure that you can carry out all of these skills reasonably well before going out to practise. Your instructor will advise you when you are ready to go out with someone else.

It is important that you learn the basic procedures in very quiet areas. Housing estates with lots of parked vehicles and other hazards are not really suitable. Your instructor will talk you through each exercise until you can manage on your own. Your instructor or supervisor should give you directions in plenty of time to allow you to carry out all of the individual skills without rushing. However, you may find that someone who isn't an ADI does not give you enough time, because of lack of experience with learners. If you find yourself becoming confused and rushed, ask your supervisor to give instructions much earlier.

Avoid talking whilst you are practising – this will only distract you. Concentrate, keep your eyes on the road and listen carefully to directions. The following are useful instructions:

- 'I would like you to take the next road on the right.'
- 'Take the second road on the right; this is the first one.'
- 'At the end of the road, turn left, please.'

To help you prepare for this stage, you can also read:

- *The Official DSA Guide to Driving: The essential skills*, Part 5 – Starting to drive.
- *The Official DSA Guide to Learning to Drive*, Section 2 – Moving away and stopping, Section 2 – Safe positioning, Section 2 – Mirrors – vision and use, Section 2 – Signals.

Learn *Highway Code* rules:

- 159–61 Moving off, normal driving position and use of mirrors.
- 238–45 Parking.

Starting the engine and preparing to move off

Go through the cockpit drill that you learned in Stage 2. Once you are correctly seated you can learn how to start the engine and get the feel of the clutch and accelerator pedals by practising finding the biting point.

Starting the engine

Before turning the ignition key it is important to make the safety checks of 'parking brake and neutral'. You must make sure the car is secure and that it won't move when you switch on the engine. If your car is in gear or if the handbrake is not properly set, when you switch on the engine you could move unexpectedly. Check that the parking brake is on firmly. Now check that the gear lever is in the neutral position. When you move the gear lever from side to side, it should feel quite free. If you are driving an automatic, check that the selector lever is in the P (park) or N (neutral) position.

The starter or ignition switch is normally on or near the steering column and usually combines an anti-theft steering lock. Most cars have an ignition switch with three positions. The first releases the anti-theft lock, the second position switches electrical power to the car's instruments and controls, and the third position operates the starter.
Place the ignition key in the switch and turn it to release the anti-theft steering lock. You may need to turn the steering wheel slightly whilst you do this.

Turn the key until you see some red warning lights appear on the instrument panel. The battery symbol is the ignition warning light. It only illuminates when the battery is not being charged by power from the engine. This light should go out soon after you start the car. The oil can symbol is the oil pressure warning light. It should also go out soon after you start the engine. If the red lights do not go out you should switch off and investigate. Driving with any red light displayed on the dashboard usually indicates a mechanical fault that could damage the engine or compromise your safety.

If your car runs on diesel, you may have to wait until the pre-heater warning light goes out before you can switch on the engine.

Turn the key gently to operate the starter. When the engine starts release the key. If the engine does not start you might need to gently squeeze the accelerator pedal and try again. Do not pump the pedal, as this can flood the engine and make starting even more difficult.

Most modern cars have an automatic choke. This allows more fuel to flow into the engine in cold weather to help it start. If you're in an older car, you may need to pull the choke out manually, but remember to push this in once the engine is warm.

Once started, the engine should run smoothly without you having to press the accelerator pedal. The engine is said to be running at **tick-over** speed.

To stop the engine, simply turn the key anticlockwise. If you were leaving your car you would then remove the key and set the anti-theft lock by turning the steering wheel slightly until the lock engaged.

How to find the biting point

Finding the biting point

With the engine running, press the clutch pedal fully down with your left foot and keep it pressed down. With the palm of your hand, select first gear. Then you need to **set the gas**. This means pressing the accelerator pedal lightly with your right foot until you get an even hum from the engine. You should only need to press the pedal down about the thickness of a £1 coin. Then hold your right foot steady. The engine speed should only be about half as fast again as the tick-over speed.

Raise the clutch pedal slowly by bending your ankle. Keeping your heel down will give you more support and positive clutch control. It may feel a little awkward at first, particularly if you have small feet or are in a car with high pedals. As you raise the clutch, listen for a slight drop in the engine speed. When you hear or feel this, you have found the holding point and should keep the pedal still. If you come off the clutch pedal a little further, you may see the bonnet begin to rise. When you try this exercise with the parking brake released you will find the car begins to creep forward as you lift the clutch pedal just beyond the biting point.

Push the clutch pedal down again and release the accelerator. Put the gear lever into neutral and relax your feet.

Setting the gas and holding the clutch at biting point for too long is a fault, which will waste fuel and wear the clutch unnecessarily. For this reason, as you get more experienced, you will learn to check all round before preparing the car to see that there will be a safe opportunity to move away reasonably soon.

Practise this exercise until you are confident you can find the biting point. If you let the clutch pedal up too far or too quickly the engine may stall. If this happens, go through your safety checks again (parking brake and neutral) before restarting the engine.

Assessment – starting the engine and finding the biting point

Moving off and stopping

Now you know how to prepare the car for moving off. The next step is to learn the routine for moving away safely and how to stop in a safe place without causing danger or inconvenience to others. Initially, your instructor will get you to move off in first gear, drive a little way down the road and then stop again at the kerb.

Using the clutch to manoeuvre at slow speed

Before practising moving off it is worth learning how to make the car creep forward slowly and stop it again using the clutch pedal. Choose a level road and prepare the car to move off by selecting first gear, setting the gas and finding the biting point. Keep your feet still and, when safe, release the parking brake. If you have correctly found the biting point, the car shouldn't move. If it starts to creep forward, you need to push the clutch pedal down very slightly to stop it again. Practise using the clutch pedal to move the car forward a couple of metres by raising the clutch pedal slightly and then stopping it again by dipping the clutch pedal back to the biting point. This procedure is known as clutch control and will help you to move off smoothly.

Moving off

Check in your mirrors and all round before moving away

Take an initial look to the front and in the mirrors for traffic and pedestrians and then get ready to move. Remember to look ahead and to the sides of the car. As well as other vehicles, look out for pedestrians and cyclists who are in or approaching your blind spots. What are they going to do? Might someone be about to cross the road ahead of your car?

You normally move off in first gear, so you can prepare the car by selecting the gear, setting the gas and finding the biting point as above. Hold the clutch pedal still whilst you make your safety checks.

Make sure it's safe to move off. This means applying the mirrors–signal–manoeuvre routine. Check your mirrors and look all round to make sure there is no other road user in your blind spots.

You must then decide if a signal is necessary. You will need to give a signal when moving away if it will help, warn or inform another road user of what you intend to do. Timing the signal is important. You should not signal too early, too late or for too long. There is more about signalling later in this chapter.

Give a signal if needed; then be ready to release the parking brake.

Make a final safety check over your right shoulder to make sure there is no other road user in your blind area. If safe, release the parking brake and squeeze the gas pedal a little more. The car should start to move forwards. Smoothly raise your left foot fully from the clutch pedal as you build up speed.

You will need to steer to your normal driving position – about a metre from the kerb. Turn the wheel slightly right as you move

It is very important to make a final safety check over your right shoulder before moving off

off. When you reach the correct road position, turn the wheel slightly left so that you end up steering a straight course.

It can be difficult to judge road position at first. Don't look at the kerb or the road just in front of the bonnet. Avoid staring at nearby objects; it will only make you steer towards them. Look well ahead to where you want the car to go. Plan your course well ahead by memorizing the position of any obstructions. Rely on your side vision to sense your position in the road and to judge the clearance you are leaving between your car and parked vehicles. Look ahead at the space at the side and in front of any obstruction – this will help you give enough clearance.

Stopping on the left

Except in an emergency, the routine for stopping is always the same. Select a safe place to stop and use the MSM routine.

Check your mirrors and give a left indicator signal if necessary. Steer gently towards the kerb, remembering to correct the steering as you approach so you don't bump it.

Pivot your right foot from the accelerator pedal to the footbrake. Follow the rule of progressive braking: apply light pressure at first, gradually increasing pressure as the car slows.

Except in an emergency the procedure for stopping is always the same

Just before the car stops, you will need to push the clutch pedal down fully with your left foot so that the engine doesn't stall. For a smooth stop you should be easing the pressure on the footbrake as the car comes to rest. With practice you should be able to stop parallel to the kerb with the steering set straight.

Cancel the indicator signal if you've given one; then apply the parking brake and select neutral before taking your feet from the pedals.

Changing gear

First gear provided the power you needed for pulling the weight of the car away. As you build up speed you don't need so much power, so you can change up through the higher gears. To gain confidence, practise gear changes on fairly quiet, level roads.

Changing up

First to second

The procedure for changing up from a low to a higher gear is always the same.

To change from first to second, grip the wheel a little more firmly with your right hand and, keeping your eyes on the road, cup your left hand over the gear lever ready. Push the clutch down quickly and at the same time take your foot off the gas pedal. Using gentle pressure, move the gear lever from first into second.

Second to third

Raise the clutch smoothly to the top and then press the accelerator gently to increase the engine speed. Put your left hand back on to the wheel.

Second gear will allow you to accelerate a little more until you are ready to move to third and so on. Remember to use the palm of your hand to move the gear lever.

Changing down

The procedure for changing down from a high to a lower gear will depend on whether or not the car has been slowed by braking. As a general rule, you should use the footbrake to reduce speed before changing down to the appropriate gear. However, braking need not always precede a downward

gear change. You may slow down simply by easing off the
gas as you approach a hazard.

To practise changing down the gears you will need to
move off and build your speed up until you are driving at
about 30 mph in fourth gear. Your supervisor should help by
keeping a lookout, making sure it is safe for you to carry out
each step of the exercise.

Fourth to third

Changing down whilst slowing down

Remember to grip the steering wheel a little more firmly with your right hand.
When safe, ease off the accelerator pedal and begin gentle braking so that
the car slows to about 20 mph. Keeping your eyes on the road, cup your left
hand over the gear lever ready. Push the clutch down quickly and at the
same time move the gear lever from fourth into third. Raise the clutch
pedal smoothly and return your right foot to the accelerator pedal or continue braking as appropriate. Bring your left hand back to the steering wheel.

Check the mirror to make sure it is safe and repeat the exercise, slowing
to around 10 mph and changing from third to second gear.

Block gear changes

You don't need to change down through the gears in order. It is preferable
when slowing down to brake to the desired speed and then select the
appropriate gear. Move off and build up your speed until you are travelling
at about 30 mph in fourth gear. Check the mirrors to make
sure it is safe and brake gently to slow the car down to
about 10 mph. Release the brake and change from fourth
gear into second.

If safe, build up your speed, changing up through the gears,
until you reach about 30 mph again. Keep practising until
you can carry out the exercise smoothly and confidently.

Fourth to second

Changing from third to first gear

To practise this exercise you will need to move off and build up your speed
until you are driving along at about 20 mph in third gear. If safe, brake
gently to slow the car down until you have almost stopped. Push the clutch
down, keep it down and release the brake so the car keeps rolling forwards
very slowly. Just before the car stops, change from third gear into first.

When safe, accelerate gently to build up speed again. Change up through the gears until you reach about 20 mph in third so that you can practise again. Keep practising the exercise until you feel confident.

Changing down under acceleration

Sometimes you need to select a lower gear because you anticipate needing more power. You might need to have a reserve of power to overtake another vehicle, or you could be approaching a hill and need more power for the upward slope.

Cup your left hand on the gear lever ready, push the clutch pedal down fully and at the same time keep a little pressure on the accelerator pedal. Select the appropriate lower gear, and then raise the clutch pedal smoothly as you increase pressure on the accelerator. You will practise this exercise in the next stage.

Knowing when to change gear is just as important as knowing how to change. Listening to the engine will help the driver know when to change. With experience you will learn to anticipate hazards in the road ahead and select appropriate gears for the conditions.

It is inadvisable to drive for prolonged periods with your left foot resting on the clutch pedal. Try to get into the good habit of placing your left foot on the floor away from the clutch pedal after each gear change.

Stopping smoothly at a fixed point

To practise this exercise you must find a fairly straight, quiet road with plenty of distinctive features such as telegraph poles or trees. The object will be to stop with your front bumper level with one of these. You will need lots of practice so that you can consistently bring the car to a smooth stop at the required place.

When safe, move off and build up your speed to about 25–30 mph with third or fourth gear selected. Your supervisor should look ahead and select your stopping place. Check your mirrors and, when safe, cover the brake. This will have a slight braking effect as the engine begins to slow down. Use this to help you judge how much braking pressure you will need. To begin with, squeeze the brake very gently. Gradually press it harder until you appear to be stopping short of the required position.

Gradually ease the braking pressure and push the clutch down. This will allow the car to roll up to the stopping point. Select first gear ready for moving away.

As the car comes to a rest with the front almost level with the stopping point, set the gas and find the biting point ready to move the car off again.

Notes:

Notes:

Notes:

Assessment – moving off, changing gear and stopping

Choosing a safe place to stop

When stopping at the kerb, choose a safe place, not too close to a junction or bend or near to the brow of a hill, for example. You should also try not to inconvenience other road users, for example by parking too close to, or across, an entrance to property or a driveway.

You also need to think about what is on the opposite side of the road and, if you can, avoid parking opposite a junction or another stationary vehicle or obstruction.

Find a straight part of the road and, putting the mirrors–signal–manoeuvre routine into practice, stop as close to the kerb as you can without touching it. Of course, you must obey any parking or waiting restrictions

Look out for signs and road markings when choosing a safe place to stop

Parking your car in a unsafe place can cause danger by forcing others on to the wrong side of the road when they can't see approaching traffic and approaching drivers can't see them

in force at the time and place you are stopping. Take heed of road signs and markings.

More about signalling

Giving appropriate signals at the correct time and place and correctly interpreting the signals of other road users are important for the safety and convenience of all road users.

Purpose of signals

Signals are used to let other road users know what you intend to do or to warn them of your presence. Signals give advance warning to other road users that you intend to perform a manoeuvre. Remember that your signals are not instructions to other road users and do not give you the right or make it safe to perform your planned manoeuvre.

When to signal

Signal timing is important. Your signals must be given in good time before your manoeuvre and for long enough for their meaning to be clear to other road users. Your signals must not be given too soon or another road user could be confused. Although you should normally follow the MSM routine, there are occasions when the signal may need to be delayed, for example when there are several side roads close together. Take particular care when intending to stop on the left beyond a side road on the left. Signalling too soon may lead an emerging driver to assume you are going to turn.

How to signal

You should normally give signals by direction indicators and/or brake lights. Your signals must be readily recognized by other road users. For this reason, you should only use those signals shown in *The Highway Code*.

Before giving a signal you should ask yourself whether it is necessary, when it should be given and when it will be safe to make your move. You can only answer these questions properly by making proper use of the driving mirrors. Remember the routine: mirrors–signal–manoeuvre.

Signals by indicator

These can be given when intending to turn left or right, change lane, overtake or stop at the side of the road and will give warning to traffic ahead and behind, providing that their view of your vehicle is not obscured.

Brake light signals

These illuminate when you have applied a little pressure to the footbrake and warn following traffic of your intention to slow down or stop. Early and progressive braking is important to give following drivers time to react.

Signals are normally given by indicators and/or brake lights

Signals by arm

Arm signals can be given when mechanical signals are not used or have failed and when necessary to reinforce direction indicator and stop light signals. You should not as a routine give both arm and mechanical signals, but there are circumstances where it could be useful to do so, for example when you are the lead vehicle on approach to a zebra crossing.

Unnecessary use of signals

There are good reasons for not giving signals when to do so would not help another road user. Apart from unnecessary wear and tear on your vehicle, you could cause confusion.

There are times when you may need to use an arm signal

When deciding whether a signal is necessary, think about how close you are to junctions and bends, anticipating that another road user could appear just as you are about to make a manoeuvre.

In traffic queues, ask yourself whether it's necessary to keep an indicator signal flashing.

Remember to cancel direction indicators when your manoeuvre is complete – they may not always cancel themselves.

It isn't usually necessary to signal to pass parked vehicles. Take up position in good time to maintain a steady course.

You should not signal carelessly, should not mislead others by giving the wrong signal and should never wave a pedestrian across a road.

Warning others of your presence

Flashing headlights are a warning of presence

Flashing headlights and sounding the horn warn other road users of your presence rather than of your intentions. The flashing of headlamps by another driver should not be taken as an invitation for you to proceed. If you see another vehicle flashing headlights you must decide on whether it is safe for you to proceed, and be sure of the other driver's intentions.

The horn is usually operated by a stalk control or a push-switch on the steering wheel. You must NOT sound the horn in a moving vehicle in a built-up area between 11.30 pm and 7.00 am. You must NOT sound your horn in a stationary vehicle unless in danger from another vehicle that is moving nearby. Be considerate; using the horn inappropriately can cause danger or alarm, particularly when there are pedestrians, cyclists or animals nearby. Your instructor will show you how to operate the horn in your vehicle.

Hazard warning lights

Don't use hazard warning lights to excuse inconsiderate or illegal parking

These are activated by the switch in the cockpit and cause the indicator lights on both sides of the car to flash at the same time. They should only be used to inform other road users that you are temporarily blocking the free flow of traffic. You must not use hazard warning lights as an excuse for illegal or inconsiderate parking. They should not be used when the vehicle is moving except briefly on fast roads such as motorways if you have to slow suddenly for an accident or traffic queue ahead.

Reversing lights

Reversing light signals warn other road users of your intention to reverse. White reversing lights at the back of your car are activated whenever you select reverse gear. This is particularly important for parking in reverse gear on busier roads. Selecting reverse gear promptly will help other road users anticipate your intention.

Exercises

These exercises will help you gain confidence with steering.

Exercise 3.1 – Anticipating when to turn the wheel

Find a quiet road with some sharp bends.

When approaching left bends, move your left hand towards the top of the wheel ready to pull it down to steer round the curve in the road.

When approaching right bends, move your right hand towards the top of the wheel ready to pull it down to steer round the curve in the road.

Exercise 3.2 – Steering with one hand

Although you should keep both hands on the wheel as much as possible, there are times when you need to change gear or operate the lights, wipers and other controls.

Find a straight, quiet road where you can steer with one hand while you practise using these controls. You can also practise opening and closing the windows.

Exercise 3.3 – Giving arm signals

Practise giving arm signals for left and right turns and for slowing down.

Exercise 3.4 – When to check the instruments

The instruments help to keep you informed of the condition of your car. Ignoring warning lights can result in breakdowns or serious damage.

When checking them, look well ahead and glance quickly at one instrument at a time. Only do this when there is nothing much happening on the road and you can spare the time.

You should stop and get help: if the brake warning light comes on; if the temperature gauge shows the engine is overheating; or if the oil pressure is low.

Find out from your car's handbook what all of the symbols on the dashboard mean.

Checkpoint 3

1   Before starting the engine you should ensure that:
    Choose two answers
    a. the parking brake is applied
    b. you have selected first gear
    c. the gear lever is in neutral
    d. the hazard lights are on

2   Starting the engine with the car in gear could:
    Choose one answer
    a. waste fuel
    b. damage the gearbox
    c. cause the car to move unexpectedly
    d. ruin the starter motor

3   You are about to start the engine and see this light on the instrument
    panel. You should:

    Choose one answer
    a. switch off immediately
    b. check you have enough petrol for your journey
    c. wait for the light to go out before operating the starter
    d. start the engine promptly before the light goes out

4   After starting the engine you see that this warning light doesn't go out. You should:

Choose one answer

a.   drive to the nearest service station for immediate help
b.   report the fault when your car goes for its next service
c.   switch off the engine and investigate
d.   drive to a fuel station and pick up some oil

5   Before moving off from the left, you must always:
Choose three answers

a.   check the interior mirror
b.   check the exterior mirrors
c.   select first gear
d.   look over your right shoulder
e.   give a signal

6   For moving off you should: *Choose two answers*

a.   always use first gear
b.   normally use first gear
c.   use second gear for some down slopes
d.   never use second gear

7   When preparing to change gear you should: *Choose two answers*

a.   look at the gear lever
b.   put your hand to the gear lever in readiness
c.   grip the steering wheel more firmly with your right hand
d.   move your right hand to the top of the steering wheel

8   To move the gear lever smoothly you should: *Choose one answer*

a.   'palm' your hand towards the position of the gear you need
b.   grip the lever as tightly as you can
c.   push the lever as quickly as you can
d.   allow the clutch pedal to come up during the gear change

9 To steer accurately you should look:

Choose one answer

a. well ahead at where you want the car to go
b. towards the kerb to help guide you
c. at the central white line
d. at the road surface just ahead of the bonnet

10 When driving along a straight road you should position the car:

Choose one answer

a. about a metre away from the kerb
b. as close to the kerb as you can
c. about a metre from the centre line
d. as close to the centre line as you can

11 Parking near bends and hill crests:

Choose three answers

a. is inconsiderate
b. is dangerous
c. puts others at risk
d. is only advisable on multi-lane roads
e. is fine if you use your hazard lights

12 You are looking for a place to park and see this road marking. You should:

Choose one answer

a. drive on because no parking is allowed
b. check for nearby signs showing when parking restrictions are in force
c. park on the lines and switch on your hazard lights
d. park on the lines and look for the signs showing when restrictions are in force

13 Red lines at the edge of a road indicate:

Choose one answer

    a. cycle lanes
    b. that parking is allowed
    c. that both parking and loading restrictions are in force
    d. that you are in a congestion charging zone

14 To stop smoothly and accurately at the left kerb, you should:
Choose two answers

    a. brake gently and early
    b. put the clutch pedal down as soon as you start braking
    c. look towards the kerb
    d. ease the pressure on the footbrake just as you are stopping

15 Before leaving your car, you should always:
Choose two answers

    a. apply the parking brake
    b. put on your parking lights
    c. switch off the engine
    d. switch on the hazard lights

16 If you park near junctions, you will:
Choose three answers

    a. make other drivers' observations more difficult
    b. make it difficult for pedestrians to cross the road
    c. cause danger and inconvenience
    d. make it easier for you to move off again

17 Hazard warning lights: *Choose one answer*

    a.   must never be used when the vehicle is moving

    b.   should only be used on moving vehicles

    c.   can be used when broken down and temporarily obstructing traffic

    d.   can be used to excuse poor parking

18 You see the driver ahead giving this signal and should expect the vehicle to:

Choose one answer

    a.   slow down

    b.   turn left

    c.   turn right

    d.   stop

19 An approaching driver flashes his or her headlights. You should take this to mean: *Choose one answer*

    a.   it is safe to proceed

    b.   you need to stop

    c.   a warning of presence

    d.   a fault with your car

20 You see white lights illuminated at the back of a stationary vehicle ahead. This means: *Choose one answer*

    a.   the vehicle is parked

    b.   the driver has left the vehicle unattended

    c.   the driver is intending to reverse

    d.   it is safe to pass the stationary vehicle

You will find the answers on page 423.

Scores:	First try	Second try	Third try

Record your scores in Appendix 2 (page 426).

Stage 4
Learning to plan ahead and gaining more control

Up to now your driving instructor will have been guiding you through everything you needed to do. This should have helped you 'get things right first time' and to build up your confidence.

So far during your driving lessons, your ADI will have been checking all around to make sure that everything you do is safe and is not affecting others. When you are practising privately, your supervisor should be doing the same.

In this stage you will learn to take more responsibility for safety by planning your approach to hazards and keeping a safe distance from other vehicles and road users around you. You will gain more confidence by learning how to control the car on hills and how to be able to stop the car quickly and safely in an emergency.

To help you prepare for this stage, you can also:

- Revise *The Official DSA Guide to Driving: The essential skills*, Part 5 – Starting to drive.

- Read *The Official DSA Guide to Learning to Drive*, Section 2 – Anticipation and planning, Section 2 – Use of speed, Section 2 – Other traffic.

Before going out to practise, read the section of *The Highway Code* dealing with traffic signs and signals, and learn the *Highway Code* rules:

- 103–12 Signals.
- 117–22 Braking.
- 126 Stopping distances.

Taking responsibility

As your car control skills improve, your instructor or supervisor will be encouraging you to be more aware of what else is happening around you so that you can start dealing with hazards.

In driving terms, a hazard is any road feature or situation that could cause you to change your road speed or position. A hazard is therefore any situation in which there may be a danger to yourself or any other road user, such as:

- road features, for example bends, junctions and hills;
- temporary features, such as parked vehicles and road works;
- moving hazards: pedestrians, cyclists and drivers;
- surface conditions: surface type and weather conditions that affect grip and stability.

The hazard routine – MSPSL

You already know this routine as mirrors–signal–manoeuvre! A manoeuvre is any change in position or speed, so we expand the MSM routine to:

Mirrors
Check the position and speed of following traffic in good time!
Just looking is NOT enough; act sensibly on what you see!

Signal
Ask yourself 'Will a signal help another road user?'
If you need a signal, give it in good time.

Position
If necessary, steer to a new course or road position.
Position in good time so that others can anticipate what you intend to do.

Speed
Slowing down, ease off the accelerator and/or brake. If you need to speed up, accelerate smoothly.
If necessary, change gear for greater control.

Look
Look well ahead. **Assess** the situation. **Decide** on what you need to do. **Act** promptly on your decision to wait or proceed.

The MPSL routine

You will use the MSPSL routine very often as you drive and adapt to changes going on around you. You must decide whether signals, repositioning and speed changes are necessary for each hazard and may need to repeat the routine as each situation develops or as new hazards arise.

Get into the habit of beginning the routine early when approaching bends, junctions and other hazards such as obstructions in the road. When you look in the mirrors, try to judge the speed and position of vehicles behind. In the early stages, your instructor/supervisor should help you to judge whether your manoeuvre will be safe. Decide whether a signal will help to warn or inform others about your actions. Allow time for them to see and respond to your signals.

Positioning your car early helps to confirm your signals and intentions. The correct position provides you with the best view and safety margins. Others can see you, and you can see them, so your view of any possible danger is improved. Try to get your car into position well before you reach a turn or other hazard. This will cause the least inconvenience to the flow of traffic.

Approach junctions and other hazards slowly enough to look for a safe opportunity to proceed. To do this, you will need to slow down before reaching the junction, giving you time to select an appropriate gear ready to accelerate away.

Remember, the brakes are for slowing and the gears for going. Slow down before changing down. If you need to change gear, do it as you finish braking or after you have released the footbrake.

Approaching hazards too fast will result in frequent and unnecessary stops because you won't have time to look properly on the approach. Start looking early as you approach a junction. Make sure you can see properly before deciding to go forward. Give yourself time!

The MSPSL routine is crucial to **defensive driving**. This means:

- putting safety first;
- always taking effective observation;
- planning ahead and anticipating the actions of other road users;
- not relying on other road users to do the right thing;
- driving responsibly and carefully;
- driving with courtesy and consideration for others.

Defensive driving involves more than control of the car; it involves keeping control of your own feelings and being patient with others on the road. You must not drive in such a way as to give offence to other road users or provoke a hostile response. Think of the risks to yourself of letting situations get out of control.

Safety margins

Driving too quickly for the conditions and driving too close to a vehicle ahead are major causes of road accidents. Avoiding these faults is simply a matter of applying common sense and realizing your own and your vehicle's limitations.

The Highway Code says that you should never drive so fast that you can't stop in the distance you can see to be clear ahead. So what factors affect your stopping distance and how can you judge it?

The stopping distance is the distance travelled between seeing a hazard and stopping the car and is made up of **thinking** and **braking** distances. The diagram shows minimum thinking and braking distances and how these compare to car lengths for an average-sized car.

20 mph   6m + 6m = 12m

30 mph   9m + 14m = 23m

40 mph   12m + 24m = 36m

50 mph   15m + 38m = 53m

60 mph   18m + 55m = 73m

70 mph   21m + 75m = 96m
Thinking Distance   *Braking Distance*

Your overall stopping distance is made up of 'thinking' and 'braking' distances

Your thinking distance is the time taken between seeing the hazard and pressing the footbrake. It usually takes just a little over half a second (the time it takes to check your mirrors) for a driver to react to a hazard ahead, and in this time your car will travel about 3 metres per 10 mph of speed.

Braking distance depends on the size and weight of your vehicle and is proportional to the square of road speed. The stopping distances shown are the minimum possible for an alert driver on a level road with good brakes and tyres. Your overall stopping distance will be affected by:

- your health and concentration (thinking distance);
- the condition of your vehicle (brakes, steering and suspension);
- tyres (type, condition and pressure);
- the size and weight of your vehicle and the load it is carrying;
- the gradient of the road – it will take longer to stop going downhill;
- the type and evenness of the road surface;
- the weather conditions – if it is wet your tyres have less grip on the road surface and you need to allow twice the distance. It can take up to 10 times longer to stop on ice!

It is essential that as a driver you can judge a safe **separation distance** between yourself and the vehicle ahead. The only safe gap is your overall stopping distance; anything less is a risk. However, in heavy traffic it may not be practicable without wasting valuable road space. Therefore your separation distance should NEVER be less than your thinking distance, and much more in poor conditions.

A reasonable rule to apply is a gap of about 1 metre for each mile per hour of speed for good conditions. You can estimate the distance by keeping a two-second time gap from the vehicle ahead.

To judge your separation distance from the vehicle ahead, note when it passes a fixed feature such as a road sign or marking ahead. Count two seconds by saying to yourself either 'One thousand and one, one thousand and two' or 'Only a fool breaks the two-second rule.'

After 1 second

If you reach the fixed feature before the two seconds are up, you are too close and should drop back. Remember to allow at least twice the distance, a four-second time gap, in poor weather conditions when the road surface is wet.

After 2 seconds

The 'two second' rule

Too close!

Keep well back so you can see clearly ahead

By following other vehicles at a safe distance you can help avoid accidents with vehicles ahead and behind.

Stay even further back from large or slow-moving vehicles. This improves your view of the road and of traffic ahead and helps you to anticipate the actions of the driver in front. You get more time to respond.

When other drivers are following you too closely, drop even further back from the vehicle ahead. This gives you more breathing space and extra time to brake gently. In turn this gives the drivers behind more time to respond.

Passing obstructions

Give adequate clearance! What if a car door opens?

The less clearance you can give, the slower you need to go

As well as keeping a safe distance when you are following other vehicles, you need to keep clear of parked cars and other obstructions.

When driving along you would normally keep about a metre from the left kerb. When passing parked cars you need to allow the same clearance in case a car door opens or someone steps out. Look well ahead and steer out into position early so you can follow a smooth line past parked cars.

If the road is too narrow or you can't give a metre clearance because of approaching traffic, you need to slow down. The closer you need to get, the slower you should go. As a guide, allow a minimum of a third of a metre clearance for every 10 miles an hour of speed.

Your instructor or supervisor will help you judge separation distances and clearance as you gain driving experience.

How to follow and pass cyclists safely

Stay well back from cyclists until you can give them at least 2 metres clearance without endangering oncoming drivers. Following in this position makes passing safer. Remember that cyclists can wobble or move sideways without warning to avoid drain covers and so on. Think of the consequences if a cyclist fell off as you were passing. Allow enough space for this to happen without you running over them.

If you must overtake with less clearance, then slow right down.

Notes:

Notes:

Notes:

Assessment – allowing clearance to other vehicles

Dealing with hills

Facing uphill, your vehicle will naturally tend to roll backwards unless you stop it from doing so by means of the brakes or use of **clutch control**. Over-anxiety about rolling back can be a major cause of loss of control on uphill junctions, and it is a good idea to learn to control the car on hills fairly early in your course of lessons. The following exercises should give you confidence with uphill starts.

Exercises

Exercise 4.1 – Using the clutch to hold the car on an uphill slope

For this exercise you need to practise on a fairly quiet road with a slight uphill slope. You need plenty of space ahead and behind.

With the engine running, select first gear, set the gas and find the biting point. You will need to set a little more gas than you would for a level road. If there are no other road users nearby, release the parking brake. Keep your feet still and hold the car stationary for a few seconds.

If the car moves forwards, press the clutch down a little. If it rolls back, keep calm and raise the clutch pedal slightly. When the car is still, apply the parking brake, push the clutch pedal down as you come off the gas, select neutral and rest your feet. Practice until you are confident you can use clutch control to hold the car still with the parking brake released.

Exercise 4.2 – Regaining control when rolling backwards

Keep tight control of the clutch

This exercise should help to increase your confidence by showing how easy it is to regain control and stop the car rolling. Make sure the road behind is clear for some way back.

Follow the procedure in Exercise 4.1 so that the car is still; then push the clutch down slightly until the car starts rolling backwards. To regain control, raise the clutch smoothly until you can feel the car stopping.

It is important to control the clutch very gently. If you let the pedal up too far or too quickly it may stall the engine or cause the car to jump forwards. At junctions this could be more dangerous than rolling back a little. Keep tight control of the clutch.

Exercise 4.3 – Creeping forwards on an uphill slope

Follow the procedure in Exercise 4.1 so that the car is still. Gently raise the clutch pedal a little so that the car begins to move forwards. You may need to add a little more gas as you move. Move forwards 2 or 3 metres; then stop again by dipping the clutch pedal back down to the biting point. If you push the clutch pedal down too far the car will roll back, but you already know how to stop that happening!

Practising Exercises 4.1 to 4.3 on steeper gradients will give you the confidence you need to deal with uphill slopes at junctions.

Moving off uphill

Follow the routine for moving off on a level road that you practised in Stage 3. Remember to check the 'blind areas' before moving off. You will need to allow for a bigger gap in the traffic to move into, because it will take you longer to build up speed going uphill. You may also need to press the accelerator

pedal a little more than for a level road. If the car jerks, you need to let the clutch up more slowly or press the accelerator a little more. If the engine roars, use less pressure on the accelerator or let the clutch up a little further.

The engine has more work to do when driving uphill. This means you will have to accelerate for longer in the lower gears and make upward gear changes promptly so that the car doesn't slow excessively when you push the clutch pedal down.

Moving off downhill

It is easier to move off downhill, because the weight of the car will help move it forward. To practise, park on a quiet road facing downhill. Prepare the car by selecting first gear, or second if on a steep slope. Apply the footbrake to hold the car and release the parking brake. Raise the clutch to just below the biting point. You will have to 'feel' for this, as the change in the engine note will be less noticeable. Use the MSM routine; complete your safety checks and signal if necessary. Ease off the footbrake to let the car roll forwards. Raise the clutch pedal smoothly as the car begins to move and accelerate when safe.

When moving off downhill there are times, such as in heavy traffic, at junctions, or when moving out from behind parked vehicles, when you will need to restrain the speed and move off very slowly. To do this you must keep the clutch just below the biting point and use the footbrake to prevent the car rolling away too quickly.

Practise your clutch control on level roads and on uphill and downhill slopes.

Assessment – clutch control and hill starts

More about hills

Now that you know how to move off on a gradient it is time to practise dealing with hills as you drive. A hill is a hazard, so make use of the MSPSL routine described on page 64. Look for road signs that may tell you how steep the slope is.

Going uphill

On approach, check your mirrors, assess the slope and look out for slow-moving and heavy vehicles. Decide whether you may need to change to a lower gear. If so, it is best to do so before you start to climb.

Remember, in comparison with driving on a level road:

- it is more difficult to increase or maintain your speed;
- your brakes will slow the vehicle sooner;
- you can brake later to stop the car;
- pressing the clutch down will cause your car to slow more;
- releasing the gas pedal will cause your car to slow more;
- you will need to make gear changes more promptly to avoid the car slowing too much.

On the hill, increase your separation distance. The vehicle ahead could slow suddenly. Holding back may mean that you don't have to stop every time the traffic ahead does so.

Going downhill

On approach, check your mirrors, assess the slope and consider changing to a lower gear. In a lower gear the engine will help control the speed of the car and you will not have to rely so heavily on the brakes.

Remember, in comparison with driving on a level road:

- it is more difficult for the engine to hold the car back;
- your brakes will take longer to slow the vehicle;
- you must brake sooner to stop the car;
- pressing the clutch down will cause your car to gather speed;
- releasing the gas pedal will cause your car to slow less;
- you will need to make gear changes more promptly to avoid the car building up too much speed.

On the hill, increase your separation distance. The vehicle ahead could slow suddenly. Holding back will give you more time to stop, which will give more warning to traffic following you.

Hazards on hills

Approaching junctions and other hazards on a hill requires extra care. Use the MSPSL routine in good time; position to get the best view without baulking other traffic.

At the brow of a hill, remember that your view of the road ahead will be restricted. Keep well to the left and remember to ease off the gas, as your engine will have less work to do. Beware of oncoming traffic; someone could be trying to overtake.

Parking is more difficult on a slope; you will need more room to manoeuvre. You should leave a bigger gap so that others can manoeuvre safely around you.

Facing uphill:

- With a kerb, leave your front wheels pointing to the right.
- Without a kerb, leave your front wheels pointing to the left.
- Make sure the parking brake is firmly applied.
- Leave your vehicle in first gear (or, in automatic transmission, select park).

Facing downhill:

- With or without a kerb, leave your front wheels pointing to the left.
- Make sure the handbrake is applied.
- Leave your vehicle in reverse gear (or, in automatic transmission, select park).

How to stop in an emergency

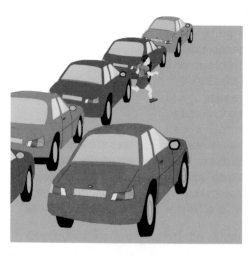

Quick reactions are important in an emergency

Anticipation and good forward planning help you to avoid emergencies. The earlier you spot any possible danger, the sooner you can act on it. Taking early precautions, such as slowing down, will make it less likely that you need to brake hard at the last moment. Even experienced drivers sometimes find themselves having to stop quickly because something unexpected happens, for example a child running into the road.

In a real emergency it is vital that you react quickly, and you won't have time to check the mirrors before braking. Make sure you are using them often as you drive along so that you are aware of what is happening behind.

Make sure you know how to stop quickly before you go into heavy traffic. You can practise the emergency stop on quiet, fairly wide and straight roads.

Before you move away, your instructor or supervisor will demonstrate a signal to be given for the stop and, after you move away to practise, will ensure there are no other road users about before giving it.

As soon as you see the danger you need to brake firmly. Follow the rule of progressive braking, but, unlike the case in a normal stop, you will not need to ease off the footbrake as the vehicle stops.

Exercises

Exercise 4.4 – Stopping promptly

Your first attempts at stopping promptly should be carried out at fairly low speeds. Just practise stopping with a little more than the pressure needed for a normal stop.

When your instructor gives the signal to stop, respond at once and pivot quickly to the footbrake. Leave the clutch pedal alone until just before stopping. This aids braking and also provides the vehicle with more stability. If you leave the clutch pedal alone until the last moment, the engine will help the car to slow down. You will also reduce the chances of skidding, as the road wheels are less likely to lock if they are still being 'driven' by the engine.

The braking force will throw extra weight to the front wheels and you will find the car more difficult to steer

Whilst braking, keep both hands firmly on the steering wheel. You may need to steer to avoid injuring another road user.

After coming to a complete stop, apply the parking brake. Remember, you were in your normal driving position on the road before you stopped. Before moving away again, check all around the car that it is safe by looking back over both your right and left shoulders.

Exercise 4.5 – Stopping quickly as in an emergency

Repeat Exercise 4.4, gradually increasing the speed and the braking pressure until you can stop the car quickly and without skidding or swerving. It may feel as if your car travelled a long way before coming to a stop. If you do cause a skid, use the skid recovery method described in the next section to regain control.

Skidding

Always be aware of road surface conditions

Drivers cause skids; they don't just happen. Keep your car in good mechanical order, drive safely and adjust to the conditions when driving. Always be aware of the road surface; if the surface is loose, wet or icy, your tyres will have less grip. Road signs might tell you that the surface ahead is poor, but you can't rely on road signs to tell you about the weather!

Skids happen when you try to change speed (accelerating or braking) or direction so suddenly that the tyres lose their grip with the road. Uncontrolled braking is one of the main driver faults that result in skidding.

The brakes of a car are most effective when the wheels are almost locked. When braking, the weight of the car is thrown forward, reducing the grip of the rear wheels and making them more likely to lock. This can cause a rear-wheel skid, and the rear of the car may swing round as it tries to catch up with the front.

To recover from the skid, remove the cause – release the footbrake to allow the wheels to turn again, and then reapply the brake if necessary, with less pressure. If the rear of the car slides, you will need to steer when you have released the footbrake. Steer to straighten the car. Take care, because over-correction can lead to a skid in the opposite direction.

Very harsh braking, even on a dry road, can cause a four-wheel skid and loss of all control of steering and braking.

Skids caused by acceleration

Sudden or harsh acceleration can cause wheel spin to the front or rear wheels depending on whether engine power is transmitted to the front (front-wheel drive) or rear (rear-wheel drive).

To recover from the skid, remove the cause – release the accelerator to allow the wheels to grip the road again. If the car slides sideways do not try to steer until some grip has been regained.

Notes:

Notes:

Notes:

Assessment – stopping promptly and avoiding skids

Planning ahead to avoid danger

Knowing how to stop in an emergency doesn't excuse you from planning sensibly to avoid danger and conflict with others.

Watch out for signals given by the drivers of vehicles in front, and anticipate their actions. When a signal is flashing, the driver is almost sure to slow down for the manoeuvre. Expect this and carry out your MSPSL routine.

If the vehicle ahead is turning right, position your car well to the left and decide whether or not there is room to pass on the nearside. Remember, the other driver may have to wait for oncoming traffic. Be prepared to slow down and wait if the space is too small to get through safely.

If the driver in front is signalling left, the vehicle may be either stopping or turning. Move into an overtaking position, but hold well back, as drivers waiting in the side road may emerge.

Even when you are sure the driver in front is turning, he or she may still have to stop and wait if the side road is blocked or if there are any pedestrians crossing. Keep well back.

Checkpoint 4

1 At 30 mph your thinking distance is:
Choose one answer

    a.   9 m (30 ft)
    b.   14 m (45 ft)
    c.   18 m (60 ft)
    d.   21 m (70 ft)

2 At 30 mph your overall stopping distance is:
Choose one answer

    a.   9 m (30 ft)
    b.   14 m (45 ft)
    c.   18 m (60 ft)
    d.   23 m (75 ft)

3 At 70 mph your overall stopping distance is:
Choose one answer

    a.   38 m (125 ft)
    b.   53 m (175 ft)
    c.   75 m (245 ft)
    d.   96 m (315 ft)

4   Signs giving orders are normally:
Choose one answer

a.   rectangular
b.   triangular
c.   circular
d.   hexagonal

5   Compared to a dry road, on a wet road the gap between you and
the vehicle ahead should:
Choose one answer

a.   remain the same
b.   be halved
c.   be at least doubled
d.   be two seconds

6   In an emergency you should:
Choose one answer

a.   brake gently and quickly
b.   brake immediately
c.   brake harshly and gradually
d.   try to lock the wheels

7   An anti-lock braking system (ABS):
Choose two answers

a.   will always prevent skidding
b.   will help maintain steering control during hard braking
c.   needs you to pump the brake for it to work
d.   will not always prevent skidding

8 A solid white line across the end of a road means you must:

Choose one answer

a. stop at the line
b. not park in that road
c. go if the way is clear
d. apply the parking brake

9 Double broken lines across the end of a road mean:

Choose one answer

a. stop before you reach the line
b. stop at the line
c. give way to traffic in the major road
d. go if the way is clear

10 To stop in the shortest possible distance, you should brake:
Choose one answer

a. as hard as you can with the clutch down
b. until the wheels lock up
c. firmly and push the clutch down just before you stop
d. gently and then as hard as possible

11 Braking in an emergency, you should:
Choose two answers

    a. keep both hands on the wheel
    b. brake hard and change down a gear
    c. brake but do not touch the clutch
    d. brake firmly and push the clutch down at the last moment

12 Areas of white diagonal stripes on the road are used to:

Choose two answers

    a. separate opposing streams of traffic
    b. help speed up the traffic flow
    c. protect right-turning traffic
    d. show you where to position to turn right

13 You should drive at a speed:
Choose two answers

    a. dictated by the road signs
    b. such that you can stop in the distance you can see is clear
    c. dictated by the road conditions
    d. to keep up with the other drivers

14 Coasting is travelling in neutral or with the clutch down. It means:
Choose two answers

    a. engine braking is eliminated
    b. your speed downhill can increase quickly
    c. you will achieve more fuel economy
    d. the appropriate gear may be more difficult to select

15 Skids may be caused by the driver:
Choose three answers

    a. planning too far ahead
    b. driving too fast for the conditions
    c. steering too harshly
    d. accelerating too harshly
    e. driving too slowly for the conditions

16 The correct routine for approaching hazards is:
Choose one answer

  a. MPSL
  b. MSPSL
  c. MSMPL
  d. MSLPS

17 This sign means:

Choose one answer

  a. no right turn
  b. keep right
  c. turn right ahead
  d. one-way street ahead

18 If you saw this sign you would:

Choose two answers

  a. expect a steep downhill gradient ahead
  b. anticipate changing to a lower gear to give more power
  c. prepare for an uphill gradient
  d. consider selecting a lower gear for speed control

19 You are the driver of the red car shown.
The broken white centre line means:

Choose one answer

a. it is safe to overtake
b. there are no hazards ahead
c. you may park at certain times
d. you may cross the line only if safe

20 You see this sign ahead and should:

Choose two answers

a. ignore it because it is intended for cyclists
b. check your mirrors
c. anticipate cyclists ahead
d. expect cyclists to keep to their path

You will find the answers on page 424.

Scores: First try   Second try   Third try

Record your scores in Appendix 2 (page 426).

Stage 5
Road positioning and turning corners

By now you will have had to negotiate some junctions with guidance from your instructor. In this stage you will learn how to correctly approach and turn bends and junctions, putting the MSPSL routine into practice.

Practise in a quiet area with fairly wide roads, rounded corners and not too many parked cars. When you can cope confidently with the simpler junctions, progress to those with sharper corners and roads with a little more traffic.

It is useful at this stage to get some practice driving in and out of built-up areas so that you get used to changes in road and traffic conditions. You will need to adhere to different speed limits, so make sure you know the relevant road signs and speed limit rules from *The Highway Code*. Knowing the speed limits for different types of vehicle will help you anticipate possible problems ahead.

Don't attempt too much too soon. If things go wrong, it will shatter your confidence. Your supervisor must be sure you can cope before taking you on very busy roads, to junctions on hills and to those where your view is restricted.

To help you prepare for this stage, you can also read:

- *The Official DSA Guide to Driving: The essential skills*, Part 7 – On the road, and Part 8 – Junctions.

- *The Official DSA Guide to Learning to Drive*, Section 2 – Safe positioning, Section 2 – Junctions.

Before going out to practise, learn/revise *Highway Code* rules:

- 124–25 Speed limits.

- 127–32 Lines and markings on the road.

- 144–47 General advice.

- 152–54 Driving in built-up areas and country roads.
- 159–61 Moving off and driving along.
- 170–72 Road junctions.
- 179–81 Turning right.
- 182–83 Turning left.

Road positioning

Unless you intend to overtake or turn right, or road markings, traffic conditions or road layout dictate otherwise, you should observe the rule of keeping well to the left, usually about a metre from the kerb. This will help the free flow of traffic and allow drivers of faster vehicles to overtake if they wish to. Don't weave in and out when passing lines of parked cars or other obstructions. Take a smooth line past a series of obstructions.

You should not drive too close to the left. This could:

- endanger or frighten pedestrians or splash them in wet weather;
- reduce your control of the car, as the surface may be uneven or littered with road hazards;
- result in you hitting the kerb and damaging your tyres;
- mislead other road users into believing you are going to turn left or stop on the left.

You should not drive too close to the middle of the road. This could:

- endanger yourself and approaching traffic;
- mislead other road users into believing you intend to turn right;
- hinder the free flow of traffic and prevent others from overtaking.

Lane discipline

Lanes are marked to guide the flow of traffic and make best use of the road space available:

- Where lanes are marked, position centrally in your lane.
- Unless road markings, road layout or traffic conditions dictate otherwise, you should normally drive in the left-hand lane.

Keep to the centre of your lane

- Where the road is wide enough for lanes but they are unmarked, think in terms of lanes and position accordingly.

You should not weave from lane to lane, straddle two lanes or lane lines, change lanes at the last minute or drive in the wrong lane for your intended route.

Judge your position by looking well ahead. With practice, positioning will become second nature and you will find yourself fitting in with other traffic without conscious effort.

Dealing with bends

Look out for warning signs that tell you there are bends ahead

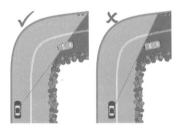

Positioning towards the left gives you a better view in a right-hand bend

Apply the MSPSL routine on approach. You will not need an indicator signal to follow a bend, but good positioning will help keep you safe and give you the best view of the road ahead.

Slow down in good time and select a lower gear if needed to give you more control. You should not be braking as you steer round a bend. For best grip, the engine should be 'under acceleration'. This doesn't mean that you should increase speed in the bend; it simply means that the engine should be pulling the car.

In a right-hand bend, position towards the left of your lane. This will:

- increase your zone of vision into the bend;
- keep you out of the path of approaching traffic;
- give you more time to deal with any other hazard in the bend.

In a left-hand bend, keep to the centre of your lane. This will keep you out of the path of approaching traffic.

Do not get too close to the left. This would severely restrict your view of the road ahead and give you little time to deal with hazards in the bend.

As you come out of a bend, check your mirrors again and make progress by building up to a speed appropriate for the road and traffic conditions.

Positioning too close to the left in a left-hand bend will restrict your view

Assessment – positioning and bends

Dealing with junctions

A junction is any point where two or more roads meet. Junctions include T-junctions, Y-junctions, crossroads, staggered junctions and roundabouts.

The key to dealing with all junctions safely is to apply the MSPSL routine. Your instructor or supervisor should give you plenty of time to plan your approach. Road signs and markings, traffic flow joining, leaving or crossing the road, a change in the building line, and gaps in lines of parked vehicles will all help you locate a junction ahead.

Assess the junction. The more information you have on approach, the better prepared you will be to make your turn.

Look for the speed, type and density of traffic on the road you are joining, the width and gradient of the road and the presence of other road users, particularly pedestrians. Look out for other road users ahead of you in your own road and in the road you will be joining.

Turning left into a side road

Use the MSPSL routine as follows:

Turning left

- **Mirrors:** When you first see the junction you should check the mirrors to assess the speed and position of following traffic.

- **Signal:** Give a left indicator signal to let others know that you intend to turn. Timing the signal is important. If you give your signal too soon, another road user may think you intend to stop or turn into property bordering the road. If there are side roads before the junction you want, take particular care in timing your signal.

- **Position:** Your normal driving position about a metre from the kerb is correct for a left turn. If you do need to change course slightly, first check your exterior mirror in the direction you intend to move.

- **Speed:** Once in position you will need to adjust your speed. Ease off the gas pedal to begin with, but use the footbrake in good time so that following traffic has enough time to react to your stop light signals. When you are travelling slowly enough, select the appropriate gear.

- **Look:** As you are slowing down and changing gear, you should still be watching the corner for more information. Look as far into the new road as you can, and then decide whether or not it is safe to proceed. Look out for any danger from emerging traffic, or obstructions just around the corner. Be particularly careful about pedestrians.

Anticipate the point of turn when the front of your car reaches the corner. You must not turn too soon because of the danger that the rear wheels may take a short cut across the kerb. Neither should you swing out just before turning; you could move into the path of other vehicles.

Steer smoothly so that you follow the line of the corner. Once in the new road, check your mirrors again to make sure it is safe to build up speed again. Remember to check that your indicator signal has cancelled.

Turning right into a side road

The main danger when turning right is from oncoming traffic. You must normally let approaching vehicles go first. Slow down and hold back until they have passed the junction. If you are going to reach the point of turn first, stop and wait just short of it. Use the MSPSL routine on approach.

Check mirrors and give your right indicator signal in good time.

Positioning to turn right

Steer to take up a position as close to the middle of the road as is safe. This usually means positioning just left of the centre of the road and may leave room for following traffic to overtake on your left. If there are no markings to guide you, then imagine the centre line for yourself. When turning right, if there are obstructions such as parked cars on the right-hand carriageway, you will need to keep more to the left to give clearance for approaching traffic and any vehicles emerging left at the junction.

When you are travelling slowly enough, select the appropriate gear. Look as far into the new road as you can, and ahead, to decide whether or not it is safe to proceed.

Turning right

Priority

Traffic emerging from the side road should give priority to you. If you need to stop for approaching traffic, you must keep to your own side of the road. Stop in position so that the front of your car is just before the centre of the road you intend to turn into. Do not proceed until you are sure it is safe. If in doubt about going, be patient and wait. Your instructor will guide on judging whether or not it is safe to proceed.

When safe, steer smoothly so that you end up in your normal driving position in the new road. Check your mirrors again to make sure it is safe to build up speed, and make sure that your indicator signal has cancelled.

Turning right, if you can't safely cross the path of approaching traffic, wait in position on your side of the road

Point of turn

You should begin turning in good time to avoid the danger of over-steering or clipping the kerb in the new road. How soon you begin turning will depend on the widths of the roads you are leaving and entering and on what else you can see. Move up to the point of turn and make sure you can see into the new road before turning. As a guide, the front of your car should be about level with the centre of the road you are joining before you commence the turn.

Dangers when turning right

Watch out for vehicles approaching the end of the road, and avoid cutting the corner by turning too soon. This could endanger you and others by putting yourself into the path of an approaching vehicle.

Sometimes obstructions in the side road may force you to turn earlier. If this is the case, don't start your turn until approaching vehicles are clear.

Turning right, avoid cutting the corner

Pay attention when turning right where your view of oncoming traffic is limited.

Cross oncoming traffic safely when turning right. Sometimes your view ahead may be restricted near bends and hill crests. There may be an approaching vehicle just out of sight. Try not to rush across.

Before you commit yourself to the turn, stay in your position as close to the middle of the road as is safe until you can see into the new road. Go a little further forward before turning if necessary.

Pedestrians and cyclists

Give way to pedestrians crossing any road you are turning into. If a pedestrian has started crossing, you should hold back until the pedestrian is safely clear of your path. Watch out particularly for those with their back to you. They may not have seen or heard you and could walk into the road without looking. In some instances, where they are walking towards the road, it may be appropriate to sound the horn lightly.

Deal safely with vulnerable road users at junctions

It is dangerous to overtake cyclists as you approach to make a left turn. You would have to cut back in and could hit the cyclist or cause him or her to fall off. Hold back and let the cyclist clear the junction before you start to turn.

Choosing the correct gear at junctions

Anxiety about which gear to select on approach to junctions can be a distraction. Your instructor may advise that second gear is the most versatile, but this may not always be appropriate. The gear you select will depend on the safe speed for the corner. The safe speed depends on how far ahead the driver can see and the angle through which you need to turn.

A wide, gentle turn with a clear view can be taken at a higher speed than a narrow road with a restricted view, so third gear may be appropriate. You may select first gear if the angle of your turn into the new road is very sharp or your view restricted.

Whichever gear you select, remember it is safe to miss out a gear on approach. You do not need to change through the gears in order.

The gear you select on approach to a corner will depend mainly on how much you can see

Once you've selected a gear, make sure you actually use it! You must not 'coast' around the corner with the clutch down. Coasting reduces your control of both braking and steering. When making the turn, the engine should drive your car. This means that you should have enough gas set to be just pulling the car around the corner.

Notes:

Notes:

Notes:

Assessment – approaching and turning into side roads

Approaching T-junctions at the end of a road

Whilst some T-junctions on quieter roads may be unmarked, most are clearly marked as either 'Give way' or 'Stop'. Look out for signs and road markings as you come up to the end of a road to identify the type of junction.

Give way signs and markings tell you that you must give priority to traffic on the main road and stop if necessary to let it pass.

Stop signs and markings tell you that you must stop before the solid white line to assess the situation before joining the main road.

Your instructor may refer to T-junctions as either 'open' or 'closed'. At an open junction, your line of sight into the major road will be fairly clear of obstructions so that you can see other traffic. At closed junctions, the building line, fences, hedges and so on will restrict your line of sight.

At 'closed' junctions your line of sight will be restricted

Coming up to a T-junction, use the MSPSL routine you've already learned. Approach the ends of roads slowly enough to give yourself plenty of time to look into the main road. Whether the junction is open or closed, you should scan left and right as you approach it to build up a picture of the traffic flow and other hazards in the main road.

Emerging

This means leaving the minor road to join the main road. Your zone of vision will get wider as you approach the end of the road. The diagram shows that you will not be able to decide if it is safe to emerge until your eye line is level with any obstructions.

Keep a special lookout for cyclists or motorbikes travelling along close to the kerb.

When you are approaching the end of a road, watch out for others who may turn in too soon and cut the corner. Larger vehicles may need more room to turn. Be prepared to hold back for them.

Make sure you have looked both ways before moving into major roads. Be particularly careful turning left that you will not put yourself into the path of any vehicle approaching from the left. The driver may be passing an obstruction and positioned in your intended path. It is very dangerous to emerge left whilst looking right.

Parked vehicles and pedestrians standing near the junction can seriously restrict your view of traffic travelling along the main road.

At a closed T-junction, you can't make a decision to emerge until your eyes are level with the obstructions

Be prepared to hold back for traffic turning into the minor road

Check that it is clear to the left and right before emerging

If your view is restricted, 'peep and creep'

To assess the situation properly you will probably need to stop. In these situations, and at stop junctions, use clutch control to creep forward into position for the best view. Lean forward in your seat so that the front of your car doesn't need to stick out so far. A good way to remember this is 'peep and creep'.

Whatever the type of junction, you must not cause other traffic to swerve or slow down as you join the major road. Whether you are turning left or right, remember it will take you time to build up speed in the line of traffic you are joining. Turning right, you will be crossing in front of vehicles approaching from your right. Make sure you can clear their path safely.

If an approaching vehicle is signalling to turn left, wait until you are sure the driver is turning before you emerge.

Practise emerging left and right at junctions. As you gain confidence, practise emerging on uphill and downhill junctions.

At Y-junctions, position to get the best view into the major road

Turning right from different positions

At Y-junctions your view to the left can be severely restricted because of the angle at which the two roads meet. Position so that you are at or near a right angle to the major road. This will give you a wider zone of vision at the junction.

Turning right at the end of a narrow road, you will need to leave enough space for traffic turning in. You may have to keep well to the left to achieve this. You will still be following the rule of *positioning as close to the middle of the road as is safe*.

Emerging from a narrow road, leave enough room for traffic to turn in

Pedestrians at junctions

Pedestrians are very vulnerable at junctions, and you will need to anticipate their movements. Take particular care with infirm, elderly or young people. If a pedestrian has started to cross the road you are entering, you must always give way to him or her. If a pedestrian hesitates after stepping on to the road, try to establish eye contact and allow the pedestrian time to decide whether to proceed or wait. You must not wave a pedestrian to cross; you could be inviting him or her into the path of another vehicle!

When approaching T-junctions, look out for pedestrians and give way to any who may be crossing the end of the road. Be particularly careful when approaching busy shopping streets.

Give priority to pedestrians

Notes:

Notes:

Notes:

Assessment – emerging safely at junctions

Checkpoint 5

1   The correct position to take for turning left is about:
   Choose one answer

   a.   half a metre from the kerb
   b.   a metre from the kerb
   c.   a metre and a half from the kerb
   d.   2 metres from the kerb

2   The correct position for normal driving is:
   Choose one answer

   a.   as close to the kerb as possible
   b.   in the centre of your side of the road
   c.   half a metre from the kerb
   d.   about a metre from the kerb

3   If pedestrians are crossing the road you are turning into you should:
   Choose one answer

   a.   sound your horn loudly
   b.   hold back and give way to them
   c.   keep moving at the same speed
   d.   wave them across so they know what you are doing

4   Where there is a stop sign at the end of a road you:
Choose one answer

    a. needn't stop unless pedestrians are crossing
    b. need only stop if you see other traffic
    c. must stop at the line until it is safe to proceed
    d. should keep moving if the road is clear

5   Approaching a left bend you should take up position:
Choose one answer

    a. half a metre from the kerb
    b. towards the centre of the road
    c. in the centre of your lane
    d. as close to the kerb as possible

6   In a built-up area with street lights, the speed limit is usually:
Choose one answer

    a. 45 mph
    b. 40 mph
    c. 35 mph
    d. 30 mph

7   When you see a national speed limit sign on a single carriageway
road, the limit for cars is:

Choose one answer

    a. 40 mph
    b. 50 mph
    c. 60 mph
    d. 70 mph

8 You must not exceed the maximum speed limits for:
Choose two answers

   a. the type of road you are on
   b. the type of vehicle you are driving
   c. your age group
   d. the age of your vehicle

9 If you are waiting to emerge into a main road and you cannot see because of parked vehicles you should:
Choose two answers

   a. wait for several seconds and then go
   b. stop at the line and wait until you can see
   c. creep slowly forwards until you can see past the obstructions
   d. lean forward in your seat if needed to help you see

10 The main danger when turning right from a main road into a side road is:
Choose one answer

   a. following traffic
   b. oncoming traffic
   c. traffic ahead of you waiting to turn
   d. traffic emerging from the junction

11 When turning right at the end of a narrow road you should position:
Choose one answer

   a. just to the left of the white line
   b. as close to the white line as you can
   c. well over to the left
   d. about a metre from the kerb

12 The speed limit for large goods vehicles travelling in built-up areas is:
Choose one answer

   a. 20 mph
   b. 25 mph
   c. 30 mph
   d. 35 mph

13 The speed limit for cars towing trailers on single-carriageway roads outside built-up areas is:
Choose one answer

a. 35 mph
b. 40 mph
c. 45 mph
d. 50 mph

14 When turning right you should position:
Choose two answers

a. well over to the left
b. well over to the right
c. as close to the middle of the road as is safe
d. in any space marked for traffic turning

15 Before turning left you should not:
Choose two answers

a. position a metre from the kerb
b. overtake
c. swing out to the right
d. pass parked cars without signalling

16 A sign like this means:

Choose one answer

a. maximum speed 30 mph
b. no vehicles over 30 metres length
c. end of minimum speed limit
d. maximum speed for cyclists 30 mph

17 A sign like this means:

Choose one answer

a. bend to the left ahead
b. series of bends ahead
c. move left ahead
d. junction ahead

18 White reflective studs mark the: *Choose one answer*

a. left edge of the road
b. middle of the road
c. lanes for traffic
d. edge of the carriageway at lay-bys

19 You are waiting to turn right and your view ahead is restricted by a bend. You should: *Choose two answers*

a. move further forward for a better view if needed
b. turn in as slowly as possible
c. be prepared to cut the corner
d. make sure you can see into the new road before turning
e. turn in as quickly as possible

20 Approaching a side road to turn left you see a cyclist ahead and should: *Choose one answer*

a. overtake the cyclist quickly before the junction
b. sound your horn as you get close to the cyclist
c. not overtake the cyclist
d. expect the cyclist to dismount so you can pass

You will find the answers on page 424.

Scores:	First try	Second try	Third try

Record your scores in Appendix 2 (page 426).

Stage 6
Manoeuvring
at low speed

This stage explains how to carry out manoeuvring exercises at low speed. Start practising these as soon as you feel confident with your clutch control skills. By the time you reach Stage 8, you should be able to carry out all of these exercises with reasonable accuracy and safety.

In this stage you will be using reverse gear. Only reverse where it is safe, legal and convenient. Remember, when you are manoeuvring, other road users and pedestrians have priority. You must take responsibility for checking all around so that you know you will not be inconveniencing them.

Whilst practising, make sure that you will not inconvenience other road users by blocking driveways and entrances. When choosing a safe place for a manoeuvre, look out for pedestrians, particularly children playing in the road. Whilst reversing, your rear view will be limited and you may not be able to see small children behind your car. You should choose a place where other road users would not have to manoeuvre dangerously to get by. For these reasons you should choose reasonably wide and quiet roads, where visibility is good.

Avoid repeated practice of manoeuvres at the same place. You could annoy local residents, particularly at popular locations for driving school cars.

Initially, your instructor will help by keeping a lookout. When practising with others in the early stages, encourage your supervisor to help with your observations.

To help you prepare for this stage, you can also read:

- *The DSA Official Guide to Driving: The essential skills*,
  Part 9 – Manoeuvring.
- *The DSA Official Guide to Learning to Drive*, Section 2 – Turning the vehicle around, Section 2 – Reversing, Section 2 – Parking.

Before going out to practise, learn *Highway Code* rules 200–03 on reversing.

Exercises

Exercise 6.1 – Revise low-speed clutch control

Revise using the clutch to manoeuvre at slow speed, which you learned in Stage 3 (page 48), and practise again for a few minutes on a quiet road. Begin practising driving slowly forwards and then stopping again by dipping the clutch pedal down.

Keep tight control of the clutch

Exercise 6.2 – How to move out from behind a parked vehicle

When you are confident at controlling the car at low speed, you need to combine this skill with brisk steering so that you can turn the car in a restricted space. To practise, find a vehicle parked on a wide, level road and pull up about 3 metres (10 feet) behind it. You will need to control the clutch to move off more slowly than usual. Take extra observations to the front and rear before you move off, and make a final check of the blind areas before you pull out.

Consider whether you will need a signal to warn oncoming drivers, as well as any approaching from behind. Remember that it will take you longer to move out from behind another vehicle. Make allowance for this so you don't cause other traffic to slow as you move off.

Use a slipping clutch as practised in Exercise 6.1 to keep the car creeping very slowly. Turn the wheel briskly to the right as soon as the car is moving. When sure that the front of your car will clear the parked vehicle, turn it back to straighten the car. Remember to look where you want the car to go.

Keep the car moving slowly and steer briskly

When confident, try the manoeuvre starting closer to the parked vehicle as you might have to in a residential street with lots of parked cars. When you have mastered the exercise on a level road, practise on up-and-down slopes, remembering to use the footbrake to control the speed on the downhill ones.

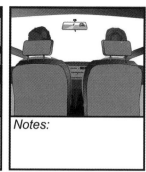

Notes:

Notes:

Notes:

Assessment – moving off at an angle

Using reverse gear

Practise on a quiet road. It is important to look where you are going.

When reversing, turn round slightly in your seat until you can see the road clearly through the back window. You may remove your seat belt for reversing if it is restricting you. Remember to put it on again before driving away.

You may place your right hand towards the top of the wheel, at the 12 o'clock position, and your left hand low on the wheel. If you find it difficult or uncomfortable to hold the wheel in this way, place your left arm on the back of your seat or the passenger seat.

When reversing you will find it helpful to steer a little sooner than seems necessary, because the back wheels don't turn. You should always turn the wheel in the direction you want the back of the car to turn. To make the car move towards the kerb, steer towards it. To make it move away from the kerb, steer away from it. It is important to move slowly so that the steering has time to take effect.

Exercises

Exercise 6.3 – How to reverse in a straight line

Parallel to the kerb

Moving away from the kerb

Moving towards the kerb

When reversing it is easier to judge whether you are moving towards the curb or away from it by looking well back down the road

Before starting this exercise, make sure you are parked parallel to the kerb with your front wheels set straight. Look back through the rear window. You should be able to see the kerb on both sides.

Select reverse gear, set the gas and find the biting point. Have a good look round just as you would for moving away.

Keep a special lookout for pedestrians before you start moving backwards.

Look well down the road to the rear as you are reversing.

Use clutch control to move slowly back, and keep checking to the front and rear for approaching traffic.

It is much easier to judge whether you are moving towards the kerb or away from it by looking well back down the road.

Looking at where the kerb intersects the back window doesn't help! There is relatively little change in what you see.

Practise reversing slowly in a straight line, and then try turning a little towards and a little away from the kerb. This will give you a feel for the steering and practice in judging where the back of the car is going.

Notes:

Notes:

Notes:

Assessment – reversing in a straight line

Exercise 6.4 – How to drive into a parking space between two vehicles

Look and plan ahead for a suitable parking space. It will need to be at least two and a half times the length of your car. Remember to put the MSM routine into practice. Slow down almost to a stop just before the space, keeping about a metre (a yard) out from the parked vehicles. Remember to go far enough forward to allow for the back wheels to cut in when you steer left.

Steer briskly into the space until your front wheel nears the kerb; then steer right to bring it into line. When you stop you should be parallel to the kerb with your front wheels set straight.

If necessary, reverse a little to leave yourself enough room to pull out again safely. Don't forget to look through the rear window when you are reversing.

Secure the car with the parking brake and select neutral. Remember to check that your indicator signal has cancelled.

If you are leaving your car, make sure you check it's clear before opening your car door – remember that approaching drivers will find it more difficult to see you if you are parked between other vehicles.

Notes:

Notes:

Notes:

Assessment – driving into a parking space

Exercise 6.5 – How to turn the car in the road

This exercise is useful if you need to turn the car round to go back the other way when there are no convenient places for reversing.

Your first attempts at this exercise should be carried out on fairly wide and level road. Make sure there are no obstructions such as trees or street lights on the pavement nearby.

Keep away from parked cars and other obstructions in the road that might make it difficult for you to see and be seen.

Turning in the road

Choose a safe, legal and convenient place

As you near the right kerb, turn the steering wheel to the left

Get the car ready for moving off in the normal manner, with the clutch slightly below the biting point. Check ahead and behind for approaching traffic. Look out for pedestrians nearby. You don't want to cause alarm or danger by driving towards them during the manoeuvre. If necessary, drive on to a safer place.

A–B: When you are sure it is clear and safe, look across the road where you intend to go. Bring the clutch pedal up to the biting point so the car begins to creep slowly forwards. As soon as you are moving, steer briskly to the right until it is in 'full lock'. Use the clutch pedal to keep the car moving slowly.

When you are about a metre from the right kerb, start turning the wheel back to the left. As you near the kerb, push the clutch down and brake to stop. You should end up near to the kerb with the front wheels pointing a little left ready for the next part of the manoeuvre. When stopped, you may need to apply the parking brake, depending on the camber (the slope of the road towards the gutter).

B–C: Select reverse gear and prepare the car for moving. Check all around. When you're sure it's safe, look over your left shoulder through the rear window. Creep slowly back, turning the wheel briskly to the left. When you have driven over the centre of the road, look over your right shoulder so that you can judge your distance from the kerb and turn the wheel briskly to the right.

You should end up near to the kerb with the front wheels pointing a little right ready for the next part of the manoeuvre

Be ready to brake if the car rolls down the camber. Keep turning the wheel to the right and stop just before reaching the kerb. Apply the parking brake if needed to stop the car rolling.

C–D: Select first gear and get ready to move. Check all around for others. When you are sure it's safe, look well down the road and creep slowly forward turning the wheel to the right until you are in the normal driving position. Straighten the wheel, carry out the normal MSM routine and pull in and park on the left.

If you don't manage to complete the manoeuvre in three movements, don't worry. Simply repeat the second and third movements.

Dealing with others during the manoeuvre

As you cross the road, look round at intervals to ensure that you remain aware of other road users. If you just started moving and you see another vehicle approaching, stop and let it go. If you are already halfway across and see another vehicle approaching it is usually wiser to complete your move to the other side of the road. Otherwise you could be blocking both carriageways.

Practise until you are confident with the 'turn in the road'. With experience you should be able to complete the manoeuvre on narrower roads.

Notes:

Notes:

Notes:

Assessment – turning in the road

Exercise 6.6 – How to reverse into a side road on the left

This manoeuvre is useful for turning round to travel in the opposite direction or for reversing into your driveway or bays in car parks. It takes practice to master this manoeuvre. Don't worry if you can't get it right first time. Start from a fairly wide road on a corner that isn't too sharp.

A–B: With safety in mind, you need to plan this manoeuvre as you approach the side road.

As you drive past the road, check for any parked cars or other obstructions that could make your manoeuvre unsafe. If necessary, move on to another location to practise.

Using the MSM routine, drive past the corner until you can see it in the interior mirror and stop on the left about half a metre from the kerb.

Reversing into a side road on the left

B–C: Turn in your seat so that you can see well down the road through the middle of the rear window. You may remove your seat belt if you feel restricted. When you have checked that it's safe all around, use clutch control to creep slowly back.

As you reverse towards the corner, the kerb will disappear from view in the rear window. You are now close to the point of turn. It is very important to look all around to the front and sides to make sure there

Anticipate the point of turn when you see the kerb disappear from view in the rear window

The front of the car will swing out as you steer left

will be no danger to other road users. As you steer left the front of your car will swing out!

As you look over your left shoulder again, you will see the kerb come into view in the bottom corner of the side window. If sure it is safe, you can begin steering to the left. Keep checking that it's safe and keep steering to the left until you see through the rear window that the car is straight in the new road. The amount of steering you need will depend on how sharp the corner is.

Keep looking well down the road through the middle of the rear window. This will help you judge whether the car is parallel with the kerb. An occasional glance into the nearside door mirror will help you judge your distance from the kerb. If you want the car to go nearer to the kerb, turn the wheel towards it. If you want to take the car away from the kerb a little, turn the wheel away from it. Any adjustments in steering at this point should be very slight. If you misjudge and bump the kerb or get too close to it, pull forwards a little and then reverse again to correct your position.

Follow the line of the kerb when it reappears in the side window

Make sure you finish your reverse in a safe place, far enough away from the junction to allow others to use it properly. As a guide, you need to be far enough back so that when you move off again you can position correctly for turning right at the junction.

If you removed your seat belt for reversing, make sure you put it on again before driving away.

Dealing with others during the manoeuvre

If your manoeuvre is going to affect other road users, remember they have priority. Be prepared to stop and let them make the decision to proceed or to wait for you.

Be prepared to pull forward to allow emerging traffic to use the junction

Give priority to pedestrians crossing at the junction. If you have started reversing and a pedestrian approaches, stop and give him or her the opportunity to cross.

If you see another vehicle approaching from behind, you may have to move forward to the start position to allow the vehicle to use the junction safely.

To build up your confidence, practise reversing to the left at different junctions.

Notes:

Notes:

Notes:

Assessment – left reverse

Exercise 6.7 – How to reverse into a road on the right

This exercise is useful for turning the car round where there are no convenient places on the left or for reversing into your driveway or into bays in car parks.

Judging the point of turn in a right reverse is easier because you can see the kerb.

A–B: Select a corner where your manoeuvre will be safe, legal and convenient. Use the MSM routine and take up a position as if you were going to turn right. If there are other road users around, you may have to delay your signal, as otherwise they may think you are turning right.

B–C: Wait for any oncoming traffic at the point of turn and look into the road

Reversing into a side road on the right

for any obstructions that would make your manoeuvre unsafe. Steer over to the right and stop a little out from the kerb about two to three car lengths past the corner. Take off your seat belt if you need to. You may want to open your window to see the kerb.

C–D: Select reverse gear and prepare to move. Remember, you are manoeuvring on the wrong side of the road. You are more vulnerable; keep looking all around, and respond to others. When you're sure it's clear, move slowly back. You should be looking over your left shoulder as you approach the corner, but look round to the right periodically to check your position and judge when to turn.

Just before turning, look all round again, remembering that the front of your car will swing out as you steer right. Look over your right shoulder as you steer, and follow the kerb. How much steering you need will depend on how sharp the corner is.

When you have turned the corner, look over your left shoulder again. This will help you judge whether or not your car is straight in the new road. You will also be able to see what is happening behind you and to respond to others.

When your car is straight, turn the wheel to the left sufficiently to keep it straight. Remember, any final adjustments should only be slight. Check your distance from the kerb by using your nearside door mirror.

To complete the exercise, drive far enough into the side road so that you have room to get back on to the left side of the road to approach the junction properly. This will also allow others to use the junction safely.

The right reverse manoeuvre is particularly useful when driving a van, because your view to the rear and sides is too restricted to reverse left safely. If the van has no rear windows, you would need to rely more heavily on your side mirrors to look out for others as you manoeuvre.

Just as in the left reverse, you must give priority to other road users when you make this manoeuvre.

Notes: Notes: Notes:

Assessment – right reverse

Exercise 6.8 – How to reverse into a parking space at the kerb (parallel parking)

Parallel parking

Compared to driving forwards into a gap between two other vehicles, you need less space using reverse gear. Start practising this manoeuvre only when you can carry out the previous reversing exercises reasonably well. Choose a quiet area to practise. Make sure you will not be disrupting the traffic and that the place you choose is legal and safe. By the time you master the exercise you should be able to reverse into a space about one and a half times the length of your car.

Use the MSM routine to position your car for the exercise.

Position your vehicle alongside and parallel with the parked car so that the back of your car is slightly forward of the parking space. You should be between half a metre and a metre from the parked car, with your front wheels set straight. Keep your foot on the brake and select reverse gear so that following traffic can see your reversing lights.

Have a good look all round to make sure there is no danger to other road users before you begin to reverse. When you are sure it is safe, reverse slowly, looking back through the rear window until the rear of your vehicle is level with the beginning of the space. This is the point of turn. Look round to check it is safe before steering left – the front of your car will swing out.

Steer briskly to the left to turn the back of your car towards the middle of the parking space. Once you have a good angle, turn the wheels right again enough to straighten them. As a guide you will need to do this when you can line up the right side of your car with the nearside headlamp of the vehicle behind.

Steer briskly at the point of turn

Move slowly into the space until you are sure you are clear of the vehicle ahead. As a guide, you ought to be able to see the bumper of this car over the top of your bonnet. At this point, check that you will be reasonably close to the kerb and, if so, steer briskly to the right to bring the front of the car into the space.

Straighten the wheels when you have a good angle

When your vehicle is almost parallel with the kerb and still moving very slowly, steer left to bring all the wheels parallel to the kerb.

Carrying out this manoeuvre slowly will allow you more time to see how the car is responding to your steering and will also give you plenty of time to make any necessary adjustments. It also means that you will be able to respond properly if there are other road users about.

Once you are in the space, pull forward so that you are positioned centrally and apply the parking brake.

Notes:

Notes:

Notes:

Assessment – parallel parking

Exercise 6.9 – Reversing into a parking bay

In car parks it is usually easier and safer to reverse into a parking bay than to drive forwards into a space. Depending on the layout of the car park and available space you may employ one of two methods to park:

- Reverse turning into the space. Drive past the parking space and then reverse (either left or right) to get into the space. You will probably use this method when the access way to the parking bays is of limited width.

Reverse turning into a space

On approach, check that the parking space is clear of obstructions and that it is wide enough for your vehicle. A badly parked car in the next bay might make it difficult for you to park or open your car door. Select reverse gear promptly when positioned for the manoeuvre so that following drivers can anticipate your move. Keep tight control of the clutch and reverse slowly into the space, keeping a good lookout for pedestrians.

Park centrally in the bay. If you misjudge, pull forward a little and then reverse to correct your position. When stopped, apply the parking brake.

- Turning on approach. If space permits you can turn the car as you approach the space so that you are in a better position to reverse into it.

Angled approach

It doesn't matter which method you choose or whether you reverse to the right or left. The important thing is to make sure you complete the manoeuvre safely by keeping a good look-out for other vehicles and pedestrians.

Be considerate when parking in bays. Don't occupy bays set aside for the disabled or parents with children when you are not entitled to use them. Park squarely so that you don't make it difficult for others to enter or exit adjacent bays.

Your instructor will be able to advise where it is safe to practise this exercise.

Notes:

Notes:

Notes:

Assessment – bay parking

Making a U-turn

Turning the car round without any reversing is only possible on very wide and quiet roads. It is not a move that others expect and can be potentially dangerous. Only make this manoeuvre when you can see the road is clear of approaching traffic and you are sure that you have enough room.

Making a U-turn safely may only be possible at a large roundabout (see Stage 7). You should avoid making a U-turn at mini-roundabouts.

You must not make a U-turn on motor-ways, in one-way streets or where signs forbid it.

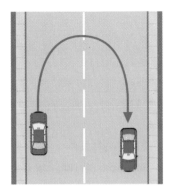

Making a U-turn

Checkpoint 6

1   Before reversing you should:
    Choose one answer

    a. sound the horn
    b. make sure the road is clear
    c. switch on the hazard flashers
    d. switch on the indicator

2   If you are unable to see when reversing you should:
    Choose one answer

    a. sound the horn
    b. get someone to help
    c. switch on your lights
    d. take a walk around the car

3   When turning the car round in the road you should:
    Choose two answers

    a. always complete the exercise in three movements
    b. keep full control of the vehicle
    c. take priority over other road users
    d. give priority to other road users

4   When turning round in the road you should: *Choose two answers*

    a.   keep the car moving slowly
    b.   keep the car moving quickly
    c.   turn the steering wheel slowly
    d.   turn the steering wheel briskly

5   When parallel parking between two vehicles you should:
Choose one answer

    a.   centre your car in the space
    b.   park your car close to the one in front
    c.   park your car close to the one behind
    d.   finish half a metre from the kerb

6   When reversing you should normally: *Choose two answers*

    a.   take priority over other road users
    b.   give priority to other road users
    c.   ignore the other road users
    d.   let the other road users decide

7   Reversing into a road on the right is useful when:
Choose two answers

    a.   the road is very wide
    b.   you are in an estate car
    c.   you are in a van
    d.   you can't see through the rear window

8   Parallel parking between two vehicles will require a space of at least:
Choose one answer

    a.   three times the length of your car
    b.   two and a half times the length of your car
    c.   twice the length of your car
    d.   one and a half times the length of your car

9   When using a driveway you should: *Choose two answers*

    a.   drive across the footpath quickly
    b.   drive across the footpath slowly
    c.   reverse in so that you can drive out
    d.   drive in so that you can reverse out

10 You must not reverse: *Choose two answers*

   a. further than is necessary

   b. less than is necessary

   c. from a main road into a side street

   d. from a side street into a main road

11 When reversing you should: *Choose three answers*

   a. use your mirrors when necessary

   b. look out for pedestrians

   c. only look through the side windows

   d. mainly look through the rear window

   e. never use your mirrors

12 When reversing you should: *Choose one answer*

   a. look at the kerb as a guide

   b. use a marker in the rear window

   c. look where you want the car to go

   d. mainly use the mirrors

13 Markings on the kerb like this mean:

Choose one answer

   a. no parking

   b. no waiting

   c. loading restrictions in force

   d. loading and unloading permitted

14 When reversing into a side road you see a pedestrian about to cross at the junction. You should: *Choose two answers*

   a. continue and expect the pedestrian to give way

   b. stop until you are sure of the pedestrian's movements

   c. allow the pedestrian to decide whether to wait or proceed

   d. sound your horn as a warning before continuing the manoeuvre

15 A sign like this means:

Choose one answer

a. no U-turns
b. reversing forbidden
c. no right turn ahead
d. restricted turning space ahead

16 When manoeuvring in a confined space you should:
Choose two answers

a. turn the wheel whilst stationary
b. use clutch control to maintain low speed
c. avoid dry steering
d. rely on your mirrors to check it's safe behind

17 When positioning to reverse round a corner you should:
Choose two answers

a. not worry about using the MSM routine
b. be careful when timing your signals
c. position as close to the kerb as possible
d. position a little way from the kerb

18 A marking like this in a parking bay means:

Choose one answer

a. disabled drivers only
b. bay reserved for disabled badge holders
c. space reserved for wheelchairs
d. you can park in the space if no disabled drivers are about

19 You turn into a side street and see this sign. You realize you have taken the wrong route and should:

Choose one answer

a. reverse out of the side road
b. make a turn in the road
c. find a side road to reverse into so you can turn round
d. drive on because it would be illegal to turn round

20 When deciding on a place to manoeuvre you should:
Choose two answers

a. consider the safety of other road users
b. not worry about causing temporary inconvenience to others
c. make sure your intended manoeuvre is legal
d. be more concerned with car control than observation

You will find the answers on page 424.

Scores: First try   Second try   Third try

Record your scores in Appendix 2 (page 426).

Stage 7
Gaining experience and using common sense

By now you should be confident with your car control skills and ready to drive in busier traffic conditions and deal with more complex junctions. In this stage you will also learn more about dealing safely with others on the road.

Build up your confidence and experience by taking things one step at a time. Get plenty of practice on as wide a variety of roads as possible. If you live in a rural area, your instructor may advise you to have longer lessons to incorporate these. If you live in a town you may have to learn to deal with these situations earlier in your course of driving lessons.

To help you prepare for this stage, you can also:

- Revise *The Official DSA Guide to Driving: The essential skills*, Part 7 – On the road, and Part 8 – Junctions.

- Read *The Official DSA Guide to Driving: The essential skills*, Part 10 – Defensive driving.

- Read *The Official DSA Guide to Learning to Drive*, Section 2 – Roundabouts, Section 2 – Dual carriageways, Section 2 – Pedestrian crossings, Section 2 - Independent driving.

Learn the following *Highway Code* rules:

- 133–43 Lane discipline.
- 170–90 Road junctions.
- 191–99 Pedestrian crossings.
- 291–99 Railway level crossings.
- 300–07 Tramways.

Lane discipline at junctions

Where there are two lanes, or room for two lanes that are not marked, unless road markings or signs show otherwise, when intending to:

- turn left – keep to the left-hand lane;
- follow the road ahead – keep to the left-hand lane;
- turn right – move to the right-hand lane in good time.

Abide by lane markings

Where there are three lanes, unless road signs and markings indicate otherwise, when intending to:

- turn left – keep to the left-hand lane;
- follow the road ahead – keep to the left-hand or middle lane;
- turn right – move to the right-hand lane in good time.

How to choose the most appropriate lane for turning left or right

Look and plan well ahead, and get into position as soon as you can. At some junctions the road markings do not follow the normal rules. Where there are two or more lanes marked for the direction you wish to take, choose the most convenient one. To do this you need to know where you should be positioned at the next junction. Look and think ahead. If you don't have knowledge of the local area you should take note of route direction signs that may guide you.

Unless you need the right-hand lane at the next junction it is normally better to select the left lane. This will avoid you having to change lanes after the turn. If you select the right-hand lane for the turn, check carefully to the left after the turn to

Look and think ahead to get into the correct lane for your route

make sure there is no one in your blind area before returning to the left lane.

Acceleration and deceleration lanes (slip roads) allow you to join or leave a road without hindering the through flow of traffic. Get into position early and use these lanes to build up speed when joining a road or slow down when leaving at a junction.

Deceleration lane

One-way streets

Look out for signs telling you that you are joining a one-way street or system. Get into position in good time on approach to and once in the one-way street:

- To enter a one-way street by turning right, turn directly into the right-hand lane.
- To enter a one-way street by turning left, turn directly into the left-hand lane.

In the one-way street, unless road signs and markings say otherwise, when intending to:

- turn left – keep to the left-hand lane;
- follow the road ahead – use any convenient lane;
- turn right – move to the right-hand lane in good time.

Early positioning in one-way streets is important because traffic flows quickly and is permitted to overtake on the left or right. Take particular care and check mirrors well before changing lane.

Multi-lane roads

Unless road signs and markings permit otherwise:

- On three-lane carriageways, drive in the left-hand lane. Use the middle lane only to overtake, and remember that you have no more right to use that lane than traffic approaching from the opposite direction.

Where there are four or more lanes, do not use the lanes on the right-hand half of the road.

Dual carriageways

- Drive in the left-hand lane normally.
- Use the right-hand lane for overtaking or turning right.

On a three-lane dual carriageway you may stay in the middle lane if there are slower vehicles in the left lane, but must return to the left lane when you have passed them.

Notes: *Notes:*   *Notes:*

Assessment – lane discipline

Dealing with pedestrian crossings

There are three main types of pedestrian crossing:

- zebra crossings, which are uncontrolled;
- traffic-light-controlled crossings, which may be at ordinary traffic lights or under the direct control of pedestrians, that is pelican, puffin and toucan crossings;
- supervised crossings, which are controlled by a police officer, traffic warden or school crossing patrol warden with a manual stop sign.

Look and plan well ahead for pedestrian crossings. There may be warning signs if a pedestrian crossing ahead is obscured from a driver's view. The 'Pedestrian crossing' warning sign is usually placed in advance of   a zebra crossing, whilst a 'Traffic signals' warning sign quite often advises of a light-controlled crossing ahead.

On approach to zebra and pedestrian-controlled crossings, you will notice an area marked by white zigzag markings on the road. You must not park or wait in this area or overtake the lead vehicle approaching the crossing. When driving in lanes of traffic, where there are vehicles in another lane waiting to let someone cross, you may pull level with the lead vehicle but must not proceed in front of it.

In slow-moving traffic and traffic queues, keep pedestrian crossings clear.

Zebra crossings

Be ready to slow down and stop on approach to zebra crossings

Look out for the yellow flashing amber beacons marking zebra crossings. Use the MSPSL routine. Check mirrors when you see the crossing. Look for people standing near or moving towards crossings, and try to work out in advance whether they are likely to cross. Check what is happening behind, and be ready to slow down. You must be travelling at such a speed that you can pull up safely if a pedestrian steps out. Never accelerate towards a pedestrian crossing hoping to beat the pedestrian to it!

Take care if your view of the crossing is blocked

If your view of either side of the crossing is blocked, slow down as if people were crossing. Be ready to stop until you can see it is safe to continue.

Where you see pedestrians waiting to cross, check your mirrors and slow down. If you hold back early enough they may have time to go before you reach the crossing. Try to make eye contact with anyone waiting. This helps reassure them that they have been seen.

If you have time, give an arm signal for slowing down. This lets the pedestrian know what you are doing and also warns oncoming drivers that you are stopping. Do not give any kind of invitation for people to cross. Other drivers may not be stopping.

Some pedestrians find it more difficult than others to cross the road. Be patient and allow extra time for the old and infirm. People with prams cannot put a foot on to the crossing to claim priority. They will have to push the pram out. Others with small children also need more time. Young people are often impulsive and may dash out on to the crossing.

If the pedestrians are walking from your right to left, wait until they are on the pavement before moving away. If they are walking from left to right, give precedence to them, but you don't need to wait until they are completely across before you proceed.

Do not startle or try to hurry pedestrians by edging forwards or revving your engine. If you are stopping for more than a couple of seconds, apply the parking brake.

Remember before moving away to check to the sides for other pedestrians in your blind spots.

If a zebra crossing has a central reserve, each half is a separate crossing and you only need to give way to people on your side of the road. Beware, however, people running towards the crossing on the right-hand carriageway; you should still be prepared to slow down and stop.

Treat a zebra crossing with a central refuge as two separate crossings

Pedestrian light-controlled crossings

Pelican crossing

These are recognized by the traffic light signals and a yellow box on the pole, where special signals for the pedestrians are operated by a push-button.

At pelican crossings, the sequence of lights differs from that at other traffic lights. Instead of the red and amber signal, there is a flashing amber phase.

This has the same meaning as the flashing yellow beacon at a zebra crossing – you must give way to people on the crossing. A straight-line pelican crossing that has a central reserve is still one crossing and you must give way to people crossing from your right even during the flashing amber phase.

At puffin, toucan and equestrian crossings there is no flashing amber phase. Instead, sensors must detect that the crossing is clear before the traffic light signals will change to permit traffic to cross.

At toucan crossings cyclists are allowed to ride across. They are found in places where cycle lanes have to cross busy roads and junctions. On approach to a toucan crossing you may see a cycle lane. Equestrian crossings are similarly designed for use by riders with horses.

At staggered light-controlled crossings you only need to give precedence to users on your side of the road.

Staggered crossing

When light-controlled crossings are clear and signals permit, you may move on but must make sure that nobody is about to step on to the crossing. Always be ready for the possibility that a pedestrian could rush on to the crossing at the last second. You must still give precedence to pedestrians on the crossing even if traffic control signals indicate that you can proceed.

Supervised crossings

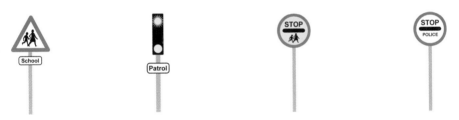

Near schools these may be preceded by warning signs – look out for the twin flashing light beacon at the beginning and end of the school day. The signs may have supplementary plates to identify the danger ahead. You must obey the manually operated signal given by the school patrol warden. Police or traffic wardens may also use a manually operated stop sign.

Assessment – pedestrian crossings

How to approach traffic lights

Look and plan well ahead and anticipate lights changing. All colours except green mean stop, and you should always be travelling at a speed at which you can pull up safely.

Working things out as you approach will help speed up your reactions. Check your mirrors to see how close following vehicles are and how fast they are travelling. Continually assess what you will do if the lights change.

When approaching a red light, check your mirrors and start slowing down. If the light stays red, you

Remember the traffic light sequence

will be able to stop comfortably. Apply the parking brake and select neutral. If the light changes to green you may continue, but, remember, green means go only if it is safe. Check for vehicles from all directions and watch for oncoming drivers turning across your path.

A green light can change at any time. When approaching, be aware of what is happening behind, slow down and be ready to stop if the light changes. If the green light stays on, continue, but remember to check in all directions.

Look for pedestrians crossing the road you are taking and be ready to give way to them.

If your exit road is blocked, wait at the stop line – do not drive forward and block the junction.

What to do at filter lights

Filter lights indicate that you have priority in the direction shown by the arrow. They may be timed to control traffic congestion in peak periods. Arrows may indicate priority to left, right or ahead.

Plan well ahead and look for road markings. Avoid using a filter lane unless you intend to proceed in the direction of the arrow shown. If you find yourself in the wrong lane, continue in that direction to avoid holding other traffic up.

At a left filter, when the arrow comes on you may turn left regardless of any other lights that may be showing. Before turning, check for other traffic moving in from your offside.

Where you see a filter arrow to the right, you may turn right regardless of any other lights showing. Remember, however, that green means go only if safe. Check that any oncoming traffic is stopping before you proceed.

Where you see a filter arrow to the left, the nearside lane will normally be marked for left-turning traffic only

Assessment – traffic lights

How to deal with crossroads

A crossroads is a junction where two roads cross, although not necessarily at right angles to one another. There are basically two types of crossroads, unmarked and marked.

Treat unmarked crossroads with great care – neither road has priority. To understand this, imagine a junction with traffic lights that have failed – you would be extra careful because no driver would have priority. Approach slowly and be prepared to give way to traffic moving along the other road.

Where a crossroads sign is displayed, the broader line indicates priority through the junction

Marked crossroads may have Stop or Give way signs, traffic lights and/or yellow box road markings.

Whether you are approaching on the minor or the major road, use MSPSL on approach and take effective observation before entering the crossroads. You need to look at the road ahead as well as to the right and left. This is particularly important when waiting to emerge on to the major road but applies equally when driving ahead at crossroads on the major road. Remember that a driver in the minor road, in the absence of crossing traffic, may not even realize he or she is about to enter a crossroads and come straight out without looking.

Choosing the most appropriate lane for going straight ahead

Use common sense to position for going ahead at crossroads

You should follow the general rule of keeping to the left to go ahead at crossroads, leaving the right lane clear for traffic wishing to turn right. However, looking and planning ahead will help you select the most appropriate lane for going straight ahead at busy junctions.

If the road ahead narrows at a crossroads, or if the road ahead is offset to the right (staggered junction), you may need to position in the right lane. You must of course obey any road signs or markings that are there to guide the traffic.

Where there is a queue of traffic waiting to turn left and you anticipate being able to proceed safely, you may position in the right-hand lane to follow the road ahead. The same applies where there are parked cars or other obstructions on approach or at the opposite side of the junction. In these situations you need to use your common sense in deciding on the most suitable approach position.

Turning at crossroads

A crossroads has four entry points, and this can sometimes lead to confusion over priority. The problem here usually occurs when you are waiting to join or cross the major road when there is other traffic on the opposite side of the junction. If you intend to go ahead or turn left and the approaching traffic wishes to do likewise, there is no reason, providing the main road is clear, why you should not both go at the same time.

If one of you wishes to turn right and the other wishes to go ahead, remember that the driver turning right is crossing the path of the approaching vehicle and should give priority to the driver wishing to follow the road ahead. You should try to establish eye contact with the other driver if you are unsure of his or her intentions. Remember, it is unwise to rely on the other driver's signals or lack of them. Consider the other driver's road position, where he or she is looking, and the direction the vehicle's front wheels are facing to help you anticipate the other driver's most likely path.

If both of you wish to turn right, the main road is clear and there is sufficient space, then you may both proceed at the same time. There are two ways to deal with this situation, regardless of whether you are turning from the major or the minor road.

You can turn offside to offside so that you pass behind the other vehicle. This method gives you a clear view of approaching traffic.

Both turning right – offside to offside gives a better view of approaching traffic

You can also turn nearside to nearside, although this method does not give you as good a view of oncoming traffic. Motorcyclists and cyclists are particularly vulnerable in this situation – take care!

Turning nearside to nearside can restrict your view of oncoming traffic

Either method is acceptable and will be determined by the layout of the road, the course that the other driver decides to take and any road markings dictating the position to take. In busy traffic, where space is limited, turning nearside to nearside may have to be the choice to avoid blocking the junction. Whichever method you use, prior to making your turn you should check your mirrors again, especially if you have had to wait for a safe opportunity to proceed.

How to deal with box junctions

If your exit road is not clear, wait at the stop line until you can move through the junction without blocking it.

If you are turning right and the exit road is clear, you may enter the box and wait in the centre for any oncoming traffic to pass.

Obey the rules for yellow box junctions to keep the junction clear

Be prepared to give way to oncoming traffic

When turning right at crossroads with traffic lights, oncoming vehicles usually have a green light at the same time. Watch out particularly for traffic that is likely to travel straight through the junction or turn left. You must give way to these vehicles, as they have priority.

Wait just short of the point of turn for a suitable break in the traffic. If it is very busy, you may have to wait for the lights to change before you get an opportunity to turn. When this happens you should normally clear the junction as quickly as you can. Make sure, however, that the oncoming traffic is stopping before you proceed.

Notes:

Notes:

Notes:

Assessment – crossroads

Dealing with roundabouts

Roundabouts are designed to aid the free flow of traffic at busy junctions, allowing it to cross or merge with traffic from other roads without necessarily stopping. The general rule is to 'give way to traffic from the right'. Long before you reach a roundabout, look for information signs that may show the layout of the roundabout, and make a mental note of the position of your exit road.

Procedure on approach to roundabouts

Use the mirrors–signal–manoeuvre routine. Unless road signs and markings, traffic conditions or the layout of the roundabout dictate otherwise, follow the normal rules for positioning on approach as you would at any junction.

When turning left (blue car 'A' in the diagram), approach in the left lane. Signal left and keep to the left lane through the roundabout. Keep the left signal on until you are into the exit road.

When following the road ahead (green car 'B'), you should normally approach in the left lane and stay in it through the roundabout. As you pass the first exit check the mirrors and give a left signal to indicate you are leaving by the next one.

When turning right (red car 'C'), use the mirror–signal–manoeuvre routine to get into the right-hand lane on approach. Keep the right signal on and stay in the right-hand lane into and round the roundabout. As you

It is important to take the correct route on approach and through roundabouts

are passing the exit prior to the one to be taken, check for vehicles in the nearside lane (left mirror) and make sure it is safe to cross it. Change to a left indicator signal and leave by the next exit. You should normally leave in the left lane if it is clear.

If using a roundabout to make a U-turn, approach as if turning right and use MSM before signalling to leave the junction as described above.

Helping the free flow of traffic

The layout of some roundabouts can make it difficult to judge which lane to take on approach. As a guide, imagine the roundabout as a clock face, with you approaching from the six o'clock position. If your exit road is past 12 o'clock and there are no other road markings to guide you, approach in the right-hand lane.

Keep scanning to the right and left as you approach roundabouts. Try to time your arrival to coincide with a gap in the traffic, but give way to any traffic approaching from your right. Look across the roundabout, watching for traffic already moving through it. This will help you anticipate whether traffic on your immediate right will be prevented from joining the roundabout.

Build up and maintain a reasonable speed on roundabouts. Failing to do this, especially when you are in the right-hand lane, may result in other drivers passing on your nearside. Always check for vehicles on your left before leaving a roundabout. If the left-hand lane of the exit road is blocked or there are vehicles in the lane to your nearside, leave in the right-hand lane.

If there are three lanes on approach, use the left to turn left, the right lane to turn right and the left or middle lanes to follow the road ahead. If there are more than three lanes on approach, use the clearest suitable lane. Look well ahead for road markings giving directions that vary from the basic rules. Get into position early and stay in the middle of your lane.

Mini-roundabouts

Apply the same rules as at any other roundabout. Note, however, limited space means that:

- you have less time to signal to leave the roundabout;
- larger vehicles may not be able to avoid driving over the roundabout road marking;
- you should not enter the roundabout unless certain that other vehicles on it will be able to clear the route you intend to take.

At double mini-roundabouts and multiple roundabouts, follow the normal rules of priority and treat each roundabout separately.

Mini-roundabout

Double mini-roundabout

Other roundabouts

Exceptional round-abouts have road markings (give way lines) that indicate that traffic on the round-about must give priority to traffic entering the roundabout.

Spiral roundabouts may be used at major junctions where there is heavy through-flow of traffic. Lanes within the roundabout are

Exceptional roundabout

Spiral roundabout

marked in a spiral pattern to help drivers select and stay within the correct lane for their route.

Assessment – roundabouts

Driving along dual carriageways

When driving on dual carriageways you should use your mirrors even more frequently. Look well ahead for problems, and anticipate what may happen. Respond early, giving those behind you time to act. Look for:

- obstructions in your lane;
- vehicles ahead slowing down;
- vehicles turning through central reserves;
- traffic joining the carriageway.

Turning right on to dual carriageways

Dual
carriageway
ahead

When turning right on to dual carriageways, decide if there is enough room in the central reserve to offer your car protection from traffic moving along the new road. If the central reserve is wide enough to wait in, make sure you position correctly to avoid problems for drivers turning right off the dual carriageway.

If the central reserve is too narrow, treat the carriageway as one road

If the central reserve is wide enough you can cross the first carriageway and then wait for a suitable gap in the traffic

Dealing with level crossings

Advance warning of a gated level crossing

Advance warning of a level crossing without gates or barriers

At level crossings, the road crosses a railway line. Trains can't stop or give way to road traffic! If you see a sign for a level crossing, use the mirrors–signal–manoeuvre routine on approach. A sign should tell you what kind of crossing it is. There may also be distance countdown markers if the crossing is near a bend.

Most crossings have full or half-barriers and may be controlled by traffic lights and an audible alarm, operated either by

Countdown markers to a concealed level crossing

an attendant or automatically as the train approaches the crossing. Approach carefully and cross with care.

At any level crossing you must not:

- drive on to the crossing unless the road is clear beyond it;
- drive 'nose to tail' over the crossing;
- stop on or just after the crossing;
- park close to the crossing;
- start crossing once the lights, alarm or barriers operate;
- zigzag around half-barrier crossings.

How to deal with gated level crossings

An amber light and ringing sound will be followed by a flashing red light if a train is approaching. The barriers will then come down. You must stop. The red light will continue flashing whilst the barrier is down. If another train is approaching the lights will continue to flash and the barriers will remain down.

Don't try to beat the barriers!

If you have already started crossing and the lights begin to show or the alarm sounds, you *must* keep going.

The cross symbol outlined in red is used at all level crossings without a gate or barrier

How to deal with ungated level crossings

Some level crossings do not have gates or barriers. These will have either traffic lights or 'Give way' signs. Obey the traffic signs. Look both ways, and listen for approaching trains.

Railway telephones

Where provided, you must use the railway telephone to inform the signal operator if:

- you have an accident or break down on the crossing;
- you need to check it is safe to cross;
- you need permission to use the crossing, ie you are:
  - driving a large vehicle;
  - driving a slow-moving vehicle;
  - driving a vehicle with limited ground clearance.

Breakdowns and accidents at level crossings

If you are involved in an accident on a level crossing, or your car breaks down:

- *as your first priority* get everybody out of the car and clear of the crossing;
- if available immediately use the railway telephone to inform the signal operator;
- *obey instructions that you are given*;
- if it is possible and there is time, move the vehicle clear and inform the signal operator on the railway telephone;
- if a train approaches or the lights and audible alarm operate, *get clear*; the train will not be able to stop.

Dealing with tramways

Tramways or light rapid transport (LRT) systems are becoming more common in British towns and cities. Apart from the tracks on the road surface, warning signs, diamond-shaped signs and traffic lights showing white symbols for tram drivers will all tell you that trams are operating. Where a tramway crosses your road, treat this in the same way as a level crossing. Look out for:

- tram lanes – marked by white lines and/or a different type of road surface;
- traffic lights;
- tracks crossing the road;
- the road narrowing;
- pedestrians running to catch trams.

Do not enter a lane or road reserved for trams. You *must not* drive between trams and the left kerb or park in a way that would obstruct a tram or force other drivers to do so.

The white symbol at these traffic lights gives instructions to tram drivers only. The instruction given may differ from that given to drivers by the traffic lights

Checkpoint 7

1   On a multi-laned road you should normally drive:
   Choose two answers

   a.   in the centre lane
   b.   in the left lane
   c.   in the centre of your lane
   d.   as close to the lane markings as you can

2   When following the road ahead at a roundabout with two lanes, you should normally:
   Choose two answers

   a.   use the left-hand lane
   b.   use the right-hand lane
   c.   use the lane with least traffic
   d.   look for signs and markings

3   For leaving roundabouts you should normally:
   Choose one answer

   a.   use the left-hand lane
   b.   use the right-hand lane
   c.   check over your right shoulder
   d.   take the lane with least traffic

4 If you are in the wrong lane at a junction you should:
Choose one answer

a. follow the directions for that lane
b. stop and wait until you can move over into another lane
c. signal and move over quickly
d. ask a police officer for instructions

5 On one-way streets you should expect:
Choose one answer

a. pedestrians to be looking the wrong way
b. vehicles overtaking on both sides
c. fewer road signs and markings
d. oncoming vehicles to take priority

6 This flashing amber light at a pelican crossing means:

Choose one answer

a. the driver has priority
b. pedestrians have priority
c. pedestrians should now start to cross
d. you should wait for pedestrians within 50 metres of the crossing

7 Following the road ahead at traffic lights, your exit road is blocked. You should:
Choose one answer

a. move into the junction to wait
b. wait at the line until the exit is clear
c. move forwards and wait behind the queue
d. change lanes quickly to avoid waiting

8 When turning right at traffic lights you should:
Choose two answers

a. give way to oncoming traffic
b. wait at the stop line for a break in the traffic
c. proceed because you have a green light
d. proceed on green only if it is safe

9 A green filter arrow means:

Choose one answer

a. you may proceed only when the main green light shows
b. you may proceed if safe, regardless of the other lights
c. all the other lights will be red
d. it is safe for you to proceed

10 The first thing to do if you break down on a railway level crossing is:
Choose one answer

a. get all passengers out of the car
b. try to push the car over the crossing
c. telephone the signal operator
d. try to find out what the problem is

11 You should treat a zebra crossing with a central refuge:
Choose one answer

a. as one crossing
b. as two crossings
c. the same as a single crossing
d. the same as a pelican crossing

12 At level crossings, the flashing red light means:

Choose two answers

a. stop and wait
b. another train may be coming.
c. you have 15 seconds to cross
d. the gates will fall in 15 seconds

13 When turning right on to a dual carriageway you should:
Choose two answers

a. work out if the central reserve is wide enough to wait in
b. check that the road to the right is clear and move to the centre, regardless of the width of the central reserve
c. wait until it is safe to cross both carriageways before you move, regardless of the central reserve
d. make sure no one is turning through the central reserve

14 The road used by trams is often marked with:
Choose one answer

a. white dots
b. white lines
c. yellow hatch markings
d. yellow lines

15 The shape of signs for trams drivers is:
Choose one answer

a. circular
b. diamond
c. square
d. triangular

16 In areas where there are trams you should:
Choose two answers

a.   sometimes give way to trams
b.   always give way to trams
c.   never give way to trams
d.   not try to race or overtake trams

17 Toucan crossings are shared by:
Choose one answer

a.   car drivers and pedestrians
b.   pedestrians and cyclists
c.   cyclists and motorcyclists
d.   motorcyclists and pedestrians

18 Puffin crossings are designed to:
Choose two answers

a.   enable people with animals to cross in safety
b.   improve road safety
c.   reduce unnecessary delays to traffic
d.   stop traffic for longer to allow people with disabilities to cross

19 At puffin crossings an electronic device:
Choose two answers

a.   detects when cars are approaching
b.   detects when pedestrians are on the crossing
c.   can speed up the green light for drivers
d.   delays the green light for pedestrians

20 The zigzag lines at all pedestrian crossings mean you must not:

Choose two answers

a. stop
b. park in the marked area
c. overtake the lead vehicle in the marked area
d. drive over the zigzag lines

You will find the answers on page 424.

Scores: First try   Second try   Third try

Record your scores in Appendix 2 (page 426).

Stage 8
Learning to anticipate problems and avoid accidents

One life lost in an accident is one life too many. Road accidents cost far too many lives, leave a great number of people seriously injured and cost millions of pounds every year.

It has been shown that, by drivers learning how to anticipate and avoid problems, accidents can be reduced by as much as 50 per cent. Your car control skills should now be well developed, and you should have dealt with more types of hazards. You should also have learned from experience that other drivers don't always do what they should do. In this stage you will learn to deal with driving situations that require extra care. This stage shows you how to anticipate what might happen and explains how you can avoid accidents by driving **defensively**.

To help you prepare for this stage, you can also:

- Revise *The Official DSA Guide to Driving: The essential skills*, Part 10 – Defensive driving.

- Read *The Official DSA Guide to Driving: The essential skills*, Part 12 – All weather driving, and Part 13 – Driving at night.

- Read *The Official DSA Guide to Learning to Drive*, Section 2 – Safe positioning, Section 2 – Junctions.

Revise the following *Highway Code* rules:

- 110–11 Flashing headlights.
- 112 Horn.
- 124–25 Speed limits.
- 126 Stopping distances.

Learn the *Highway Code* rules:

- 144–48 Adapting your driving and being considerate.
- 149–50 Mobile phones and in-vehicle technology.
- 153 Traffic calming.
- 154 Country roads.
- 155 Single-track roads.
- 204–18 Road users requiring extra care.
- 219–25 Other vehicles.
- 226–37 Adverse weather conditions.

Accidents cost lives

Be prepared to give way, even if it may be your priority. No matter who causes an accident, the result is the same:

INJURY   DAMAGE   EXPENSE   INCONVENIENCE   MISERY!

Experience will teach you that other drivers make mistakes.

When you see a possible problem, check your mirrors, adjust your speed and give yourself time to react. Continually look and plan ahead. Near junctions, expect others to move into or across your path.

In areas where your view may be restricted, for example near parked vehicles, expect pedestrians to be walking or even running into the road.

Concentrate on your driving!

Traffic situations can change very quickly. If you have passengers, keep your eyes on the road when you talk to them.

In-car radio can keep you up to date with traffic problems ahead

The use of any in-car entertainment systems or telephones can also be a distraction. Radios can be useful for traffic reports and light background music. Serious listening to plays or other heavy programmes, however, can affect your concentration.

Satellite navigation systems can be an extremely useful aid, but they can also distract. If you are using this technology, make sure any settings are made *before* you start your journey, and don't rely on the navigation system to know when roads are closed or unsuitable for your type of vehicle!

Don't get distracted by in-vehicle technology

When you are driving, it is illegal and dangerous to make or receive a call on a hand-held mobile telephone. Even with a hands-free system, any telephone conversation can be a serious distraction. If you must make or receive telephone calls, find somewhere safe to pull in.

It is illegal and dangerous to use a hand-held mobile phone when driving

Changing tapes and CDs means looking away from the road and taking a hand from the wheel. It is common sense to avoid this, especially when driving at higher speeds, driving in heavy traffic, and negotiating corners and roundabouts.

Smoking can be dangerous to your health – especially if you do it whilst driving and you drop your cigarette!

Make good use of the mirrors

Act sensibly on what you see in the mirrors. Simply looking in them is not enough.

Keep regular checks all around on the speed and position of other traffic – particularly on multi-laned roads. Be aware when someone has moved out of sight into your blind areas.

Anticipate traffic joining your road and move over to make room if safe – beware of vehicles that have entered your blind spots

Think of the consequences of driving too fast for the conditions – ask yourself 'What if...?'

When you double your speed – braking distance increases by four times

Drive defensively and allow others to overtake. Leave room for them to return to the lane ahead of you.

Be sensible with your speed

You must keep within the legal speed limits, observing signs. Remember that the speed limit on a road with street lighting is 30 mph unless signs tell you otherwise. If there are no signs or street lighting, the national speed limit of 60 mph on a single carriageway and 70 mph on dual carriageways applies. Look out for national speed limit and maximum and minimum speed limit signs when you approach a new road.

Remember – a speed limit is not a target. It is the highest permitted speed for that area. This means it will not always be safe to travel up to that speed.

The speed at which you drive should depend on the road, the weather and traffic conditions. Think of the consequences of driving too fast for the conditions – ask yourself 'What if...?'

When you double your speed, braking distance increases by four times. Always travel at a speed at which you can stop safely in the distance you can see to be clear ahead!

Within the speed limit for the road you are on, you should be driving at the most appropriate speed for the conditions. Driving too slowly can be just as hazardous as driving too quickly. If you delay following traffic by driving too slowly, you can cause frustration that may tempt a following driver to make a rash move.

Be patient

In today's volume of traffic you must expect delays in your journeys. You should allow plenty of time, especially if you are driving in peak traffic hours.

Even though you have been taught to drive confidently, there are many others on the road less able than yourself. Be ready to wait patiently. If there are very few gaps in the traffic it's a waste of time losing your patience – there's nothing to be done about it. If you get annoyed it will affect your own safety and you will be tempted to take risks.

If a following driver seems too close or aggressive let them pass as soon as you safely can

If you are driving properly and keeping to the speed limits, don't let drivers behind push you. Keep calm and, if they get too close, drop a little further back from the vehicle ahead of you to increase your braking distance. If you feel threatened, it may even be sensible, when it is safe, to pull in to the left and let the drivers behind get by.

Notes:

Notes:

Notes:

Assessment – use of speed

Dealing with oncoming vehicles

In Stage 4 you learned how to pass parked vehicles safely by slowing down if needed to give adequate clearance. When there isn't enough space for you and an approaching vehicle to pass, one of you will need to hold back. Use the MSPSL routine as you approach the hazard.

You should normally give priority to the approaching driver if the obstruction is on your side of the road, but don't assume priority if the obstruction is on the other side. If you are looking well ahead and anticipate the problem, you should be able to slow down early enough to give the oncoming driver a clear path without you having to stop.

If it is necessary to stop, take up a sensible hold-back position well back from the obstruction and not too close to the kerb. This will allow you to see ahead clearly and enable you to change course gradually to steer clear of the obstruction. When the approaching traffic has passed, check your mirrors again before moving on and if necessary give a signal. Take care as you pass the obstacle – pedestrians may step out!

Give priority to approaching traffic if an obstruction is on your side of the road

Always be prepared to give way to oncoming drivers, even though it may be your priority. Look well ahead and, when you see a vehicle parked on the other side of the road, expect oncoming drivers to keep coming. Check what is happening behind and ease off the gas. This will give you time to work out whether the other driver is going to make you wait or whether you can keep moving.

Choose a 'hold-back' position to give you best view of the road ahead

Sometimes it is sensible to give priority even when the obstruction is on the other side of the road. Be considerate towards drivers of large vehicles, particularly on hills.

If there are obstructions on both sides of the road, neither you nor the oncoming driver has priority. In these situations the defensive

Be considerate towards drivers of larger vehicles

driver would not rely on the oncoming traffic to stop. If you are prepared to give way then you are in charge of the situation.

Where there are lines of parked cars on each side of the road, you may need to pull into a gap between cars or wait opposite a gap so that approaching traffic can pull in to let you pass. In these situations your speed should be kept down and, if there is only room for one vehicle to go through and you can see traffic approaching, always look well ahead for a suitable

gap. Remember that there is little point in you pulling into a gap if there is not enough room for traffic following you to do the same. The driver of an approaching vehicle should anticipate this problem, and you can only do likewise if you check your mirrors in good time!

Using your mirrors may help you anticipate what the approaching driver intends to do!

Drivers often flash headlights in these situations – make sure you are clear about the other driver's intentions before reacting to a flashing headlight signal!

In towns where traffic-calming measures are in force, you might see signs indicating priority where the road is narrowed. Always be ready for an approaching driver trying to make a dash for the gap!

In rural areas, be prepared to meet traffic where the road narrows or where there is a bend ahead – larger vehicles may be forced on to your side of the road.

When you are approaching arch bridges or other height restrictions, remember that larger vehicles may have to move to the centre of the road to pass safely beneath the obstruction – be prepared to give way.

At arch bridges large vehicles may have to move to the centre of the road

Notes: Notes: Notes:

Assessment – meeting traffic

Overtaking

Overtaking at the wrong place or time can put you on a collision course with oncoming traffic. Before deciding to overtake, ask yourself if the benefit is worth the risk:

- Is it safe?
- Is it lawful?
- Is it necessary?

Think about the distance you will and also about the time you will need to overtake and get back in safely. Consider also the distance that will be covered by any oncoming vehicles.

Do not overtake where bends or hill crests restrict your view, or when you are approaching pedestrian crossings and junctions. Take particular care where there is 'dead ground' – a dip in a road that could hide an oncoming vehicle.

There is little point if you will be turning off shortly, if there is a line of traffic ahead and you will have to slow down, or if the vehicle ahead

If it is necessary to overtake you need to choose a safe place and should ask yourself whether a better opportunity might occur ahead, for example approaching a wider stretch of road or a dual carriageway

is driving at the speed limit. Look at the road layout ahead – will there be safer opportunities to get past if you wait a minute or so?

Consider what the other driver may be doing:

- Will he or she pull out to pass a parked car or cyclist?
- Is he or she signalling to turn?

Last, but not least:

- Is it safe behind?
- Is someone overtaking you?

Getting into position to see ahead before overtaking

You will need to use the MSPSL routine several times when overtaking.

To get a good view of the road ahead, stay well back, matching the speed of the vehicle you want to overtake. When possible, particularly with large vehicles, check the mirrors and position so that you can look along the nearside of the vehicle ahead.

Check along the nearside of the vehicle you intend to overtake

When overtaking, avoid staying in another driver's blind area for too long

Check the mirrors again and, if safe, move over to look along the offside for a long straight stretch of road that is free of oncoming vehicles, obstructions and side turns.

If it appears safe ahead and behind, select a lower gear to give you a reserve of power; be ready to accelerate quickly. Apply MSPSL again – look in the mirrors to check that it is still safe, and signal to let others know of your intentions. Pull out on a smooth line that will give adequate clearance to the vehicle ahead. Overtake as promptly as you can. Try not to stay in the other driver's blind area for too long. As you clear the vehicle, look out for other traffic, or pedestrians in the road ahead hidden from your view before you started to overtake. Use the MSPSL routine again to pull back on to your side as soon as you safely can. Don't cut in too soon – you could force the driver you've just overtaken to brake sharply. Once in your normal road position, check your mirrors again and make progress. Having overtaken, you should not then cause the following driver to slow down, unless some unforeseen danger arises in the road ahead.

Notes:

Notes:

Notes:

Assessment – overtaking

Common dangers at junctions

You shouldn't always expect drivers turning right to wait for you.

When you see a vehicle approaching with a right indicator signal on, try to work out its speed. If it does not appear to be slowing down enough, check to see what is happening behind and ease off the gas. Hold back if you think it will turn in front of you.

If you're driving ahead at traffic lights, watch for drivers turning across your path. They may not have seen you.

Be prepared for drivers turning across your path

Watch out for drivers emerging from side roads. Even when you're driving along major roads, you should expect drivers to emerge from side roads. As you're driving along, check your mirrors regularly and look ahead for roads to the left and right.

Emerging drivers may respond to other road users' signals without thinking!

Look for drivers approaching the junctions at high speed. They may not look properly and may pull out in front of you simply because they didn't see you.

Emerging drivers may be distracted by other traffic and not see you. Anticipate danger if approaching traffic seems to be inviting emerging drivers to pull out.

When you are approaching side roads, always be aware of what is behind you, particularly before you decide to turn. Follow the mirrors–signal–manoeuvre routine and take a final look in the appropriate door mirror before turning right or left. Remember, if you use your mirrors properly and react to what you see in them, you shouldn't get caught out by vehicles overtaking you.

When you are waiting in traffic, make sure you leave side roads and other main entrances clear for others to drive in and out.

If you are waiting to emerge from a side road, try using eye contact and smiling. This often encourages others to let you in.

Changing lanes in heavy traffic

Look and plan well ahead, reading the signs and markings. This will help you get into the correct lane in good time. If you do find yourself in the wrong lane in heavy traffic, avoid trying to change lanes quickly.

Take care switching lanes in heavy traffic – check your mirrors for cyclists and motorcyclists who may be moving faster than you

Use MSPSL and try to make eye contact with a driver already in the lane you wish to take. When you are sure the other driver is letting you in, move over gradually and acknowledge the courtesy. Before you move, however, check in your door mirrors for cyclists and motorcyclists driving between the lanes – they may be able to travel faster than other vehicles in congested conditions.

Avoiding accidents with vehicles to your sides

Anticipate the course taken by large vehicles and hold back if necessary

Make sure other drivers are aware of your presence. Avoid driving in the blind areas to their sides.

Look well ahead for obstructions and anticipate when vehicles ahead will need to change lanes. Check your mirrors regularly and be ready to let people into the lane ahead of you.

Their size makes it difficult for larger vehicles to negotiate some turns. They often need to swing out to the right before turning left, or position well over to the left before turning into narrow roads or entrances on the right. When you see large vehicles signalling to turn, keep well back and allow them plenty of space and time.

Larger vehicles often take unusual courses through bends and roundabouts. Anticipate this, keep out of their blind areas and hold back for them when necessary.

Dealing with buses

Buses stop frequently, often with little warning. Stay well back from them and watch for:

- last-minute signals for stopping;
- passengers standing on the bus ready to get off;
- people waiting at bus stops ahead.

Take care near buses and watch out for pedestrians

When you think a bus will be stopping:

- check your mirrors;
- keep well back; and
- position to the offside in case you can get by when it stops.

When passing buses, be aware that passengers may be walking into the road in front of it. Look out for people crossing the road to catch the bus – they may not be paying attention to the traffic! When coming up behind stationary buses, watch for indicator signals. Be prepared to give way where it is safe, particularly in towns.

Dealing with emergency vehicles

Pay attention at all times and stay alert. If you listen to any in-car entertainment, don't have it so loud that it could mask outside noises such as sirens. Use your mirrors regularly, and look and listen. If you hear an emergency vehicle approaching, consider its route. Be ready to take any necessary safe action to let it pass.

Respond safely and promptly to emergency vehicles – remember that someone's life may be at stake

Think before you act – in busy and narrow roads it may be better to keep moving to create a clear path.

Whilst emergency vehicles showing blue lights – police, fire and ambulance services – are permitted to break a speed limit or go against a red

THINK! ✗
Don't react without first checking your mirrors.

✓ Do try to create a clear path for emergency vehicles.

traffic light, their drivers must give priority to others who are obliged to keep within the law. Don't endanger yourself or others when trying to create a clear path for emergency vehicles.

If you see blue lights flashing in your rear-view mirror, stay calm and look ahead for a safe place ahead to move over.

If a police officer wants you to pull over and stop, he or she will usually flash his or her headlights and/or give a left signal or point to the left. If this happens, pull up when you safely can, switch off your engine and wait for the officer to come to you.

Vulnerable road users

Anticipate dangers when your view ahead is restricted by the road layout

There could be anything around a bend or over a hill. Wherever you can't see the road ahead, anticipate that there will be some sort of problem and then you will be ready for it when it appears.

When you are approaching bends and hill crests, especially where there are no pavements, expect to meet people walking in the road. Check your mirrors and be prepared to slow down so that you will be able to stop within the distance you can see is clear.

Areas where there are lots of parked vehicles hide all sorts of problems from the driver. Remember, you may have to drive well below the speed limit in built-up areas. You need to:

- look though car windows for signs of movement;
- leave plenty of clearance, allowing for doors opening;
- look out for hidden junctions – others may be emerging;
- watch for pedestrians walking between parked cars;
- allow for the actions of cyclists.

A high proportion of pedestrians killed in road accidents are either under 15 or over 60. They often misjudge the speed and distance of traffic and may step unexpectedly into the road.

Be patient with the elderly and people with disabilities. Give them plenty of time and don't harass them. Watch out at all times for pedestrians in or near the road, particularly when driving:

- in shopping areas;
- near schools;
- near junctions;
- around ice cream vans and other mobile shops;
- near bus stops.

There won't always be signs warning you of pedestrians in the road. Look well ahead and be prepared to slow down, leaving plenty of clearance in case anyone steps into the road. Sometimes a light tap on the horn can draw attention to your presence. Be particularly careful near schools; not all older children feel the need to cross safely with the crossing patrol. Younger children tend to be impulsive, particularly when they've just come out of school. Check the mirrors, slow down and be ready to stop.

There won't always be signs warning you of pedestrians in the road!

Cyclists and motorcyclists are more difficult to see. When emerging from junctions, watch for cyclists and motorcyclists riding close to the left, particularly when there are lines of parked vehicles close to the junction. Make sure you look properly whatever the conditions, but especially in poor light and bad weather.

Take a good look for cyclists and motorcyclists when emerging at junctions

Cyclists don't always check behind before they pull out to pass obstructions. Check your mirrors, slow down and expect them to steer out at the last moment. The closer you get to them, the more cyclists will wobble. Allow them plenty of room. If you can't give them at least 2 metres clearance, then slow right down so that you can stop safely if they cycle into your path for any reason.

In queuing traffic, check your mirrors for cyclists before moving off

Horses are easily frightened by vehicle noise

When you have been waiting in a traffic queue, check your mirrors for cyclists before moving off. Take particular care if you have been queuing to turn at a junction.

Horse riders need extra care. Make sure you have enough room before you pass them. Check your mirrors, and slow down well before you reach them even if they are on the other side of the road. Drive quietly past, leaving as much room as possible. Expect to see horse riders near riding schools and on rural roads. Take heed of any signals a horse rider may give you.

Notes:

Notes:

Notes:

Assessment – vulnerable road users

Avoiding accidents on country roads

Concentrate and plan well ahead. Remember, speed limits are the maximum allowed for the road – not targets! It is a sobering thought that loss of control on country roads is one of the commonest causes of death amongst young and inexperienced drivers. Drive at a speed at which you can stop within the distance you can see is clear.

The countryside holds different dangers from towns and cities. You never know what there may be around the next bend. Drive more slowly on narrow roads, through villages and near farm entrances. Expect to see wild and domestic animals on the road. Expect to meet large and slow-moving farm vehicles.

The countryside holds different dangers from towns and cities

Be prepared to give way. On single-track roads there are sometimes pulling-in places. Plan well ahead and work out whether you will need to pull into one on your side or wait opposite one so the approaching vehicle can pull in.

Be patient when following slow-moving vehicles. Do not overtake until you are absolutely sure that it will be safe. In rural areas, expect mud in the road in wet weather.

Make sure you can be seen

Lights should be used, not only when it's too dark or foggy for you to see properly, but to help others see you.

When daylight conditions are poor, or in heavy rain and snow, use dipped headlights so others can see you!

When daylight conditions are poor, or in heavy rain and snow, use your dipped headlights. When visibility falls to below 100 metres, use your fog lights. These should not, however, be used at other times. When used at the wrong time, high-intensity rear lights can mask the brake lights so that following drivers have little or no warning that you may be slowing down. Front fog lights can dazzle and annoy oncoming drivers – use them properly.

Avoiding accidents at night

In darkness keep a good look out for pedestrians who may be wearing dark clothing

It's much harder to see at night. Your view may be masked by shadows, particularly at dusk. Watch out for cyclists riding without lights and pedestrians wearing dark clothing, particularly where there is no footpath or you are approaching a junction.

Use dipped headlights in built-up areas so that you can see and be seen.

Use full headlights where the street lighting is poor. Be ready to dip them for oncoming drivers and when you are following other vehicles so that they don't cause dazzle in the mirrors.

Fog, snow and ice

Only drive in poor weather conditions if your journey is absolutely necessary.

If you must drive in fog, use dipped headlights. If visibility is really bad, switch on the fog and high-intensity rear lights. To keep down condensation in your car, use the demister and rear screen heater. A slightly open window will not only help this but also help you hear other traffic before you can see it.

Driving in fog during the hours of darkness requires extra care

Don't be tempted to follow others too closely in fog – remember, they may brake suddenly. Keep your distance. Drive at a speed at which you can stop safely, and remember that not all other drivers will be using their headlights.

Watch out for obstructions in the road, and drive at a distance at which you can stop safely. Signals for passing parked vehicles and other hazards will become more necessary, as it is more difficult for following drivers to see obstructions.

Don't use full beam headlights in fog. At night your forward vision would be seriously reduced

When waiting to turn right into minor roads in fog, it may help to keep your foot on the brake pedal – this will give you an extra set of lights to the rear.

Driving in fog at night is particularly dangerous. Avoid the temptation of clinging to the tail lights of the vehicle ahead. Use dipped headlights in fog at night – if you try to use full beam, reflection from the mist will seriously reduce your forward vision.

In freezing conditions, avoid accelerating or braking on exposed parts of the road such as bridges. There could be black ice, which is almost impossible to detect.

In snow or icy conditions you should:

- slow down early using light pressure on the brake pedal;

- accelerate gently and stay in the highest gear possible;

- when driving uphill try to keep moving steadily by keeping well back from the vehicle ahead;

- remember that road markings may be hidden.

Avoiding problems by reading the road ahead

Always read the road well ahead and take the weather conditions into consideration.

Check your mirrors and slow down when you can see the road surface deteriorating. Keep off soft verges and look out for mud, gravel or chippings. When it rains after a long spell of dry weather, a combination of oil, dust, rubber and water can make the surface very slippery.

In the autumn, watch for damp patches under trees, where leaves can also make the surface slippery. In the winter, these areas will hold frost longer than the parts of the road the sun has reached.

Driving in windy conditions

When overtaking high-sided vehicles, expect to feel the wind throwing you off course as you pass by. This will be even worse in high exposed places, such as bridges. Hold the steering wheel firmly to compensate.

When driving in lanes, anticipate other road users being

affected.

Driving through floods and fords

Look well ahead for signs, and always be aware of what is behind. At some fords there are gauges to tell :ep the water may be. Slow down, change into first gear and, using a slipping clutch, keep the engine revs up. Look for any camber in the road, and drive slowly through at the shallowest point.

Ford

When you reach the other side you need to make sure the brakes are dry. Drive very slowly and press the brake gently with your left foot.

Avoiding aquaplaning

Aquaplaning can happen when a cushion of water is built up in front of fast-moving tyres. If the tyres cannot displace the water, they may ride up on to it, losing contact with the road surface. The steering will become light, and you could also lose your braking control.

To avoid aquaplaning:

- keep your tyres in good condition and properly inflated;
- make sure your brakes are well maintained;
- plan well ahead, adapting your speed to suit the conditions;
- take into account the road and weather conditions.

Checkpoint 8

1 If you must drive in fog:
  Choose three answers

  a. drive nearer to the centre line
  b. use dipped headlights
  c. use full beam headlights

    d. keep your footbrake on when waiting to turn right off a main road

    e. allow more time for your journey

2 When driving near animals you should be ready to:
Choose two answers

    a. slow down or stop

    b. sound your horn

    c. drive quickly away

    d. give lots of clearance

3 If you park on the road at night, you use your sidelights:
Choose two answers

    a. on a road with a speed limit of less than 30 mph

    b. on a road with a speed limit of more than 30 mph

    c. if parking within 10 metres of a junction

    d. if the road is poorly lit

4 You should only flash your headlights:
Choose one answer

    a. when you want another driver to give way to you

    b. when you are giving way

    c. to let others know you are there

    d. to encourage pedestrians to use zebra crossings

5 You should be careful and considerate to other road users. You should:
Choose two answers

    a. expect others to take the correct action

    b. expect others to make mistakes

    c. always be ready to give way

    d. only give priority when you have no choice

6 Staying well back from a slower-moving vehicle will:
Choose three answers

    a. give you a better view ahead

    b. help you to anticipate its actions

c. make it more difficult to overtake

d. make it safer to overtake

e. waste road space

7 Wind or side draught can affect your car:
   Choose two answers

   a. in high exposed places

   b. if you drive at high speed with your sunroof open

   c. mainly in built-up areas

   d. after overtaking a large vehicle

8 If a following driver becomes impatient when you are waiting to emerge into a busy road, you should:
   Choose one answer

   a. pull out as quickly as you can

   b. keep calm and wait for a safe gap in the traffic

   c. take as long as you can to teach the other driver some manners

   d. put on your high-intensity rear lights to distract the other driver

9 Driving on a fairly narrow road, you see ahead a large vehicle emerging from a road on the right. You should:
   Choose three answers

   a. expect the large vehicle to swing out into the road

   b. ignore the situation because the other driver should give way

   c. check your mirrors and steer well in to the left

   d. hold back and give the other driver plenty of room

   e. sound your horn and maintain your course

10 Elderly pedestrians are particularly vulnerable. They:
   Choose two answers

   a. should be able to judge your speed

   b. may not be able to judge your speed

   c. could step out into the road

   d. should be encouraged to hurry across the road

   e. tend to be impulsive and make a dash for it

11 If you see someone with a white cane with a red band, he or she is:
   Choose one answer

a. deaf and blind
b. deaf and mute
c. blind and mute
d. fitted with a hearing aid

12 If a pedestrian is hit by a car travelling at 20 mph, the chance of the pedestrian being killed is:
Choose one answer

a. 1 in 10

b. 1 in 20
c. 1 in 30
d. 1 in 40

13 You should only use a hand-held mobile phone when:
Choose one answer

a. driving on motorways
b. driving in towns
c. you are stopped in a safe place
d. you want to answer a call

14 What does this sign mean?

Choose one answer

a. high-grip surface ahead
b. slippery road
c. danger of ice
d. off-road vehicles only

15 When an emergency vehicle approaches you should:
Choose two answers

a. try not to panic
b. stop your car immediately
c. speed up to get out of the way
d. pull on to the footpath to get clear
e. check your mirrors before deciding on the safest course of action

16 Driving after snowfall, you see this road sign at a junction ahead.
You should:

Choose one answer

a. keep going slowly past the sign
b. stop and check for traffic on the main road
c. ignore the sign
d. report the danger to your local highway authority

17 Fog lights should be used:
Choose one answer

a. whenever you need to use headlights
b. when you drive in rural areas at night
c. only in foggy weather
d. whenever visibility is less than 100 metres

18 In wet weather your tyres:

Choose one answer

a. have less grip on the road
b. have more grip on the road
c. need to be inflated to a higher pressure
d. need to be inflated to a lower pressure

19 Before driving away in icy conditions you should:
Choose two answers

a. clear a patch in the windscreen
b. clear the front and side windows
c. clear all of the windows
d. demist the windows thoroughly

20 You are driving on a narrow rural road and see this sign. You should:

Choose three answers

a. check your mirrors because of the hazard
b. not worry, as you are on the road with priority
c. beware of emerging traffic
d. be prepared to stop if necessary
e. position towards the centre of the road
f. maintain your speed and sound your horn

You will find the answers on page 425.

Scores: First try   Second try   Third try

Record your scores in Appendix 2 (page 426).

Stage 9
Driving at higher speeds, basic maintenance and dealing with emergencies

By now you should be able to drive confidently in most of the situations covered in the previous eight stages and may have done some driving on higher-speed roads. At this stage your instructor should be making sure you can drive safely and confidently at higher speeds. You may have to take longer lessons to get to areas where there are dual carriageways that carry the national speed limit. Driving on this type of road will prepare you for motorway driving. Although as a learner you are not allowed to drive on motorways, you do need to know the rules. Not only will this prepare you for your theory test, but it will mean that as soon as you have passed the test you will be able to apply those rules.

It is your responsibility as a driver to ensure that the car you are driving is roadworthy. Of course, if you are taking professional tuition in a driving school car you should expect your instructor to take care of it. He or she should show you how to carry out basic safety checks on your vehicle that will be important when you are practising in your own vehicle. You should know how to carry out simple tasks, including:

- checking tyre pressures and tread;
- changing wheels;
- checking oil and water levels;
- checking and replacing bulbs.

You will be asked questions on these and other vehicle checks in the theory test and may be asked to show or describe how you would perform some of these tasks in your practical test. You should also know what to do in cases of breakdowns and other emergencies.

To help you prepare for this stage, you can also:

- Read *The Official DSA Guide to Driving: The essential skills*, Part 11 – Driving on motorways, Part 14 – Basic maintenance, Part 15 – Breakdowns, Part 16 – Accidents and emergencies, Part 17 – Eco-safe driving and the environment, and Part 18 – Avoiding and dealing with congestion.

- Read *The Official DSA Guide to Learning to Drive*, Section 2 – Safety checks, Section 2 – Independent driving, Section 2 – Environmental issues, Section 2 – Passengers and loads, Section 2 – Security.

- Read *The Highway Code*, Annex 6 – Vehicle maintenance, safety and security, and Annex 7 – First aid on the road.

Learn the following *Highway Code* rules:

- 253–73 Motorways.
- 274–87 Breakdowns and accidents.
- 288–90 Road works.

Planning your journeys

During your final preparation for your practical driving test you should learn how to navigate without prompts from your supervisor or instructor. This should help prepare you for some driving alone after you have passed. Here are some tips for preparing for a journey:

- Allow yourself plenty of time. In today's congested traffic you cannot depend on getting to your destination in the shortest possible time. The later you are, the more frustrated you will become, to the point where you may even be tempted to take risks.

- Plan your journey. Organize yourself with a route plan, noting down all the road numbers and names of towns. Start out early, making sure you allow time for road works and other problems. A route card only takes a few minutes to prepare, and if you have internet access it is easy to download route plans and information. It is worth doing this even if you have satnav technology in your vehicle.

- Learn how to read and follow road signs. Keep up to date with traffic news by tuning your car radio to local stations or having the traffic announcement (TA) system switched on.

- Keep your concentration to a maximum. If you are going a long distance, take plenty of breaks. Keep the temperature comfortable and not too stuffy. Listen only to light programmes on the radio or music centre. Remember, fiddling about with discs and tapes can be a distraction whilst you are driving.

- Mobile phones. In emergencies, mobile phones can be extremely useful (particularly if you are a lone female driver). Remember, however, that they should only be used when you are stationary.

Lane discipline

When you drive on any type of dual carriageway or motorway, make sure you keep to the correct lane. People not driving in the left lane when it is reasonably clear cause many of the hold-ups that occur on these roads.

Remember, on a three-lane motorway you should:

- use the left lane for normal driving unless there are a number of slower-moving vehicles – you may then use the centre lane;

- use the centre lane as above, but return to the left lane when it is clear;

- use the right lane for overtaking only.

Look and plan well ahead, using your mirrors to keep aware of what is happening all around all of the time. Work out in good time whether the traffic ahead in the left and centre lanes is moving more slowly and you need to consider overtaking. This will allow you more thinking time after checking the mirrors to work out whether or not your manoeuvre will be safe.

Anticipate drivers ahead preparing to overtake, and be prepared to act. You may either slow down a little or, if safe, move over to the next lane on your right. Expect people to be joining the motorway from slip roads and, if you have time and it is safe, be prepared to move over to allow them on to the main carriageway.

When approaching your exits, look for the signs and plan ahead so that you can get over in good time without causing problems for other drivers. You will see advance warnings for motorway exits usually at one mile and half a mile before the turn-off. These may be at the side of the carriageway or they may be overhead gantry signs. By the time you reach the countdown markers you should be in the left lane. Remember that the deceleration lane is for slowing down. Unless there are queues for your exit, try not to slow down drivers on the motorway.

Speed can be deceiving. Once in the deceleration lane, keep checking your speed and make sure you have full control as you approach the junction. If you have been driving at higher speeds for some time, you will think you are travelling much more slowly than you are when you first leave the motorway.

Get into the left lane in good time for your exit on motorways and dual carriageways

Reducing the risk of breakdowns

Your car should be maintained in a roadworthy condition. Before driving at any time, take a look around your vehicle for any obvious defects. You don't need to be a qualified mechanic to make some basic safety checks! These will reduce the chances of your being involved in breakdowns and accidents.

If you are capable of undertaking more than basic maintenance yourself, make sure you use only approved parts and lubricants as recommended by the vehicle manufacturer.

You don't need to be a mechanic to take care of basic maintenance

Regular checks – at least once a week

The frequency of these checks will depend on how often and how much you drive. The owner's handbook will give advice for your car:

- Fuel: Try to avoid running on less than a quarter-tank. Check your fuel as soon as you switch on. Remember, if you are travelling far, it may be a long way to the next service station.

- Oil: Check the engine oil and top up as necessary with the correct type of oil for your vehicle. When you move your car from its regular parking spot, it is worth looking to see if there are telltale oil drips that could indicate a leak. If the oil pressure warning light comes on whilst driving, stop as soon as it is safe and check the problem out. If you run your engine without oil, it could seize up.

- Brake fluid: You should be able to identify the brake fluid reservoir in your engine compartment and check the level against the 'minimum' mark. When topping up the brake fluid level, be careful not to contaminate the reservoir with dust, dirt or water.

- Windscreen wash: Make sure that there is water in the washer bottle and that the windscreen washer jets are functioning. In winter it is worth mixing an additive with water in the wash bottle so that it doesn't freeze.

- When the engine is cold, check the radiator coolant. If it needs topping up, use the correct mixture of water and coolant/antifreeze. It is best to make fluid checks on a level surface when the engine has been switched off and allowed to stand for at least 30 minutes.

- Electrics: Before driving, check that all the lights and indicators are working. Keep spare bulbs in the car. Although many car batteries are now sealed units, yours may be the type that needs checking.

Check that the electrolyte fluid level in the battery covers the plates. If necessary, top this up with distilled water.

- Visually check your tyres, looking for any obvious cuts or bulges, and check for uneven tyre wear. Remove any stones from the tread. Use a reliable pressure gauge to check that your tyres are properly inflated. You could get a puncture at any time, so check the spare as well. Check the tyre tread depth against the wear markers on the tyre. You can also use a depth indicator to measure how worn your tyres are.

Check your tyres for obvious defects and signs of uneven tread wear

Use a reliable gauge to check type pressures

Changing a wheel

You can get a puncture at any time, so it well worth knowing how to deal with it before you start driving by yourself. Read the owner's handbook for your vehicle.

When changing a wheel, as a matter of routine you should park on level, firm ground. Apply the parking brake and leave the car in gear (in an automatic, select Park). If you are on the road, switch on your hazard warning lights. Two items that are worth carrying in the car are a hazard warning triangle and a high-visibility vest. Wear the vest if you have it, and place your warning triangle at least 45 metres behind your car on the same side of the road.

Hazard warning triangles should be placed at least 45 metres behind the car but you should not use one on a motorway

Unfortunately, you never know when or where you will get a puncture. If you are on a slope, position

Changing a wheel, you need to loosen the wheel nuts slightly before jacking the car up

Refer to the vehicle handbook to locate the correct jacking points and make sure the base of the jack is on firm ground

Have everything ready before you jack the car up

a chock, brick or heavy object at each side of one of the good wheels to prevent movement. Be aware of other traffic, and try not to stand in front of your lights at night.

Place the spare wheel, jack and wheel brace (spanner) near the tyre to be changed. Slightly loosen the wheel nuts of the flat tyre before you jack the car up. If these are difficult to turn you may have to use your foot and body-weight on the lever. Make sure you support yourself as you do this, so that you are not injured.

Position the jack at a suitable point under the vehicle – refer to the owner's handbook to locate special jacking points. Make sure that the base of the jack is on a firm and level surface so that it can't tilt or collapse when the car is raised. Now raise the vehicle enough to allow room for the properly inflated tyre to be fitted.

Remove the wheel nuts and put them safely to one side where you can find them again! Remove the wheel with the flat tyre and replace it with the spare.

Fit the new wheel, locating two opposite nuts finger tight. Fit the other nuts and tighten them all lightly with the brace. Then lower the jack and tighten the nuts firmly.

Remove the chocks, and remember to replace the tools and the flat tyre in the boot. Check the pressure of the replacement tyre as soon as possible.

Instead of a full-size spare wheel, some cars have a 'space-saver tyre' or an emergency inflation kit that simultaneously re-inflates and seals the inside of the tyre. These are only intended as temporary repairs. The owner's handbook will advise you on these and may recommend a maximum speed and distance that a space-saver or re-inflated tyre can be used for until you can get a puncture properly repaired.

If you break down

If possible, try not to inconvenience others, and get your car off the road. Switch on your hazard flashers and place your warning triangle 45 metres behind the car on the same side of the road. At night, be careful not to stand in front of your lights. If you are a lone female, in quieter areas lock yourself in the car and be prepared to speak to others through a slightly open window.

If you don't have a mobile phone and there is no one around, you may have to walk for assistance yourself. Make sure you lock the car, putting any valuables in the boot.

In cases of emergency the police and motoring organizations give priority to lone women.

Before setting out on a long journey, it can be useful to let someone know your route, destination and estimated time of arrival.

If you break down on a motorway

If your car develops a problem, try to get it to the next exit or service area. If you can't do this:

- Get over to the hard shoulder as safely as possible and stop as far to the left as you can.
- Switch on your hazard warning lights.
- Try to stop near one of the emergency telephones.
- If you have a disability and can't get out of the car, display a 'help' sign and wait for the police.
- You and your passengers should exit to the nearside.
- Unless they are in real danger, leave animals in the car.
- Do not try to 'fix it' – you could put yourself in danger even changing a wheel.
- Make sure all passengers get on to the verge as far away from the carriageway and hard shoulder as possible.
- Keep children, and animals, under control.
- Walk to the nearest emergency telephone. An arrow on the post will tell you which

Marker posts are at 100 metre intervals and an arrow indicates the direction to the nearest emergency telephone way this is. This is a free service, and you will get a quicker response than by using a mobile.

- Face the traffic flow when using the telephone.

- Give full details, and inform the operator if you are a lone woman.

- Go back and wait on the verge near your vehicle.

- Should you feel threatened by someone, get in your car from the left and lock the doors. If the danger passes, get out and on to the verge again.

Emergency telephones are at about one mile intervals on the motorway. Face the traffic flow when using the phone

What to do at the scene of an accident

You never know when you're going to arrive at the scene of an accident. Could you do anything to help or would you be one of those who just stands and stares?

Keep a first aid kit in your car

Keep a first aid kit in your car where it will be easy to get at if needed – it's no good buried under your luggage!

If you get to the scene before anyone else, keep calm. The first thing to do is warn other traffic – switch on hazard lights and seek assistance. Take charge until someone better qualified arrives. Either call yourself or get someone else to phone for the emergency services.

Impose a smoking ban at the scene! Don't put yourself in danger trying to help a casualty.

People with injuries should be kept warm and calm. Talk to casualties constantly to keep them reassured. Do not give them anything to eat or drink. Only move a casualty if there is the real possibility of further danger to him or her.

Some knowledge of first aid can be very helpful – you could save a life by following some of the simple procedures outlined in Part 16 of *The Official DSA Guide to Driving: The essential skills* and in the annex of

The Highway Code. Could you save a life if you found a casualty not breathing?

If you'd like to better equip yourself for dealing with anyone injured in an accident, the St John Ambulance service runs courses all over the country – look in your *Yellow Pages.*

Are you equipped to save a life?

Reducing the risk of fire

Although the risk of fire in modern cars is minimal, it is sensible to carry a fire extinguisher – and know how to use it!

Pipes can become damaged in accidents, and fuel could leak on to electrical contacts. The engine of any vehicle involved should be switched off immediately.

If no one else has done so, impose a 'no smoking' rule at the scene. If you suspect your car may have electrical problems, get it checked as soon as possible.

It is worthwhile carrying a small fire extinguisher in your car

If you suspect there is a fire in the engine compartment at any time:

- Pull in as soon as you can and get everyone out and well clear of the vehicle.
- Call the fire services or get someone to do it for you.
- Go back and wait on the verge near your vehicle.
- *Do not* open the bonnet – try to direct a fire extinguisher through the gap created when you operate the bonnet latch release.
- Don't risk injury to yourself if the fire can't be extinguished quickly and easily. Get well clear and wait for the fire brigade. A fire in the engine compartment can completely destroy a vehicle in less than five minutes!

Breakdowns in tunnels

Tunnels present particular problems if you have a breakdown or emergency, because it can be difficult for you to get clear and others to reach you.

If you have a breakdown or accident, switch on hazard warning lights, leave your vehicle and, after dealing with any casualties, get to an emergency refuge point to call for help.

If your vehicle catches fire in a tunnel and you can still drive it, try to get it out of the tunnel before the fire gets out of control. If you can't drive clear, stop and try to put out the fire (there are fire extinguishers in tunnels). If that fails, get to a refuge point as soon as you can and call for assistance.

Dealing with road works

Delays are inevitable when the carriageway needs to be repaired. You need to take a common-sense approach to these situations and follow some basic safety rules so that accidents and further delays are avoided.

Road works are well signposted, particularly on fast and busy roads. Slow down and get into the correct lane in good time. Remember that there will be workers in the road who might not be concentrating on the traffic. Obey any speed limit that is in force, and keep a good separation distance so that you can avoid braking sharply.

On dual carriageways and motorways it is often the case that a contraflow system is in operation. This permits traffic travelling in the opposite direction to use the same carriageway. This means reduced lane widths and higher traffic density. On motorways, signs may indicate that you should use the hard shoulder as part of the carriageway. Take care in these situations – if a vehicle breaks down, there is nowhere for the driver to pull in!

Vehicle security

The theft of vehicles and their contents has now become extremely common. To reduce the risks, make sure you secure your car and its contents properly. You should:

- close all windows and sunroofs;

- retract aerials where possible;

- use a steering wheel lock;

- put valuables in the boot;

- remove the keys while in filling stations;

- get your windows etched with the registration number;

- get an immobilizer fitted;

- buy only coded audio equipment;

- use lockable fuel caps and wheel nuts if possible.

Park your car in well-lit areas if possible. If you are leaving a window open for a pet, it is sensible to fit a grille into the gap to deter any would-be thief.

Be alert: if you see anyone acting suspiciously around another vehicle, call the police.

The driver and the environment

Whilst owning and driving a car are seen by most as an essential part of modern life, you shouldn't forget that the environment suffers in consequence.

Vehicles consume energy and cause pollution. Your choice of vehicle, your style of driving and the times you choose to drive can all contribute to environmental damage and global warming:

- Think before you buy; choose a vehicle with a fuel-efficient engine. Consider alternative fuels such as LPG.

- Think before you drive; short journeys such as the 'school run' contribute to congestion and waste fuel. Wouldn't it be better to walk or use public transport?

- Think about the environment; keep your vehicle well maintained and adopt a driving style that avoids late braking and harsh acceleration. Driving in a fuel-efficient 'eco-safe' way will help the environment and help your pocket!

Checkpoint 9

1   Red reflective studs mark the:
Choose one answer

    a.   right edge of the road
    b.   left edge of the road
    c.   centre of motorways
    d.   motorway entry slip roads

2   Driving on to a motorway, you should use the slip road to:
Choose two answers

    a.   build up your speed
    b.   look for a gap in the traffic
    c.   change into fifth gear
    d.   check over your left shoulder

3   When joining a motorway you should be travelling at:
Choose one answer

    a.   50 mph
    b.   60 mph
    c.   70 mph
    d.   the speed of the traffic in the left lane of the main carriageway

4   To leave a motorway you should:
Choose two answers

    a.   keep a lookout for the signs
    b.   move to the left lane as soon as you see the 300-yard marker
    c.   move to the left lane well before reaching the exit markers
    d.   slow down as soon as you see the half-mile marker
    e.   move on to the hard shoulder as you approach the exit

5   If something falls from your car whilst you are on a motorway you should:
Choose one answer

    a.   stop on the hard shoulder and retrieve it
    b.   stop on the hard shoulder and telephone the police
    c.   leave at the next exit and telephone the police
    d.   consider it irretrievable and forget about it

6 If you see this sign above your lane on a motorway you should:

Choose one answer

a. not proceed further in that lane
b. leave the motorway at the next exit
c. ignore it, as it is a warning for high vehicles
d. slow down to less than 50 mph and continue

7 If you break down on a two-laned road you should first of all:
Choose one answer

a. telephone for the breakdown service
b. think of other traffic
c. get your passengers out
d. call home on your mobile phone

8 If you are driving on a motorway and think there may be a problem with your car, you should first of all:
Choose one answer

a. use your mobile phone to call the police
b. try to get over to the hard shoulder
c. get your passengers out of the car
d. telephone for the breakdown service

9 Anxiety and frustration when driving can be reduced by:
Choose two answers

a. starting your journey earlier
b. keeping the air conditioning on
c. taking anti-depressants
d. accepting that you will sometimes be held up in traffic queues
e. sounding your horn and flashing your headlights

10 If you break down on a two-lane highway, you should place a warning triangle:

Choose two answers

a. at least 45 metres behind your car
b. at least 45 metres ahead of your car
c. on the opposite side of the road
d. on the same side of the road

11 If you break down on a motorway you should:
Choose two answers

    a.   place a warning triangle at least 100 metres behind your car

    b.   not use a warning triangle

    c.   switch on the hazard warning lights

    d.   switch on the fog lights at night

12 When wishing to leave a motorway that is carrying freely moving traffic, you should slow down:
Choose one answer

    a.   as soon as you see the half-mile sign

    b.   as soon as you see the 300-yard marker

    c.   as soon as you move into the left lane

    d.   when you move into the slip road

13 When you see a sign for road works you:
Choose one answer

    a.   may exceed any temporary speed limit

    b.   must not exceed any temporary speed limit

    c.   may switch lanes to get into a shorter queue

    d.   may go through a red light at night if there is no oncoming traffic

14 On a three-lane motorway you see this sign on a slow-moving vehicle ahead that is in the middle lane. The sign displays flashing amber lights. You should:

Choose two answers

    a.   approach slowly and overtake on the right

    b.   keep behind the vehicle until it leaves the motorway

    c.   expect that there will be a workforce in the road ahead

    d.   approach cautiously and overtake on the left

    e.   obey the instruction to leave the motorway at the next exit

15 If you're involved in an accident causing damage to property or injury to someone you must:
Choose three answers

a. drive straight to a police station to report the incident
b. stop
c. give your name and address to anyone with grounds for requiring them
d. give the registration number and the name of the owner to anyone with grounds for requiring them
e. not give your details to anyone until you have spoken with your insurance company

16 If you cannot produce your insurance certificate at the time of an accident that involves injury, you must produce it for the police within:
Choose one answer

a. 24 hours
b. two days
c. five days
d. seven days

17 You see an accident ahead involving a vehicle displaying this sign. You should:

Choose two answers

a. stop and switch off your engine
b. stop and leave your engine running
c. use a mobile phone to call for help
d. not use a mobile phone close to the vehicle
e. not stop because of the danger

18 If you get a puncture in a tyre whilst driving you should:
Choose two answers

   a.   brake as quickly as you can
   b.   not brake suddenly
   c.   steer briskly to the left
   d.   try to keep the car straight

19 At the scene of an accident you are treating a casualty who has burns to the arms. You should:
Choose three answers

   a.   give the casualty plenty to drink
   b.   try to cool the burns with clean liquid
   c.   talk to the casualty and give reassurance
   d.   remove any clothing stuck to the burns
   e.   keep the casualty moving to prevent shock setting in
   f.   get the casualty to lie down

20 Someone is injured in an accident and has stopped breathing. The person's airway is clear, so the first thing you should do is:
Choose one answer

   a.   tilt the person's head forward
   b.   put the person in the recovery position
   c.   give chest compressions to maintain circulation
   d.   pinch the person's nose and blow into his or her mouth

You will find the answers on page 425.

Scores: First try   Second try   Third try

Record your scores in Appendix 2 (page 426).

Stage 10
The driving test and the Pass Plus scheme

Once you have passed the theory test, you should be able to concentrate on putting all of the rules you have learned into practice in preparation for your practical test.

If you've had sufficient driving lessons and plenty of practice, you should be able to carry out confidently all of the skills listed in *The Official DSA Guide to Learning to Drive*. Read Section 4 – The test and beyond for information about what to expect on your practical test.

Applying for the test

You can apply for a driving test appointment by phone, online or by post. Seek guidance from your instructor on completing the booking. If you are going to use a driving school car for your test, your instructor will need to tell you when it is available. If there is a waiting time for tests in your area, get advice from your instructor on when to apply. This will ensure that:

- you can avoid unnecessary delays;
- you don't get an appointment before you're ready;
- your instructor doesn't have another test at the same time.

When booking your test it is important to tell the DSA about any special circumstances or disability that you may have. You will still have to take the same test as anyone else, but more time will be allowed so that the examiner can talk about your disability or any adaptations the vehicle may have. If you need an interpreter to attend with you, ensure you make arrangements in good time.

Before the test

A few lessons prior to the test, your instructor will probably conduct a couple of mock tests. This will:

- ensure that you can still read a number plate at the prescribed distance;
- demonstrate what it's like to drive totally unaided;
- ensure that you both know you can deal with hazards effectively without any help;
- show up any weaknesses in your knowledge or skills.

If your instructor still has to give you help, you will not be ready to cope on your own, either during or after the test. If this is the case, it is advisable to postpone your test. You must give the DSA at least three clear working days' notice. Otherwise, you will lose the fee.

Your vehicle

Take note of the comments in *The Official DSA Guide to Learning to Drive*, Section 4 – The day of your test. If you are in a driving school vehicle, your instructor should have ensured compliance with all the requirements. If you are taking the test in your own vehicle, make sure that:

Make sure your vehicle meets the requirements for the driving test

- a valid tax disc is displayed;
- L plates (or D plates in Wales) are clearly displayed to the front and rear of the vehicle;
- your seat belts are clean and working properly;
- head restraints are fitted;
- there is an additional rear-view mirror for the examiner to use.
- If your vehicle does not comply, you will not be able to take the test and you will lose your fee.

Note that some makes and models of vehicle (such as convertibles) are considered unsuitable for a driving test because examiners have no clear view to the rear, other than by use of mirrors. Check with your instructor and the DSA if unsure about the suitability of your vehicle.

Arriving at the test centre

When your instructor picks you up on the day of your test, make sure that you have:

- the appointment card;
- your theory test pass certificate;
- your provisional driving licence.

If you have a photocard licence, you must bring the paper counterpart licence with you. If you don't have a photocard licence you must bring your paper licence and your passport as photographic proof of identity.

Your instructor will make sure that you arrive early, leaving plenty of time to park and relax. Tell your instructor in good time if you wish to use the toilet. Some test centres do not have facilities.

It is natural for test candidates to feel a little anxious. Don't worry; your instructor wouldn't let you attempt the test if you were not ready!

You must have acceptable photographic evidence of identity when you attend for your driving test

The test

Your examiner will ask you to sign a form. Your signature will be checked against that on your driving licence and other means of identification.

If you wish your instructor to sit in the car for the test, ask the examiner at this point. You will be asked whether you have any physical disabilities not declared in your application form.

Sometimes senior examiners have to accompany driving examiners on tests. This is to ensure uniformity is maintained. Try to relax, and remember that the examiner, not you, is being checked by this person.

Your examiner will do his or her best to put you at ease, and it is acceptable to chat with the examiner during your test if that helps you relax. Don't be put off if the examiner doesn't say too much – he or she doesn't want to distract you from your driving.

Your eyesight

HK55 WES

Your eyesight will be tested before you get in the car

Before you get into the car you will be asked to read a number plate. You will probably feel a little nervous, and this could affect how you see the letters and numbers. Take your time and try not to get flustered.

Vehicle safety questions

Before the driving part of the test begins, the examiner will ask you two questions related to vehicle safety. Known as 'show me, tell me' questions, these are designed to show that you know basic maintenance and operation procedures for the vehicle you are driving for the test. These checks may require you to open the bonnet of the car and identify fluid reservoirs. You are not asked to touch a hot engine or physically check any fluid levels. There are 19 questions in all, and they are asked in set combinations (see Appendix 1). As a driver, you should recognize the importance of basic vehicle maintenance and safety – do not simply learn the questions and answers by rote.

It can be dangerous to perform these safety checks if you are unsure of what to do. Your instructor will advise you how to make these checks safely on your driving test vehicle. You are recommended to wear disposable vinyl gloves for under-bonnet checks and wear a high-visibility vest when making safety checks outside the vehicle. Your instructor should be able to provide these for you.

Following the show me, tell me questions, you will be asked to seat yourself in your car whilst the examiner takes a look around to make sure it's roadworthy.

During the test

The examiner will explain the instructions that will be given. Unless you are asked to turn left or right, you should follow the road ahead or go in the direction of any signs or markings. Remember, this is all part of the test. The examiner is checking that you can read and follow signs on your own. If you see a 'Turn left' or 'Turn right' sign, obey it. Don't be tempted to ask which way to go.

During the first few minutes, the examiner should give you time to settle down. Try to relax and concentrate on what is happening on the road all around rather than wondering what the person sitting by your side is thinking.

Put everything into practice that your instructor has taught you. Show how confident you can be. Don't try to be over-careful, but take all safe opportunities to proceed. However, if you are at all in doubt, hold back.

Planning ahead

Show how well you can drive by:

Your examiner will expect you to respond appropriately to traffic signs and signals

- looking and planning well ahead;
- making good use of all of the mirrors;
- showing discrimination in the use and timing of signals;
- concentrating on what is happening all around;
- adjusting your speed well before you reach any hazards by using all of the controls gently – demonstrating eco-safe driving technique;
- allowing adequate clearance and safety margins;
- showing care and consideration to all other road users;
- anticipating and making allowance for others' mistakes.

Make proper progress: you will not impress your examiner by being over-cautious!

The manoeuvre exercises

During the test you will be asked to pull in on the left. This is also part of the test. Make sure you stop where it is safe, legal and convenient. If you are asked to pull in behind another vehicle, make sure you leave plenty of room for moving away again.

As well as making normal stops you may be asked to carry out an emergency stop. You will also be asked to carry out one of the following exercises:

- reverse to the left (or right if in a van);
- turn the car round in the road;

- reverse park behind another vehicle;
- park in a bay in the test centre car park.

You should have had plenty of practice at all of these exercises. Remember, the things your examiner will be looking for are good control, accuracy and all-round observations:

- Control: Work out what sort of gradient you are on so that you'll know whether to control the speed with the gas and clutch or with the brake. Keep the speed down so that you have full control of the steering wheel and plenty of time to keep checking for others. Maintain full control throughout and use the parking brake when necessary.
- Accuracy: Keeping the speed down should help you carry out all of the exercises efficiently. Make sure you finish all of the reversing exercises in a safe place.
- Observations: Show that you can respond safely to other road users. Remember, when you are manoeuvring, others have priority.

The independent driving exercise

For about 10 minutes of your test you will be asked to drive by:

- Following road markings and traffic signs to a destination.
- Following a series of verbal directions such as you might get if you had pulled in to ask your way to a local destination.
- A combination of the above.

This is so that your examiner can assess how you manage road systems and deal with traffic on your own.

This part of the test will begin with the examiner asking you to pull in at a safe place. He or she will explain what is required. If necessary, the examiner may use a flash card to illustrate the route you need to take. Route cards relate to the local road layout as shown in the examples below.

Do not worry if you can't remember all the directions you are given – if you need to just ask the examiner for a reminder. You could simply pull in where safe and ask, just as you would if driving by yourself. You can't fail the test for taking a wrong turn in this part of the test – your examiner will guide you back to your route.

At the end of the test

When you return to the test centre, your examiner will complete a driving test report form. This will show those items on which you made mistakes. Not all mistakes result in failure, only those that were serious or danger-ous; you will also fail if you accumulate more than 15 driver faults. Your examiner will offer you a verbal explanation. Your instructor may be present for this, providing you give your consent.

Your instructor will probably drive you home. This is normal. You will be either too excited or too disappointed to concentrate properly.

After passing

You are more likely to pass first time if you have plenty of lessons. Take your instructor's advice and only take your test when you are ready.

Your examiner will ask for your provisional licence and give you a pass certificate in exchange. Your full licence will be issued automatically by post.

In some circumstances, however, the examiner may not be able to take your provisional licence, eg if you've just married and changed your surname. In this case you would have to send your provisional licence and your pass certificate with the appropriate fee directly to DVLA, and they will issue your full licence. Exchange your provisional licence for a full licence as soon as you can – the pass certificate is only valid for two years!

If you try continually to improve your driving skills, you will find that you get many years of enjoyment from your newly acquired freedom of travel.

If you don't pass

Try not to get too upset if you don't pass first time. The examiner has seen that you are not quite ready to drive unsupervised. Those items for which you have failed will be marked on the driving test report form, and the examiner will explain these to you. Although you may be distracted by your disappointment, try to listen carefully to what the examiner says. Your instructor will advise you on any further training requirements before you take another test. It is important that you keep up with your lessons and practice so that you keep up the standard you have already reached.

The Pass Plus scheme and advanced driving tests

 By passing the practical test you have shown that you can drive to the minimum standard required by law. You are now only at the beginning of your real driving career. You should be prepared to continue learning for a long time to come. To help you with this, your instructor will be able to advise you on the elements in the Pass Plus scheme that will be of benefit and that you may not have covered during your driving lessons. It will also help reduce the risk of your being involved in a road accident.

It is far better to gain experience in different conditions and on different roads, particularly motorways, under the expert and safe guidance of a professional before you try to take on too much too soon.

The subjects covered in the Pass Plus scheme include driving in town, in all weathers, on rural roads, at night, on dual carriageways and on motorways. You can take a Pass Plus course at any time within the first 12 months of passing your practical test. Throughout the course you will be driving with these key factors in mind:

- **attitude:** responsibility for your actions and care and consideration for others;

- **skills:** observation, assessing what you see and taking the right action.

Some insurance companies offer discounts to drivers who have taken extra training under this scheme. Ask your instructor, or visit www.passplus.org.uk for details.

If you are really interested in continually improving your standard of driving you might consider taking an advanced driving test such as that offered by DIAmond Advanced Motorists. You can contact DIAmond on 020 8686 8010 or visit www.driving.org/diamond.

A final word

The authors hope you have found this book useful and that it has made your driving lessons easier and more enjoyable. We wish you success with your driving theory and practical tests. With good preparation and heeding the advice in this book, you will have made great progress towards a trouble-free driving career.

Checkpoint 10

By the time you apply for your theory test you should be able to answer the questions in all of the other checkpoints and the theory test section in Part 2 of this book. Your instructor should have been teaching you how to put all of the rules and procedures into practice.

Remember, you are not learning these rules just in order to pass your test! You need to understand them so that you can apply them and enjoy 'safe driving for life'.

This checkpoint includes questions that cover all of the syllabus for learning and also other general rules for all drivers.

1   The main items inspected on an MOT test are: *Choose one answer*
   a.   engine, gearbox, brakes and tyres
   b.   brakes, lights, steering and tyres
   c.   engine, body, brakes and tyres
   d.   paintwork, metal trims, body and tyres

2   You should check your engine oil: *Choose one answer*
   a.   before every journey
   b.   at least once a week
   c.   once a month
   d.   at service intervals

3   Lights and indicators should be checked:
    Choose one answer

    a.   before you drive
    b.   once a week
    c.   once a month
    d.   at service intervals

4   The main cause of skidding is:
    Choose one answer

    a.   a wet road surface
    b.   icy roads
    c.   high speed
    d.   the driver

5   If the rear of your car is skidding to the left you should:
    Choose two answers

    a.   brake more firmly
    b.   pump the brake on and off
    c.   steer to the right
    d.   steer to the left

6   If your wheels lock up during an emergency stop you should:
    Choose one answer

    a.   brake more firmly
    b.   use the parking brake to help
    c.   release the brake and reapply it
    d.   push down the clutch

7   Car tyres must have a tread depth of:
    Choose one answer

    a.   1.6 mm across the central three-quarters of the width
    b.   1.6 mm across the entire width
    c.   2.00 mm across the central three-quarters of the width
    d.   2.00 mm across the entire width

8 At a pelican crossing you may proceed through a flashing amber light if:

Choose two answers

   a. there is no one on the crossing
   b. you are sure no one will step out
   c. you use your horn to warn people nearby
   d. a pedestrian beckons you on

9 On the approach to a zebra crossing you should:
Choose three answers

   a. be travelling at a speed at which you can stop safely
   b. not use arm signals
   c. check your mirrors early
   d. only stop when someone steps on to the crossing
   e. be ready to stop

10 If you see a person with a guide dog waiting to cross
the road you should:
Choose one answer

   a. always wait for him or her
   b. proceed carefully
   c. wave him or her across
   d. sound your horn to warn him or her of your presence

11 Passing the line of parked cars you see a ball bounce into the road.
You should:

Choose one answer

   a. sound the horn to warn any children and then drive on
   b. slow down and be ready to stop
   c. stop and wave any children across to get the ball
   d. swerve to avoid the ball

12 So as not to frighten animals you should be ready to:
Choose two answers

   a. slow down
   b. sound the horn to warn them
   c. drive past quickly out of danger
   d. keep the engine speed low

13 If you are turning into a road where there are pedestrians you should:
Choose two answers

   a. sound the horn
   b. give way to them
   c. wave them across
   d. not rush them

14 You are approaching a T-junction at the end of a road and there are pedestrians crossing. You should:
Choose one answer

   a. hold back for them
   b. expect them to wait
   c. sound the horn
   d. flash your lights

15 You may sound the horn when stationary on the road:
Choose one answer

   a. to test it
   b. when in danger from another vehicle moving nearby
   c. between 7.00 am and 11.00 pm
   d. at no time

16 You should not sound your horn in built-up areas between the hours of:
Choose one answer

   a. 10.30 pm and 7.30 pm
   b. 7.30 am and 10.30 pm
   c. 11.30 pm and 7.00 am
   d. 7.00 am and 11.30 pm

17 If another driver makes a mistake you should:
Choose one answer

a. flash your lights
b. sound your horn
c. be ready to compensate
d. shake your head

18 If there is a solid white line along the centre of your side of the road it means:

Choose two answers

a. no overtaking on that road
b. you should not cross the line
c. you should not park on the offside
d. you may only straddle the line to overtake a vehicle travelling at less than 10 mph

19 Yellow lines along the left edge of the road mean:
Choose one answer

a. no waiting at any time
b. there are waiting restrictions in force
c. parking is only permitted at weekends
d. loading is not permitted

20 You may overtake on the left:
Choose two answers

a. in one-way streets
b. when approaching a junction
c. on three-lane motorways
d. in lanes of slow traffic when the queue to your right is moving more slowly than yours

21 You should not normally overtake:
Choose three answers

   a.   on two-lane highways

   b.   near junctions

   c.   near the brow of a hill

   d.   if there is dead ground ahead

   e.   on the right

22 Countdown markers on motorways are:
Choose one answer

   a.   white on black

   b.   black on white

   c.   blue on white

   d.   white on blue

23 Countdown markers may indicate the distance to a:
Choose three answers

   a.   motorway entrance

   b.   motorway exit

   c.   concealed level crossing

   d.   hazard

   e.   safety camera

24 Circular signs usually give:
Choose one answer

   a.   orders

   b.   warnings

   c.   information

   d.   directions

25 Triangular signs usually give:
Choose one answer

   a.   orders

   b.   warnings

   c.   information

   d.   instructions

26 At mini-roundabouts you should:
Choose two answers

    a. give way to traffic from the right
    b. give way to all other traffic
    c. beware of vehicles making U-turns
    d. expect drivers to your left to give way to you

27 When turning right at a roundabout you should:
Choose two answers

    a. keep on the right signal throughout the manoeuvre
    b. signal left after you have passed the exit before yours
    c. signal left before you pass the exit before yours
    d. stay in the left lane all the way for safety
    e. give a right signal on approach

28 If you use full beam headlights at the wrong time you could:
Choose two answers

    a. dazzle oncoming drivers
    b. dazzle the driver in front
    c. be seen more clearly
    d. make better progress

29 What hazard should the car driver be aware of?

Choose one answer

    a. oncoming traffic
    b. traffic merging from the right
    c. a pedestrian crossing ahead
    d. trams overtaking on the right

30 It has just started to rain after a long dry spell. When will the road surface be most slippery?
Choose one answer

   a. when it has rained for an hour or so
   b. a few minutes after it starts to rain
   c. when puddles have formed on the road
   d. about an hour after the rain stops

31 What hazard should the driver in this picture expect to see next?

Choose one answer

   a. cars parked facing the kerb
   b. a roundabout
   c. a police speed trap
   d. a school crossing patrol

32 What should you do if there is an obstruction on your side of the road?
Choose one answer

   a. assume priority over oncoming traffic
   b. speed up to get past the obstruction
   c. give way to oncoming traffic
   d. wave approaching vehicles through
   e. pull up alongside the obstruction if traffic is approaching

33 The good driver should always:
Choose three answers

   a. drive at the speed limit
   b. make effective use of the driving mirrors
   c. look well ahead
   d. anticipate the actions of other road users
   e. show off his or her skill

34 What should you do if you see a sign like this in icy conditions?

Choose three answers

a. accelerate
b. gently apply the parking brake
c. use as high a gear as possible
d. slow down well before the bend
e. put on hazard warning lights
f. take care with steering

35 What does this sign mean?

Choose one answer

a. no horse riders permitted
b. no horse-drawn carriages
c. beware of horse riders ahead
d. bridleway ahead, horse riders only

36 The major cause of 'L' test failure is not: *Choose one answer*

a. being properly prepared
b. passing the theory test first
c. having private practice
d. applying early enough

37 To make sure there is enough time for your test, when you apply you should declare whether you:
Choose three answers

a. have severe hearing difficulties
b. are restricted in your movements
c. have any disabilities that may affect your driving
d. have had professional tuition
e. have dual controls in the vehicle you will be using for the test

38 When preparing for your driving test you should practise:
Choose two answers

    a. on test routes only
    b. on as many types of road as possible
    c. in all sorts of conditions
    d. in daylight only

39 If you pass your test in an automatic car you:
Choose one answer

    a. may only drive automatic cars
    b. will have to take a test in a manual car within two years
    c. may drive any type of automatic vehicle
    d. may not drive any left-hand-drive vehicle

40 The main purpose of the driving test is:
Choose one answer

    a. to check on the ability of driving instructors
    b. to see that candidates can safely drive unaided
    c. to make sure that candidates can carry out reverse manoeuvres
    d. to restrict the number of drivers on our roads

You will find the answers on page 425.

Scores: First try   Second try   Third try

Record your scores in Appendix 2 (page 426).

PART TWO
DRIVING
THEORY TEST

About the theory test

When you have your provisional licence, have had some driving experience and have studied sufficiently you should apply for your driving theory test.

You can apply for a theory test appointment by phone, online or by post. Seek guidance from your instructor on when to make the booking.

If you have special needs or a language or reading difficulty, you need to tell the booking section when you make your appointment. Provision is available to cover these difficulties, and they should not disadvantage you in the theory test.

What you can be tested on

There are 50 questions in the theory element of the test. Most of these will be multiple-choice, requiring you to select one answer from four. There will also be some multiple-response questions, requiring you to select two or more answers from the choices presented on-screen. Some of the questions will display diagrams or photographic images. The questions are similar in style and content to the checkpoint questions in each stage of this book.

The theory test questions will be selected from 14 different categories relating to road safety and the legal responsibilities of the driver. Examples of the type of question from each category are shown below. Take your time and study the questions carefully. It is very easy to overlook a key word or phrase in the question and arrive at the wrong answer.

Question categories

Accidents

Do you know what to do if you are involved in or witness an accident or incident on the road? What are your legal responsibilities? How would you deal with a casualty?

Example:

Q. At an accident scene you find an adult casualty is not breathing. You should give chest compressions at the rate of:

Choose one answer

a. 200 per minute
b. 100 per minute
c. 50 per minute
d. 20 per minute

Correct answer: b.
Knowing basic first aid procedures could save a life.

Alertness

Do you understand why it is important to be observant, anticipate problems ahead and concentrate on your driving? Do you understand the effects of boredom and distraction on your driving ability?

Example:

Q. Using a mobile telephone when you are driving: *Choose two answers*

a. could cause you to lose control of your vehicle
b. may affect your vehicle's electrical system
c. could take your attention from the road
d. is fine if the system is hands-free
e. is acceptable at low speeds

Correct answers: a, c.
Driving needs your full attention all of the time. Even using a hands-free phone will distract you and could cause you to lose control of the vehicle.

Attitude

Do you understand why it is important to show courtesy and considera-tion to other road users? Do you understand the rules of priority and the dangers of close following?

Example:

Q. A car driver pulls out in front of you at a junction. You should:
Choose one answer

a. accelerate to get past safely
b. flash your headlights and swerve round the other vehicle
c. slow down and be ready to stop if necessary
d. keep close behind the vehicle so the driver knows you are annoyed

Correct answer: c.
If you are driving defensively you should expect others to make mistakes. Being tolerant keeps you and others safe on the roads.

Documents

Do you know the rules relating to driver licensing, vehicle insurance, MOT test certificates and road tax for your vehicle?

Example:

Q. Your car needs a new MOT certificate. If you drive without a current certificate:
Choose one answer

a. you could invalidate the manufacturer's warranty
b. you will have to make a SORN declaration
c. you could invalidate your motor insurance
d. your tax disc will be invalidated

Correct answer: c.
If your vehicle MOT certificate has expired, you may not drive it except to a pre-arranged appointment for repairs or a new MOT test. Without an MOT your vehicle insurance will be invalid.

Hazard awareness

Are you paying attention and planning ahead? Can you relate speed and distance? Are you fit to drive? Do you understand how tiredness, drugs and alcohol can affect your reaction time?

Example:

Q. Which three of the following may result from drinking alcohol?
Choose three answers

  a. a greater sense of self-confidence
  b. faster reaction times
  c. poorer coordination
  d. better judgement of speed
  e. reduced concentration
  f. smoother control of the vehicle

Correct answers: a, c, e.
Alcohol can cause a driver to become over-confident and take greater risks. At the same time, driving ability and reaction times are impaired by alcohol. Together these factors greatly increase the risk of a serious accident.

Motorway rules

Do you know the rules that apply to motorway driving?

Example:

Q. What is the national speed limit for cars on a motorway?
Choose one answer

  a. 50 mph
  b. 60 mph
  c. 70 mph
  d. there is no limit

Correct answer: c.
This does not mean that you should aim to travel at 70 mph all of the time. Drive at a speed that is appropriate for the road and traffic conditions on the motorway.

Other types of vehicle

Do you understand the handling characteristics and limitations on other types of vehicle so that you can respond safely to their presence on the road?

Example:

Q. In very windy conditions you are about to overtake a motorcyclist. You should: *Choose one answer*

a. pull out at the last minute
b. allow extra room as you pass
c. sound your horn as you start to overtake
d. pass slowly, keeping close to the motorcyclist

Correct answer: b.
Motorcyclists and cyclists can be easily blown off course by crosswinds and could drift into your path. As you pass, the airflow from around your vehicle could affect these vulnerable road users. Allow plenty of room.

Road and traffic signs

Do you recognize and respond appropriately to road signs and markings?

Example:

Q. You see a sign like this in a tunnel. It means:

Choose one answer

a. direction to emergency pedestrian exit
b. pedestrian access prohibited
c. warning, pedestrians in road
d. pedestrian crossing ahead

Correct answer: a.
Pedestrian exit points can be found at regular intervals in tunnels. If an incident in the tunnel forces you to leave your vehicle and evacuate, go to the nearest exit marked by this sign.

Rules of the road

Do you understand the rules and driving procedures outlined in The Highway Code?

Example:

Q. You may only wait in a yellow box junction when:

Choose one answer

a.   your exit is blocked
b.   you are in a queue of traffic going ahead
c.   crossing traffic prevents you from turning left
d.   oncoming traffic prevents you from turning right

Correct answer: d.
The yellow box marking is designed to keep junctions clear. Do not enter unless your exit is clear. You can only wait in the box to turn right if your exit is clear but you can't safely cross the path of oncoming traffic.

Safety and your vehicle

Do you know when and how to use the safety features and equipment in your vehicle? Can you identify vehicle faults and understand the importance of dealing with them? Do you know the consequences of driving a vehicle with defective equipment?

Example:

Q. Tyre pressures need to be checked regularly. What three can result from driving with under-inflated tyres? *Choose three answers*

a.   reduced tyre life
b.   poorer control when braking
c.   increased fuel efficiency
d.   lighter steering
e.   improved cornering
f.   more fuel consumption

Correct answers: a, b, f.

Tyres need to be in good condition and correctly inflated. Driving with under-inflated tyres will affect vehicle stability, increase fuel consumption and reduce the life of the tyres.

Safety margins

Do you know how long it takes to stop your vehicle at different speeds? Do you understand how road surface conditions can affect your ability to stop your vehicle? Do you know how to avoid skidding and recover from a skid if you caused one?

Example:

Q. You are travelling at 50 mph on a dry road. What is the shortest overall distance you could expect to stop in? *Choose one answer*

    a. 23 metres (75 feet)
    b. 36 metres (118 feet)
    c. 53 metres (175 feet)
    d. 73 metres (240 feet)

Correct answer: c.
As well as knowing the figures you must be able to visualize them.

Vehicle handling

Can you adapt your driving to different weather and lighting conditions? Do you know when to use your vehicle lights? How do you deal with gradients?

Example:

Q. You are driving in daylight but the weather conditions have made visibility poor. Why should you switch on your headlights?

Choose one answer

    a. so that you can see road markings close to your vehicle
    b. so that others can see you more easily

c.   to warn drivers ahead that you are following
d.   so that you can see further ahead

Correct answer: b.
If you are finding it difficult to see other drivers, they will also find it hard to see you. Using dipped headlights will make it easier for others to see you.

Vehicle loading

Do you know the rules about vehicle loading and towing? Do you understand how vehicle loading can affect stability?

Example:

Q. Towing a small trailer on a dual carriageway, you realize that it has begun to 'snake'. You should: *Choose one answer*

a.   brake firmly to reduce your speed
b.   ease off the accelerator
c.   accelerate to correct the problem
d.   put on your hazard warning lights and maintain your speed

Correct answer: b.
If you slow down gradually the problem will correct itself. Don't brake harshly – you could cause the trailer to tip over.

Vulnerable road users

As a car driver, do you understand your responsibilities towards others using the road? Do you recognize that pedestrians, cyclists, motorcyclists, children, the elderly, those with disabilities or animals or those controlling them are vulnerable groups?

Example:

Q. At a pelican crossing you have stopped for an elderly disabled pedestrian. He or she is taking a long time to cross and the lights have changed to green. You should not: *Choose three answers*

a.   wait patiently for the pedestrian to cross
b.   drive round the pedestrian to clear the crossing
c.   edge forward to hurry the pedestrian along

d. sound your horn

e. keep your parking brake applied

Correct answers: b, c, d.

Trying to hurry a disabled pedestrian along could cause him or her to stumble or fall. Be patient – the green light means you can proceed only if it is safe!

To ensure a broad range of knowledge, you will be tested with questions from each category. You might notice that some of the questions you are asked seem quite similar. This doesn't matter, and the test isn't designed to 'catch you out'. It is simply the case that some subjects can be used to test knowledge in different categories.

Case study questions

Some of the questions you will be asked may be presented as part of a 'case study'. These questions are designed to test whether you have really understood and can apply driving theory. In a 'case study' a driving scenario is set and you will be asked a number of questions about that scenario and how you would react as in the example below:

Case Study

You are going to visit your cousin who lives in the next town. You have a road atlas in your car although you have been before and know the route really well. You also have your mobile phone and have promised to call your cousin if you get delayed. On the way you find that a country lane you usually travel on is flooded and decide to turn back.

1 You are on a country lane and see that it is flooded ahead. How can you judge the depth of the water? *Choose one answer*

a. park at the roadside and wait for another vehicle to drive through

b. drive through slowly and keep checking through the side window

c. look for a depth gauge at the roadside

d. get out of your vehicle and wade in

Correct answer: c.

2 You find that you can't judge the depth of the water so you decide to turn round. The road is quite narrow. The best method of turning would be: *Choose one answer*

a. to give a signal and make a quick U-turn
b. turn around in the road using forward and reverse gears
c. reverse back down the country lane until you can find a farm entrance to turn into
d. drive slowly forward to a wider section of road to turn round in

Correct answer: b.

3   You have turned round on the narrow country because you can't follow you usual route. The best thing to do to find a new route would be to: *Choose one answer*

a. call your cousin to ask for directions as you drive back towards the main road
b. drive on slowly whilst checking your road atlas
c. find a safe place to pull in and consult your road atlas
d. wait until you are back on the main road before calling your cousin for help

Correct answer: c.

4   On the way back to the main road you are delayed by a slow-moving farm vehicle ahead. You are worried about being late and should: *Choose one answer*

a. sound your horn so that the driver of the farm vehicle will get out of your way
b. follow the farm vehicle closely so that you can overtake at the earliest opportunity
c. pull out to overtake even though the road is very narrow
d. keep well back from the farm vehicle so that you can see well ahead

Correct answer: d.

5   You decide to let your cousin know that you will be late. You should: *Choose one answer*

a. find a safe place to pull in and make a call on your mobile phone
b. rely on your hands-free kit to keep you safe whilst you make a call
c. stop and get out of your car to make a call
d. drive slowly and send a text message to your cousin

Correct answer: a.

You will only be presented with one case study in your car theory test. Five of your 50 questions will relate to that case study.

Taking your theory test

When you attend for the test you will need to bring your photocard licence and the paper counterpart with you. If you don't have a photocard licence you must bring your paper licence and passport as photographic proof of identity. If you don't have acceptable identification your appointment will be cancelled and you will lose your fee.

Make sure you arrive in good time for your appointment and have your photographic identification with you

The first part of the theory test uses touch-screen technology. You will be able to practise answering the questions using the touch screen for up to 15 minutes before you begin your test. Follow the on-screen instructions to commence.

The computer screen will display the question, the number of answers to be 'marked' and the choice of answers. The screen will also display the time remaining to complete the test. There is no need to rush. On-screen buttons will allow you to navigate back and forth through the test. You will be able to 'flag' a question if you are not sure of the answer and come back to it later.

There is also a 'review' button on-screen. If you touch the review button you can:

- view a summary showing the number of the questions you have answered, how many are incomplete and how many you have flagged;

Follow the on-screen instructions to take the theory test

- go back through all of the questions;
- have another look at questions you have flagged;
- have another look at questions you haven't completed;
- end the test.

To pass this part of the test you must score at least 43 correct answers out of 50 within 57 minutes.

Hazard perception test

After completing the theory element you will get a short break before the hazard perception test. You will see a short video tutorial explaining how the test operates and what you need to do in order to pass. The test has 14 video clips showing a variety of hazards as seen from the driver's seat of a moving car. Each clip lasts for about a minute, and you will need to click with a computer mouse when you see a potential hazard developing into a moving hazard, that is a situation in which you would have to change speed or course to deal with it.

Each time you click the mouse a flag symbol will appear on the information bar at the bottom of the screen.

Up to five marks can be scored for each hazard, and the more quickly you respond to the developing hazard the more you will score. Don't try to beat the system by repeating patterns of clicks or clicking continu-

ously; the software will identify what you are doing and award a zero score for that clip.

Remember that one of the 14 clips will feature two developing hazards, allowing you to score up to 10 points. It is important therefore to watch all of the video clips carefully right the way through.

To pass this part of the test, you must score 44 out of the possible 75 marks.

For further reference and for a small charge, there is a DVD *The Complete Theory Test*, available to readers. This comprehensive product features actual DSA revision questions and hazard perception clips with other learning support material. It can be obtained from Grade Six Supplies Ltd; tel 01353 749807; www.g6s.co.uk.

Theory test practice papers

The remainder of Part 2 contains a series of mock theory tests made up from the authors' bank of theory assessment questions. Like the checkpoint questions, this selection has similar content to the actual questions used in a DSA theory test and covers all of the question categories listed above.

At first sight some of the questions may appear not to have the correct answer amongst the choices given. In these cases you will need to apply your knowledge to select the best answer from those given. This is not an attempt to catch you out. This material was written to train you in the technique of reading and responding to multiple-choice questions, as well as ensuring that you have read and understood the appropriate literature. To this end, the level of difficulty of the questions in Part 2 is at times higher than you would find in a DSA theory test examination. Remember also that learning should be both fun and interactive, so some of the questions are designed to promote discussion with your instructor and some are designed to be humorous!

Paper 1
Theory test assessment

Case Study for questions 1–5

You are driving home along a route regularly used by cyclists. The road surface is poor in places and there are a number of potholes. You are going to turn right at a roundabout ahead and you know that shortly after that there is a zebra crossing in the high street just before you enter the housing estate where you live. The road leading to your home has a number of chicanes and speed humps.

1 You should be aware that because of the road surface cyclists ahead might: *Choose one answer*

    a. speed up
    b. mount the footpath
    c. give arm signals
    d. swerve out in to your path

2 As you approach the roundabout you notice a cyclist in the left lane giving a right turn signal. You should: *Choose one answer*

    a. keep back from the cyclist and sound your horn
    b. expect the cyclist to turn left
    c. expect the cyclist to turn right at the roundabout
    d. accelerate to overtake the cyclist quickly

3 The high street is busy and there are lots of parked vehicles. You should anticipate: *Choose two answers*

    a. that pedestrians might step out from between parked vehicles
    b. that other drivers may warn you of hidden dangers ahead
    c. no danger from pedestrians as there is a crossing ahead
    d. pedestrians wanting to cross at the zebra crossing

4   Approaching the zebra crossing you see an elderly person waiting.
     He has a white stick with a red band. You should:
     Choose one answer

     a.   assume the person will see you when you stop to let him cross
     b.   stop and be patient because he may be blind and deaf
     c.   stop and wave him across
     d.   stop and gently tap your horn to let him know it is safe to cross

5   What danger will you be particularly concerned about as you turn
     into the road you live on?
     Choose one answer

     a.   Speeding vehicles approaching
     b.   Damage to your suspension and steering
     c.   Children playing
     d.   Following traffic trying to overtake

6   You are driving the red car (arrowed) at 30 mph in the rain. You are
     about 25 metres (82 feet) from the car ahead. You should consider
     yourself:

     Choose one answer

     a.   to be a safe distance from the car ahead
     b.   to be dangerously close to the car ahead
     c.   able to stop in good time if the driver ahead had to make
           an emergency stop
     d.   to be safe providing your car has an anti-lock braking system

7   Driving at 45 mph in good conditions, what is a safe minimum
     distance to keep between you and a car ahead?
     Choose one answer

     a.   75 metres (245 feet)
     b.   45 metres (148 feet)
     c.   35 metres (117 feet)
     d.   23 metres (67 feet)

8 Why is it better to keep to the left when driving in a right-hand bend?
   Choose one answer

   a. it improves your view of the road ahead
   b. it will keep you away from pedestrians in the road
   c. it allows you take the bend faster
   d. you needn't worry about the camber

9 Approaching a level crossing you see this sign with the amber light showing and should:

   Choose one answer

   a. drive through the crossing quickly
   b. only drive through if you can see no trains approaching
   c. drive over the crossing slowly
   d. stop before the barriers

10 If you need glasses or contact lenses to read a number plate at the distance required for driving you should wear them:
   Choose one answer

   a. only when driving in poor weather
   b. only when driving in heavy traffic
   c. at all times when driving
   d. only when driving at night

11 You are about to drive home after a hard day at work but feel very tired. You should: *Choose one answer*

   a. take some 'pep pills' to stay awake
   b. not drive
   c. drive faster to lessen the danger of falling asleep at the wheel
   d. take a flask of strong coffee with you

12 *The Highway Code* advises that you MUST NOT drive in reverse gear: *Choose one answer*

   a. for longer than necessary
   b. into a side road
   c. unless you are parking
   d. unless someone is guiding you

13 How should you signal when you want to go straight ahead at
a roundabout?
Choose one answer

a. signal right on approach and then left to leave the roundabout
b. signal left on approach and through the roundabout
c. signal left just after passing the exit before the one you want to
take
d. no signal is necessary

14 On a wet road you see a motorcyclist steer around a drain cover in
a right-hand bend. Why would the motorcyclist do this?
Choose one answer

a. to avoid mounting the kerb
b. to avoid a skid on the metal surface
c. to annoy following traffic
d. to avoid splashing passers-by

15 Where should you position your car before overtaking a long vehicle?
Choose one answer

a. as close as possible to get past quickly
b. well back to get a clear view ahead
c. to the centre of the road to get a clear view ahead
d. well back and well to the left

16 A bus driver ahead signals to pull out from a bus stop. What should
you do?
Choose one answer

a. accelerate to get past quickly
b. flash your lights and overtake
c. allow it to pull away if safe
d. sound your horn if you need to stop

17 You should switch on rear fog lights when visibility drops below:
Choose one answer

a. 200 metres (660 feet)
b. 100 metres (330 feet)
c. 10 metres (33 feet)
d. your minimum braking distance

18 Bad weather can make road markings difficult to see. When this happens you should: *Choose one answer*

    a.   expect other drivers to give way when necessary

    b.   be ready to sound your horn if another driver makes a mistake

    c.   be ready to give way at a junction even if you know you have priority

    d.   not worry about traffic joining your road

19 Your car is a dark colour. Towards sunset, you would be advised to switch on your lights: *Choose one answer*

    a.   only when other drivers switch on their lights

    b.   only after lighting-up time

    c.   only when you can no longer see clearly ahead without lights

    d.   earlier than drivers of light-coloured cars

20 What does this motorway sign mean?

Choose one answer

    a.   leave the motorway at the next exit

    b.   move to the hard shoulder

    c.   move to the lane on your left

    d.   contraflow, change to the opposite carriageway

21 You see this sign as you approach a junction. You must:

Choose one answer

    a.   stop, even if the road is clear

    b.   stop only if other vehicles are nearby

    c.   stop only if you can't see the road ahead clearly

    d.   be ready to pull up sharply

22 A police officer has asked to see your driving documents but you don't have them with you. You must produce them at a police station within: *Choose one answer*

   a. 5 days
   b. 7 days
   c. 10 days
   d. 14 days

23 Before driving a friend's car you must make sure that: *Choose one answer*

   a. your own vehicle has insurance cover
   b. your use of the car is insured
   c. your friend has third-party insurance
   d. you have the insurance documents for your friend's car

24 The Pass Plus scheme is available to all newly qualified drivers and is designed to: *Choose one answer*

   a. help them supervise a learner driver
   b. help them gain more experience
   c. reduce the cost of vehicle road tax
   d. help them service their own vehicle

25 What type of vehicle would display a flashing green light?

Choose one answer

   a. a motorway maintenance vehicle
   b. a slow-moving vehicle
   c. an ambulance or fire engine
   d. a doctor or midwife on an emergency call

26 What is the purpose of the horn? *Choose one answer*

   a. to tell other road users that you intend to come through
   b. to indicate that you have right of way
   c. to warn others of your presence
   d. to show annoyance at other drivers' mistakes

27 Who has responsibility for seeing that a vehicle isn't overloaded? *Choose one answer*

    a. the owner of the vehicle
    b. the driver of the vehicle
    c. the person who has loaded the vehicle
    d. the owner of the load

28 You are driving at night in a heavily loaded estate car. What problem should you be aware of? *Choose one answer*

    a. following drivers will not be able to see your tail lights
    b. full headlights can't be used
    c. dipped headlights could dazzle oncoming drivers
    d. you will be unable to use your mirrors

29 Catalytic converters are designed to: *Choose one answer*

    a. increase fuel consumption
    b. reduce harmful emissions
    c. improve the quality of air circulating in the vehicle
    d. reduce wear and tear in the engine

30 One of the times you may use hazard warning lights is: *Choose one answer*

    a. when being towed
    b. to excuse inconsiderate parking
    c. when towing another vehicle
    d. if your car has broken down

31 When may you use the right-hand lane of a motorway? *Choose one answer*

    a. for turning right
    b. to drive faster than 70 mph
    c. to keep away from close-following traffic
    d. to overtake another vehicle

32 You may ONLY stop on the hard shoulder of a motorway: *Choose one answer*

    a. when too tired to drive
    b. in an emergency
    c. to drop off a passenger
    d. to answer a call on your mobile phone

33 Signs like these on a motorway are:

Choose one answer

a. lane closure markers
b. countdown markers to the next exit
c. distance markers to the next phone
d. a warning of speed traps ahead

34 A motorcyclist has been injured in an accident. At the scene, you should:
Choose one answer

a. remove the motorcyclist's helmet
b. move the motorcyclist off the road
c. never move the motorcyclist
d. not remove the motorcyclist's helmet

35 After a breakdown, on a single carriageway road, you should place your hazard warning triangle:
Choose one answer

a. on top of your vehicle
b. at least 100 metres (330 feet) behind your vehicle
c. beside your vehicle
d. at least 45 metres (147 feet) behind your vehicle

36 You may legally drive a car over three years old without an MOT certificate:
Choose one answer

a. for up to seven days after the old certificate has expired
b. when driving to an MOT test centre for a pre-arranged appointment
c. if you have just bought the vehicle and it has no MOT certificate
d. to go and visit an MOT test centre to make an appointment

37 You intend to carry an 11-year-old passenger in the back seat of your car. The child is under 1.35 metres (4 feet 5 inches) in height. You must: *Choose one answer*

   a. make sure that the child can fasten his or her own seat belt
   b. only do so if there is an adult sitting next to the child
   c. ensure that a suitable child restraint is used
   d. not allow the child to use a booster seat

38 You arrive at the scene of an accident. Which of the following should you NOT do? *Choose two answers*

   a. warn other traffic by switching on your hazard warning lights
   b. put yourself in danger to assist casualties
   c. offer casualties something to drink
   d. impose a smoking ban
   e. ask drivers to switch off their engines

39 Which of these signs means overtaking is prohibited? *Choose one answer*

   a.   b.   c.   d.

40 'Coasting' by keeping the clutch pedal down or selecting neutral for long periods of time is not recommended because: *Choose two answers*

   a. you will use more fuel
   b. you could cause damage to the catalytic converter
   c. you will have less steering control
   d. it will increase tyre wear
   e. it will reduce your control of braking

41 You come up behind a vehicle being driven by an elderly driver. You should: *Choose one answer*

   a. expect the driver to make a lot of mistakes
   b. sound your horn and overtake
   c. anticipate that the elderly driver may have slower reactions than yours
   d. follow closely until the elderly driver lets you pass

42 Which of these are most likely to cause you to lose concentration whilst driving?

Choose three answers

a. loading a CD into your car audio system
b. using a hands-free telephone
c. checking your mirrors
d. looking at a map
e. using the windscreen demisters

43 At an accident a casualty has stopped breathing. Your priorities should be to:

Choose three answers

a. tilt the head forwards
b. remove anything that is blocking the airway
c. check for any internal injury
d. tilt the head back to keep the airway clear
e. call for help

44 What should you do if your vehicle has a puncture on a motorway?

Choose one answer

a. stop in lane and change the wheel
b. drive slowly to the next service area or exit
c. pull up on the hard shoulder and change the wheel
d. pull up on the hard shoulder and phone for assistance

45 What does this sign mean?

Choose one answer

a. end of speed limit
b. clearway, no waiting
c. national speed limit applies
d. trams must turn right

46 You intend to turn right on to a dual carriageway with a very narrow central reservation. You should:
Choose one answer

    a.   proceed to the central reservation and wait
    b.   wait until the road is clear in both directions and then turn right
    c.   expect approaching traffic to give way as you pull out
    d.   put on your hazard lights and edge into the traffic stream

47 Before driving through a tunnel you should:
Choose one answer

    a.   switch your radio off
    b.   switch on your fog lights
    c.   remove sunglasses if you were wearing them
    d.   select a low gear

48 Your car is fitted with anti-lock brakes. This means that the tyres:
Choose one answer

    a.   will wear more evenly
    b.   will be less likely to skid
    c.   can't be over-inflated
    d.   are less likely to aquaplane

49 Which of these vehicles is least likely to be affected by crosswinds?
Choose one answer

    a.   cyclists
    b.   cars
    c.   high-sided vehicles
    d.   motorcyclists

50 After passing your driving test, you suffer ill health that affects your ability to drive safely. You:
Choose one answer

    a.   must report the fact at your local police station
    b.   should avoid driving at higher speeds
    c.   must get a certificate from your GP confirming you can drive
    d.   must inform the licensing authority

Paper 2
Theory test assessment

Case Study for questions 1–5

On your way to work you dropped your car off for an MOT test. Unfortunately, when you go to collect your car after work, you are told it has failed the test and needs a repair which the garage can't do until the following morning. You are worried because you have left everything to the last minute and also need to get the car taxed the following day.

1   When you find out that your car has failed the MOT test you should:
Choose one answer

   a.   drive it home
   b.   consider bribing the mechanic who did the test
   c.   have the vehicle scrapped immediately
   d.   confirm that you would like the repair completed the following day

2   When a vehicle passes an MOT test this means that:
Choose one answer

   a.   it meets the legal minimum standards at the time of the test
   b.   it will be legally roadworthy for the next 12 months
   c.   there will be no need to get it serviced
   d.   it can be driven safely for another three years

3   Your car is repaired the following day and you get the MOT certificate. To get the car taxed you:
Choose one answer

   a.   can apply to the MOT station
   b.   must pay online via the DVLA website
   c.   must drive to Swansea
   d.   can go to a local Post Office

4   Your vehicle insurance cover could be affected if:
Choose two answers

a. you drove your car just before the MOT ran out
b. you drove your vehicle when it was not legally roadworthy
c. you did not declare relevant information when applying for
    the insurance
d. you renewed your tax disc online

5   Which documents must you produce in order to tax your vehicle over
the counter?
Choose two answers

a. your driving licence
b. a current Certificate of Insurance
c. the old tax disc
d. your current MOT certificate

6   If you have to leave valuables in your car, the best thing to do is:
Choose one answer

a. park in a quiet area
b. park at a bus stop
c. lock them out of sight in the boot
d. leave them concealed in a bag on the back seat

7   What does this sign mean?

Choose one answer

a. no overtaking
b. give priority to approaching vehicles
c. two-way traffic ahead
d. you have priority over vehicles from the opposite direction

8   You see this sign at a junction and should:

Choose one answer

a.   ignore it and continue on your route
b.   slow down and proceed carefully
c.   stop and report the fault
d.   turn around and find another route

9   Front fog lights may only be used if:
Choose one answer

a.   you use rear fog lights at the same time
b.   visibility is seriously reduced
c.   they were fitted by the vehicle manufacturer
d.   you are driving in fog at night

10 As a driver, how can you help improve air quality in city centres?
Choose one answer

a.   by only using your car for short journeys
b.   by only using the lower gears in town
c.   by walking, cycling or using public transport
d.   by driving through as quickly as possible

11 If you have just joined a motorway you should:
Choose two answers

a.   get into the middle lane as soon as you can
b.   take a little time to get used to the traffic
c.   move into the fast lane
d.   keep to the left-hand lane
e.   set your cruise control to 70 mph

12 As a car driver why is it important to keep these road markings clear?

Choose one answer

a. so that teachers can enter the school
b. so that children can be dropped off
c. so that there is a clear view of the crossing area
d. so that school buses have a place to park

13 In very windy conditions you need to take extra care when:
Choose two answers

a. passing large vehicles
b. moving off
c. passing a cyclist
d. parking
e. checking your oil

14 At the scene of an accident you are dealing with a casualty with a back injury. You should:
Choose one answer

a. put him or her in the recovery position
b. not move him or her unless there is further danger
c. keep the casualty on his or her back and raise his or her legs
d. get him or her to sit upright

15 A Statutory Off-Road Notification (SORN) is:
Choose one answer

a. valid for as long as the vehicle has insurance
b. only valid for 12 months
c. only required for four-wheel-drive vehicles
d. only needed for vehicles over three years old

16 You are about to turn left at this junction and see the pedestrian step into the road. You should:

Choose one answer

a. sound the horn to warn the pedestrian to step back
b. expect the pedestrian to give way
c. give way to the pedestrian
d. stop and wave the pedestrian across

17 You see a pedestrian carrying a white stick with a reflective red band. This indicates that: *Choose one answer*

a. the person is deaf and dumb
b. the person is blind and deaf
c. the person is blind in one eye
d. the person is blind and dumb

18 You should only use a hand-held mobile telephone in a vehicle: *Choose one answer*

a. if stopped in a traffic queue
b. to take an incoming call
c. when parked in a safe place
d. if you need to make an urgent call

19 Whilst turning your car in the road you should: *Choose one answer*

a. keep a close watch on your mirrors
b. keep a good look out for other road users
c. use your hazard warning lights
d. make the most of driveways

20 The last thing to do before moving off from the side of the road is: *Choose one answer*

a. give a signal
b. check your door mirror
c. look over your right shoulder
d. release the handbrake

21 You are approaching an obstruction on your side of the road and see oncoming traffic. You should:
Choose one answer

a. continue as you have priority
b. hold back so that oncoming traffic can come through
c. flash your headlights and accelerate through the gap
d. give a signal and cross to the right-hand side of the road

22 Driving in icy conditions, your car's steering may feel lighter than usual. This is because: *Choose one answer*

a. your tyres have more grip
b. cold weather deflates your tyres
c. your tyres have less grip
d. your steering mechanism has iced up

23 On a fast road in good conditions, reasonable estimates for a safe distance to keep between you and the car ahead are:
Choose two answers

a. about three car lengths
b. close enough to read the number plate of the car ahead
c. a time gap of two seconds
d. 3 metres (10 feet)
e. at least a metre (3 feet) for every mile per hour of your speed

24 The barriers have just lifted at this level crossing. The driver of the blue car (arrowed) should:

Choose one answer

a. drive across nose to tail with the white car in front
b. overtake the white car in front
c. let the car in front clear the track before driving across
d. drive across very slowly and carefully

25 The national speed limit for cars and motorcycles
    on a dual carriageway is:
    Choose one answer

    a. 50 mph
    b. 60 mph
    c. 70 mph
    d. 80 mph

26 Leaving a car parked on a road, when can you keep the engine running?
    Choose one answer

    a. at any time
    b. never
    c. if you have a flat battery
    d. if you leave hazard warning lights on

27 In which of these places are you sometimes allowed to park?
    Choose one answer

    a. on zigzag lines near a zebra crossing
    b. where there are red or yellow lines at the edge of the road
    c. in the nearside lane of a motorway
    d. on a clearway

28 It is raining and spray from the vehicle ahead affects your vision.
    You should:

    Choose one answer

    a. move out and overtake
    b. get closer to the vehicle to avoid the spray
    c. signal to the driver ahead to pull over
    d. drop back to get a clearer view

29 In bad weather, which vehicles are least likely to be affected by high winds?
Choose one answer

   a. motorcycles
   b. cars
   c. bicycles
   d. high-sided lorries

30 Driving in daytime mist, you can see more than 100 metres ahead and should:
Choose one answer

   a. use fog lights
   b. keep close to the vehicle ahead
   c. switch on dipped headlights
   d. switch on hazard warning lights

31 You need to park at night in fog. The best thing to do is:
Choose one answer

   a. leave on your rear fog lights
   b. park off the road
   c. leave on your headlights
   d. leave on your hazard warning lights

32 For what two reasons would you pull into a passing place on a narrow country road?
Choose two answers

   a. to pass the time on a peaceful afternoon
   b. to turn your car in the road
   c. to allow a following vehicle to overtake
   d. to give way to another vehicle coming from the opposite direction
   e. to take a rest when you are too tired to drive

33 Normally, you should not drive with your foot down on the clutch for longer than necessary because it will:
Choose one answer

   a. reduce your fuel consumption
   b. wear out the gears
   c. reduce your control of the vehicle
   d. prevent you from changing gear

34 Which type of sign tells you NOT to do something?
Choose one answer

a.

b.

c.

d.

35 What does this motorway sign mean?

Choose one answer

a. leave the motorway at the next exit
b. move to the hard shoulder
c. move to the lane on your left
d. contraflow, change to the opposite carriageway

36 At a pedestrian crossing, what do these zigzag lines mean?

Choose one answer

a. parking limited to five minutes or less
b. slow down and use third gear
c. no parking at any time
d. you must not stop

37 To drive on a road, learners MUST:
Choose one answer

a. not have any penalty points
b. have a signed, valid provisional licence
c. take professional tuition
d. have passed the theory test

38 To supervise a learner driver you MUST:
Choose two answers

a. not have any penalty points
b. have held a full licence for three years or more
c. be an approved driving instructor
d. be at least 21 years old
e. have passed an extended driving test

39 At a pelican crossing, a flashing amber light means that you should:
Choose one answer

a. drive on
b. give way to pedestrians who are waiting to cross
c. not stop if following traffic is too close
d. give way to pedestrians already on the crossing

40 Driving along a dual carriageway at 70 mph, another driver comes up
behind flashing his or her headlights. What should you do?
Choose one answer

a. switch on your hazard warning lights
b. allow the vehicle to overtake
c. show your brake lights
d. accelerate to keep a safe gap between you

41 You are driving in a one-way street and want to turn right ahead.
What road position should you take?
Choose one answer

a. in the right-hand lane
b. just left of the centre line
c. as close to the middle of the road as is safe
d. in the lane with the fastest-flowing traffic

42 You are loading a caravan ready for a holiday trip. You should place
any heavy items: *Choose one answer*

a. as close to the front of the caravan as possible
b. as near to the back of the caravan as possible
c. as high off the floor as possible
d. as low to the floor as possible

43 You see a symbol like this flashing on your instrument panel.
    What does it mean?

Choose one answer

   a. your hazard warning lights are on
   b. your brakes need adjustment
   c. your handbrake is on
   d. your main headlights are on

44 A child under 14 years and his or her parents are passengers in the car
    you are driving. Who must ensure that the child wears a seat belt?
    Choose one answer

   a. the child's parents
   b. the child
   c. you
   d. the front-seat passenger

45 To join a motorway from a slip road you:
    Choose one answer

   a. must speed up to 70 mph
   b. should adjust your speed to match the speed of the traffic in
    the inside lane
   c. must never stop
   d. should keep to a steady 40 mph

46 Driving along a three-lane motorway, which general rule applies?
    Choose one answer

   a. the right-hand lane is the fast lane
   b. keep to the middle lane for safety
   c. keep to the left lane unless you are overtaking
   d. keep to the lane with the least traffic

47 At the scene of an accident you notice a casualty who seems to be suffering from shock. You should:
Choose one answer

    a.   offer the casualty a drink to calm his or her nerves
    b.   talk to the casualty to reassure him or her
    c.   keep the casualty moving to prevent fainting
    d.   leave the casualty alone

48 After a motorway breakdown, your car has been repaired on the hard shoulder. To continue you should:
Choose one answer

    a.   wait for a suitable gap in the traffic and then move off into the left lane
    b.   build up speed on the hard shoulder before rejoining the carriageway
    c.   keep your hazard warning lights on as you rejoin the carriageway
    d.   complete your journey on the hard shoulder

49 What is a 'red route'?
Choose one answer

    a.   a stretch of road where there have been very few accidents
    b.   a route in a city where parking and waiting are restricted
    c.   a stretch of road with an unusually high number of road signs
    d.   a road with a red tarmac surface

50 Another vehicle overtakes you and cuts in sharply ahead. What should you do?
Choose two answers

    a.   keep calm
    b.   flash your lights
    c.   sound your horn
    d.   drop back to leave a safe space between you
    e.   overtake the other driver to show how it should be done

Paper 3
Theory test assessment

Case Study for questions 1–5

You and some friends have tickets for a football match and it is your turn to drive. The journey will take about 3 hours. Your friends are excited about the day out and they have had alcoholic drinks before you set off. You have had a cold recently and are still taking an off-the-shelf remedy for your symptoms. You have a flask of coffee with you for the journey. It is raining and you have the car's demisters on full as you start the motorway section of your journey.

1   What do you need to know about the cold remedy?
    Choose one answer

    a.   whether it contains any sweetener
    b.   whether it could cause drowsiness
    c.   how effective the manufacturer says it is
    d.   where you can buy more if you run out on the way to the match

2   Your friends are singing loudly as you get on to the motorway.
    You should: *Choose one answer*

    a.   join in the fun
    b.   not join in as you are feeling unwell
    c.   ask them to keep quiet if the noise is affecting your concentration
    d.   pull up on the hard shoulder to explain your problem to your friends

3   After an hour on the motorway it is warm in the car and your friends have gone quiet. You begin to feel drowsy and should: *Choose one answer*

    a.   ask your friends to start singing to keep you awake
    b.   open a window and get some fresh air
    c.   ask your friends to pour you a coffee
    d.   turn off the demisters to cool the car down

4   You decide to pull in for break. The best plan to keep you alert for the rest of your journey is to:
Choose one answer

   a.   stop briefly on the hard shoulder and have some coffee
   b.   pull in at the next services, have a rest and pour a coffee as you set off again
   c.   pull in at the next services, drink some coffee and then have a rest before continuing
   d.   pull in at the next services and give the coffee to your friends to liven them up so that they can keep you awake

5   After resting for twenty minutes you feel drowsy but your friends are anxious to continue the journey. You should:
Choose one answer

   a.   not worry as the drowsy feeling will go once you start driving again
   b.   not drive until you feel fully alert
   c.   ask one of your friends to take over the driving
   d.   have an alcoholic drink to stimulate your senses

6   What would reduce the chances of a neck injury in a collision?
Choose one answer

   a.   anti-lock brakes
   b.   seat belt pre-tensioners
   c.   a side impact protection system
   d.   a properly adjusted head restraint

7   It has just started to rain after a long dry spell. When will the road surface be most slippery?
Choose one answer

   a.   when it has rained for an hour or so
   b.   a few minutes after it starts to rain
   c.   when puddles have formed on the road
   d.   about an hour after the rain stops

8   What is the purpose of these raised red lines on the road surface?

Choose two answers

a. they prohibit parking and waiting
b. they alert you to a hazard ahead
c. to encourage you to slow down
d. warning of a school crossing patrol ahead
e. a reminder to check your suspension

9   If you are unsure whether a medicine will affect your driving you should:
Choose two answers

a. check the label on the medicine
b. ask a friend to try driving after taking the medicine
c. ask your doctor or pharmacist
d. ask a friend to follow you as you drive
e. stop taking the medicine

10 You see this sign whilst driving your car on a single carriageway road.
What does it mean?

Choose one answer

a. it is safe to drive at 60 mph
b. the national speed limit applies
c. you may drive at 70 mph if safe
d. you must not exceed 30 mph

11 Where may you overtake in a one-way street? *Choose one answer*

a. on the right only
b. on the left only
c. you may not overtake
d. on the left or right

12   To correct a front-wheel skid caused by fierce acceleration you should:
Choose one answer

   a.   use the choke
   b.   brake sharply
   c.   ease off the accelerator
   d.   apply the parking brake

13   The best way to slow your car on a very icy road is to:
Choose one answer

   a.   coast to a halt with the clutch down
   b.   use engine braking
   c.   select reverse gear and slip the clutch
   d.   use the parking brake

14   Rear-wheel skids are usually caused by:
Choose one answer

   a.   harsh braking
   b.   coasting
   c.   steering too gently
   d.   accelerating too late

15   It is more dangerous to overtake a tram than a car because:
Choose one answer

   a.   trams are quieter
   b.   trams are very slow-moving
   c.   you could get stuck in the tracks
   d.   trams can be very long

16   Cyclists are more vulnerable than car drivers because:
Choose one answer

   a.   they have less protection in an accident
   b.   they are unable to brake firmly
   c.   they are more prone to mistakes
   d.   they can't accelerate out of danger

17 What danger should you be aware of
when overtaking a car and caravan?
Choose one answer

a.   the car and caravan may accelerate sharply
b.   the driver towing the caravan may have difficulty seeing you
c.   caravans are prone to swing wildly from side to side
d.   you will need to pull in sharply after you have overtaken

18 What does this sign mean?

Choose one answer

a.   no horse riders permitted
b.   no horse-drawn carriages
c.   beware of horse riders ahead
d.   bridleway ahead, horse riders only

19 What does this sign mean?

Choose one answer

a.   priority over approaching traffic
b.   one-way street ahead
c.   give priority to oncoming vehicles
d.   contraflow ahead

20 What does this sign mean?

Choose one answer

a.   one-way street
b.   ahead only
c.   bus lane ahead
d.   danger overhead

21 You see this pedestrian crossing the road in the zigzag area and
    should:

Choose one answer

a. show the pedestrian consideration
b. give a short beep of the horn
c. accelerate as a warning to the pedestrian
d. stop and suggest to the pedestrian that he pays more attention in
    future

22 You need to take extra care when driving near a tramway because:
    Choose one answer

a. trams may stop suddenly to let passengers get off
b. you could get stuck in the tram rails
c. it is difficult to hear trams approaching
d. trams can't stop in an emergency

23 Parking illegally on double yellow lines can impede traffic flow and:
    Choose one answer

a. reduce air quality for local people
b. is only permitted if you show hazard warning lights
c. results in reduced congestion
d. always results in prosecution

24 An overloaded trailer is:
    Choose one answer

a. not dangerous at low speed
b. a danger at any speed
c. only dangerous at higher speeds
d. only dangerous on a motorway or dual carriageway

25 You have a heavy load in your car boot and never seem to have time to unload it. You should remember that:
Choose two answers

a. the load is likely to affect your vehicle's handling
b. carrying the load will help you when braking
c. the load will give you greater stability
d. your car will not be so economical to run with the load in it
e. your tyres will wear unevenly because of the load

26 Which four of the following could cause uneven tyre wear?
Choose four answers

a. incorrectly inflated tyres
b. faulty suspension
c. hydrolastic suspension
d. power steering
e. misaligned front wheels
f. a faulty braking system

27 How would a police officer that was following you indicate that he or she wanted you to pull in?

Choose one answer

a. by using a flashing blue light only
b. by indicating and pointing to the left
c. by overtaking you and braking sharply
d. by using both a siren and flashing blue lights

28 On a three-lane motorway this gantry sign indicates that:

Choose two answers

a. you may use any lane except the hard shoulder
b. you may use all lanes including the hard shoulder
c. there is a temporary advisory speed limit of 50 mph
d. there is a temporary mandatory speed limit of 50 mph
e. there is a queue of traffic 50 metres ahead

29 Which of these types of vehicle may not use motorways?
Choose one answer

   a. farm tractors
   b. motorcyclists
   c. buses
   d. learner lorry drivers

30 Reflective amber studs on a two-lane motorway separate the:
Choose one answer

   a. lanes
   b. hard shoulder and slip roads
   c. hard shoulder and left-hand lane
   d. right-hand lane and central reserve

31 If involved in a traffic accident you: *Choose one answer*

   a. must stop
   b. need only stop if a person is injured
   c. must show your licence to any other person involved
   d. must always report it to the police

32 How should you deal with a traffic accident casualty who is bleeding heavily from a severe cut to his or her forearm?
Choose two answers

   a. keep the casualty standing
   b. apply firm pressure to the wound
   c. apply a tourniquet
   d. put the casualty's head between his or her legs
   e. raise the arm to reduce blood flow

33 If you suspect a spill of flammable liquid at the scene of an accident you should first: *Choose one answer*

   a. test the liquid with a lighted match
   b. impose a smoking ban
   c. call the fire brigade
   d. go and find a fire extinguisher

34 A cover note is a document issued before you receive:
Choose one answer

   a. your road tax disc
   b. your driving licence
   c. your insurance certificate
   d. your vehicle logbook

35 Winter conditions can affect the distance it takes you to come to
    a stop. On an icy road you should expect stopping distances to
    increase by up to:
Choose one answer

   a. 2 times
   b. 3 times
   c. 5 times
   d. 10 times

36 You should update your Vehicle Registration document (V5C) when:
Choose one answer

   a. your insurance is due for renewal
   b. you move to a new address
   c. your next service is due
   d. you are involved in an accident

37 The light sequence seen by drivers at a puffin crossing is:
Choose one answer

   a. green – flashing amber – red – steady amber – green
   b. red – flashing amber – green – steady amber – red
   c. red – red and amber – green – steady amber – red
   d. green – red and amber – red – flashing amber – green

38 You may park on the right-hand side of a road at night:
Choose one answer

   a. provided you leave sidelights on
   b. in a one-way street
   c. only if you are more than 10 metres from a junction
   d. under a street light

39 Your vehicle catches fire whilst you are driving through a tunnel. You should:
Choose one answer

   a. turn your vehicle around and drive back out of the tunnel
   b. continue through the tunnel if you can
   c. stop and then reverse out of the tunnel
   d. stop and wait behind your vehicle until help arrives

40 The driver ahead gives this arm signal. It means:

Choose one answer

   a. the driver intends to turn right
   b. the driver intends to turn left
   c. the driver intends to slow down
   d. the driver wants you to overtake

41 You are waiting to turn left at a T-junction. A vehicle is coming from the right showing a left indicator signal. You should:
Choose one answer

   a. emerge before the vehicle reaches the junction
   b. emerge and accelerate quickly
   c. wait until the vehicle starts to turn before pulling out
   d. creep forward to see but not pull out

42 Whilst driving you see this sign at the roadside and should:

Choose one answer

   a. ignore it as it is intended for cyclists
   b. drive on knowing there will be no cyclists ahead
   c. be aware that there may be cyclists in the road ahead
   d. stop because you have driven into a cycle lane

43 Before starting a long holiday journey it is a good idea to:
Choose two answers

   a. look at a map
   b. have a heavy meal
   c. plan for rest stops
   d. fit new tyres
   e. overload your car

44 In which of these places would parking be inconsiderate to others?
Choose three answers

   a. in a lay-by
   b. near the brow of a hill
   c. where the road narrows
   d. where there is tactile paving at the kerb
   e. in a multi-storey car park

45 You are approaching a roundabout and
see a cyclist signalling to turn right. You should:
Choose one answer

   a. sound your horn to warn of your presence
   b. hold back and wave the cyclist across
   c. accelerate to get past the cyclist before the junction
   d. allow the cyclist plenty of room

46 You are following a large and slow-moving vehicle on a narrow road.
The road is straight and there is a junction just ahead. You should:
Choose one answer

   a. use the MSM routine and overtake
   b. wait until past the junction before attempting to overtake
   c. sound your horn and then overtake quickly
   d. follow the vehicle until you reach a dual carriageway

47 You see someone waiting on the footpath to cross
    at a zebra crossing. You should:
    Choose two answers

    a. accelerate to get past before the pedestrian steps on to
        the crossing
    b. check your mirrors
    c. stop and wave the pedestrian across
    d. ignore the pedestrian as he or she is still on the pavement
    e. stop and let the pedestrian cross the road

48 You are carrying a child using a rear-facing baby seat and only have
    room in the front passenger seat. Before setting off you must make sure:
    Choose one answer

    a. that the seat is in the fully forward position
    b. that you deactivate any front passenger airbag
    c. that all passenger airbags are deactivated
    d. that the child has been fed and sedated

49 You are driving on a well-lit motorway at night. You must:
    Choose one answer

    a. use only your sidelights
    b. use front and rear fog lights
    c. use your headlights
    d. only use headlights in poor weather conditions

50 You are on a single-track road and see another vehicle coming
    towards you. You should:
    Choose one answer

    a. pull into a passing place on your right
    b. expect the other driver to reverse out of your way
    c. reverse so that the approaching driver can come through
    d. wait before a passing place on your right

Paper 4
Theory test assessment

Case Study for questions 1–5

James arrives at the scene of an accident involving a motorcyclist and a number of cars. James stops and puts on his hazard warning lights before going to check on those involved. There are a number of casualties with minor injuries, a motorcyclist is conscious but lying down in the road, and another casualty is at the roadside who isn't moving or making any sound. A witness is talking to the motorcyclist.

1   Apart from putting on his hazard lights, how else could James have warned other traffic about the accident? *Choose one answer*

   a. by setting off his car alarm
   b. by parking at right angles to the kerb to block traffic movement
   c. by placing a hazard warning triangle on the road
   d. by standing in the middle of the road to flag down other motorists

2   What should James have done before checking on the casualties? *Choose one answer*

   a. called the emergency services
   b. made sure that he wasn't putting himself or anyone else in danger
   c. got the names and addresses of any witnesses
   d. asked the casualties if they had any infectious diseases

3   Who should James first give his attention to? *Choose one answer*

   a. the motorcyclist
   b. the casualties with minor injuries
   c. the casualty at the roadside who isn't moving or making any sound
   d. any witnesses who may have had a shock

4   James sees the witness trying to unfasten the motorcyclist's helmet.
    He should: *Choose one answer*

    a. shout instructions on how to do this safely
    b. not worry about the motorcyclist since he is talking to the witness
    c. tell the witness to get away from the motorcyclist
    d. tell the witness to leave the helmet in place

5   James finds that the unconscious casualty isn't breathing and decides
    to give chest compressions to maintain circulation. With what
    frequency should he push down on the casualty's chest?
    Choose one answer

    a. about 10 times per minute
    b. about 20 times per minute
    c. about 50 times per minute
    d. about 100 times per minute

6   The driver of the car in front is giving this arm signal. It means:

    Choose one answer

    a. the driver is slowing down
    b. the driver intends to turn right
    c. the driver wants you to overtake
    d. the driver intends to turn left

7   Which of the following should not be kept in your vehicle?
    Choose two answers

    a. a fire extinguisher
    b. the MOT certificate
    c. a first aid kit
    d. the vehicle registration document (logbook)
    e. the tax disc

8   You are trying to move off on snow. You should:
Choose one answer

   a. use the lowest gear you can
   b. keep the engine revs high to prevent stalling
   c. use the highest gear you can for the conditions
   d. put on your hazard warning lights

9   You break down on a motorway. To call for help it may be
   better to use an emergency roadside telephone rather than
   a mobile phone because:
Choose one answer

   a. it will connect you directly to a national breakdown service
   b. it would be illegal to use the mobile phone
   c. the emergency services will be able to locate you more easily
   d. it will connect you directly to a local garage

10 At an accident you are treating a burn victim. The shortest time you
   should cool the burn for is:
Choose one answer

   a. 5 minutes
   b. 10 minutes
   c. 15 minutes
   d. 20 minutes

11 Where would you see this sign?

Choose one answer

   a. in the window of a car taking children to school
   b. at the side of the road
   c. at playground areas
   d. on the rear of a school bus or coach

12 Driving along this country road you see horses and riders approaching. You should:

Choose two answers

a. give plenty of room
b. give a light tap of your horn
c. flash your headlights
d. drive past slowly and carefully
e. speed up to get past the danger promptly
f. select a low gear and keep your engine speed high as you pass

13 As a new driver, how likely are you to have an accident compared to more experienced drivers? *Choose one answer*

a. less likely
b. more likely
c. about the same
d. it depends on your age

14 Why is it good planning to take regular stops on a long journey? *Choose one answer*

a. to reduce engine wear, particularly on fast roads
b. to avoid losing concentration
c. to check your route
d. to adjust the driving seat and mirrors

15 Approaching a sharp bend on an icy road, what two things should you do for safety? *Choose two answers*

a. keep the clutch pedal down
b. accelerate to keep the wheels gripping
c. use as high a gear as you can
d. slow down well before the bend
e. put on hazard warning lights

16 Which of the following affect your thinking distance?
    Choose three answers

    a. the weather conditions
    b. your health
    c. your distance from the vehicle ahead
    d. your concentration
    e. the speed of your vehicle

17 What is the maximum LEGAL level of alcohol you can have in your
    breath when driving?
    Choose one answer

    a. 50 micrograms per 100 ml
    b. 35 micrograms per 100 ml
    c. 100 micrograms per 100 ml
    d. 80 micrograms per 100 ml

18 On a busy road you realize you are going the wrong way. You should:
    Choose one answer

    a. pull into a side road and reverse out into the main road to turn
        round
    b. do a 'three-point turn'
    c. find a quiet road to turn round in
    d. make a quick U-turn

19 You see this sign ahead and should:

    Choose one answer

    a. slow down to 30 mph or less after you pass the sign
    b. keep to about 35 mph after the sign
    c. make sure you are travelling at 30 mph or less as you reach
        the sign
    d. assume it is safe to drive at 30 mph after the sign

20 What is the closest you should park your car to a junction?
Choose one answer

a. 5 metres (16 feet)
b. 10 metres (33 feet)
c. 15 metres (50 feet)
d. 20 metres (65 feet)

21 What will happen if you push the clutch pedal down when travelling down a steep hill? *Choose one answer*

a. your brakes will not work
b. the clutch plate will wear unevenly
c. the vehicle will slow down
d. the vehicle will speed up

22 If you have to park your car on a road in fog, what should you do?
Choose one answer

a. leave on your headlights and rear fog lights
b. leave on your sidelights
c. leave on your rear fog lights and sidelights
d. leave on your hazard warning lights

23 You are following the long vehicle towards a mini-roundabout.
You wish to turn right and should:

Choose one answer

a. pull alongside the long vehicle
b. keep back until the long vehicle has cleared the mini-roundabout
c. drive on the white roundabout marking
d. expect the driver ahead to keep left

24 You are about to overtake a cyclist. Which one of these signs would make you take special care? *Choose one answer*

a.   b.   c.   d.

25 You are driving up a steep hill on a narrow road. A lorry is coming from the opposite direction and will need to pass a parked car. You should: *Choose one answer*

   a. expect the lorry to give way to you
   b. accelerate to clear the hazard
   c. be ready to give way to the lorry
   d. flash your lights to beckon the lorry driver through

26 After you give a signal to make a right turn at a junction, why is it important to get into position in good time? *Choose one answer*

   a. to stop any other drivers from getting to the junction before you
   b. to help other road users anticipate what you intend to do
   c. to hold up following traffic if necessary
   d. to get a better view into the junction you are approaching

27 You are driving at the speed limit and a following driver wants to overtake. There is a slower vehicle ahead. What should you do? *Choose one answer*

   a. allow the following driver to overtake
   b. move to the right to prevent the following driver from overtaking
   c. ignore the following driver and concentrate on the vehicle ahead
   d. give a signal and pull out to overtake the slow vehicle ahead of you

28 Carrying a heavy load in your car will: *Choose one answer*

   a. not affect your steering
   b. not affect your steering or braking
   c. affect your braking only in a bend
   d. affect your braking only
   e. affect your car's handling, particularly in a bend

29 A breakaway cable on a caravan is designed so that: *Choose one answer*

   a. overloaded caravans can be towed more safely
   b. the caravan will slow if the towing hitch comes loose
   c. the caravan can be released when driving
   d. the caravan can be released more quickly in an emergency

30 You notice a strong smell of petrol when driving. You should:
Choose one answer

   a. speed up to increase the airflow through your car
   b. stop and investigate the problem
   c. mention it when you next have your vehicle serviced
   d. look out for a nearby fuel station

31 You are in a slow-moving traffic queue on a motorway. You may:
Choose one answer

   a. move left to overtake
   b. overtake slower queuing traffic on the right or left
   c. only overtake by moving to a lane on your right
   d. use the hard shoulder to overtake

32 Whilst driving you realize there is a fire in
   your engine compartment. You:
Choose one answer

   a. should drive to the nearest petrol station
   b. must drive to the nearest fire station
   c. must increase speed to blow out the fire
   d. should pull in and get everyone out of the car

33 Within two years of passing your driving test you get six penalty
   points on your licence. What are the consequences?
Choose two answers

   a. you would be limited to six more penalty points before losing
       your licence
   b. you would revert to provisional status
   c. you would have to retake your theory and practical tests
   d. you would be banned from driving for 12 months
   e. you would be restricted to driving a three-wheeled car

34 What does this sign mean?

Choose one answer

a.   end of two-way traffic
b.   no low bridges ahead
c.   end of motorway
d.   no motorway traffic allowed

35 What does this sign mean?

Choose one answer

a.   two-way traffic ahead
b.   end of dual carriageway
c.   two-way traffic crosses one-way road
d.   T-junction ahead

36 You are waiting in the left-hand lane at traffic lights to turn left.
At which signals can you proceed if safe?
Choose two answers

a.

b.

c.

d.

37 You hold a provisional licence for cars and want to ride a motorcycle. You: *Choose one answer*

a. may start riding immediately
b. must apply for motorcycle entitlement
c. must not ride until you have passed a driving test for a car
d. must apply for a motorcycle licence but can start riding immediately

38 Where should you normally expect other drivers to overtake you on the left? *Choose one answer*

a. on a motorway
b. in a contraflow system
c. in a one-way system
d. nowhere

39 Driving in heavy rain you realize that your steering suddenly feels very light. You should: *Choose one answer*

a. steer towards the middle of the road
b. gently increase pressure on the accelerator pedal
c. brake firmly to reduce speed
d. ease off the accelerator pedal

40 When should you use hazard warning lights? *Choose one answer*

a. when stopping briefly in a restricted parking zone
b. when your vehicle has broken down and is causing an obstruction
c. when warning approaching traffic that you intend to stop
d. when being towed

41 You are driving on the motorway when a suitcase falls from your vehicle roof rack. You should: *Choose one answer*

a. stop at the next emergency telephone and contact the police
b. stop in lane, put on hazard warning lights and reverse back for the suitcase
c. walk back up the motorway to pick the suitcase up
d. pull in at the next service area and report the incident

42 What would you expect to find at a motorway contraflow system?
Choose two answers

a. temporary traffic lights
b. lower speed limits
c. narrower lanes than normal
d. an extra-wide hard shoulder
e. faster-moving traffic

43 Planning ahead and making smooth use of the controls can:
Choose two answers

a. reduce journey times by about 15 per cent
b. increase your journey times by an unacceptable amount
c. increase fuel consumption by about 15 per cent
d. reduce fuel consumption by about 15 per cent
e. reduce the environmental impact of your driving

44 Where would you see these red and white markers?

Choose one answer

a. on approach to a ford or flood
b. at the end of a motorway
c. on approach to a concealed level crossing
d. on approach to a slip road leaving a dual carriageway

45 What could be caused by having too much oil in your engine?
Choose one answer

a. low oil pressure
b. the engine running at a higher temperature than normal
c. oil leaks
d. reduced fuel consumption

46 You are driving at night in fog. The fog clears but you forget to switch off your rear fog lights. This:
Choose two answers

a. will warn approaching traffic that there is fog ahead
b. could make other drivers think you are braking
c. will save you putting them on again later
d. could dazzle following drivers
e. may drain your battery

47 You see a cyclist in the road ahead look back over his or her right shoulder. You should anticipate that the cyclist:
Choose one answer

a. is going to dismount
b. intends to move right
c. will turn left ahead
d. will accelerate sharply

48 What is the maximum fine specified for driving without insurance?
Choose one answer

a. £100
b. £500
c. £1,000
d. £5,000

49 When following the road ahead at a roundabout you should:
Choose one answer

a. not use any indicator signal
b. indicate left before leaving the roundabout
c. indicate left when approaching the roundabout
d. indicate right on approach and then left to leave the roundabout

50 Active Traffic Management (ATM) areas on motorways may allow drivers to use the hard shoulder as a running lane. This:
Choose one answer

a. only applies to emergency vehicles
b. allows you to stop on the hard shoulder for a rest break
c. is to help ease congestion
d. is risky if there are police vehicles about

Paper 5
Theory test assessment

Case Study for questions 1–5

Nicole is a specialist nurse who must start her shift at 6.00am. This winter morning it is bitterly cold and raining as she gets into her car. On the way to work she turns right on to a main road and feels the back of her car sliding to the left. Traffic seems to be heavier and slower than usual on the main road.

1   What danger should Nicole be particularly wary of given the rain and bitter cold conditions? *Choose one answer*

   a.   snow drifts
   b.   high winds developing
   c.   rain freezing on the roads as it falls
   d.   hailstones developing

2   What could tell Nicole she was driving on black ice?
   Choose two answers

   a.   roadside signs
   b.   there would be very little road noise
   c.   the car's steering would feel very light
   d.   the car would pull to one side when braking

3   How should Nicole react to recover from the skid as she turns right?
   Choose one answer

   a.   by easing off the accelerator and steering gently left to straighten the car
   b.   by gently applying the brakes and steering to the right
   c.   by braking firmly and holding the steering wheel straight
   d.   by accelerating gently and steering more to the right

4   As there seems to be more traffic than usual, what precaution should Nicole take given the weather and surface conditions? *Choose one answer*

   a.   drive in as low a gear as possible for better control

   b.   allow less room between her and the vehicle ahead because of the traffic volume

   c.   leave a bigger gap ahead because it could take longer to brake to a stop

   d.   use hazard warning lights to stop following drivers from getting too close

5   Given the road and surface conditions, how should Nicole use the accelerator and footbrake? *Choose one answer*

   a.   firmly and promptly

   b.   firmly and slowly

   c.   gently and slowly

   d.   gently and promptly

6   What is the THINKING distance at 50 mph? *Choose one answer*

   a.   6 metres (20 feet)

   b.   9 metres (30 feet)

   c.   15 metres (50 feet)

   d.   21 metres (70 feet)

7   Which of the following affect your overall stopping distance? *Choose three answers*

   a.   the weather conditions

   b.   how soon you react

   c.   your distance from the vehicle ahead

   d.   the condition of your tyres

   e.   the gear you are in

8   Emerging at a junction with poor visibility, you should: *Choose one answer*

   a.   creep forward, looking to the right

   b.   creep forward looking to the left

   c.   creep forward looking both ways

   d.   sound your horn and pull out after a quick glance both ways

9 In heavy slow traffic, how can you lessen the risk of hitting a cyclist or motorcyclist? *Choose one answer*

   a. by making regular use of your exterior mirrors
   b. by keeping close to the car ahead
   c. by relying on cyclists and motorcyclists to take care
   d. by regularly looking over both shoulders as you are driving

10 Having just less than half the maximum legal level of alcohol in your blood when driving is: *Choose two answers*

   a. safe enough in any circumstance
   b. no guarantee that you can drive safely
   c. unlikely to affect your driving
   d. very likely to affect your driving ability

11 You have had a lot of alcohol at a party in the evening. The next morning you: *Choose one answer*

   a. should be perfectly safe to drive
   b. could still be over the legal alcohol limit for driving
   c. may feel 'hung over' but should be within the legal alcohol limit
   d. will be safe to drive after a good breakfast

12 In a narrow road you notice an oncoming vehicle and a parked car on your left ahead. Who has priority? *Choose one answer*

   a. you do if you can reach the parked car before the approaching driver
   b. the driver of the wider vehicle
   c. the driver of the oncoming vehicle
   d. the driver who is going faster or who has the larger vehicle
   e. you do unless the owner of the parked car signals to move off

13 What would you need to do after passing a sign like this?

Choose one answer

   a. gently try your brakes
   b. rev the engine to clear the carburettor
   c. perform an emergency stop
   d. consider changing your make of car

14 Front fog lights should only be used when:
Choose one answer

a. your rear fog lights don't work
b. it is foggy
c. visibility drops below 200 metres
d. visibility drops below 100 metres

15 After heavy rain you notice that water hasn't drained from the road ahead. What should you do?
Choose one answer

a. drive in second gear, slipping the clutch
b. use acceleration to keep the wheels gripping
c. drive with one foot on the brake
d. slow down and keep engine speed low

16 Approaching a mini-roundabout to turn right, you see ahead a large vehicle in the left-hand lane showing a right indicator signal. You should:
Choose one answer

a. assume the driver has signalled incorrectly and overtake
b. keep back until the long vehicle has cleared the mini-roundabout
c. flash your lights and take a short cut across the mini-roundabout
d. expect the driver of the large vehicle to keep left

17 How often do you need to check that the horn is working properly?
Choose one answer

a. every night
b. daily
c. only if you need the horn
d. before an MOT test

18 You are approaching traffic light signals to go ahead. Which signals mean you can proceed if safe? *Choose two answers*

a.   b.   c.   d.

19 The reason for giving signals is to:
Choose one answer

a. give instructions to other road users
b. help other road users anticipate what you intend to do
c. warn other road users to give way
d. ensure that you have priority

20 You live half a mile from your child's school and own a car.
You should:
Choose two answers

a. use your car to collect your child if other parents do the same
b. try to avoid using your car to collect your child from school
c. instruct your child to walk home alone
d. be aware that very short journeys are wasteful of fuel
e. only use your car if it has a catalytic converter

21 What is wrong with this car and caravan combination?

Choose one answer

a. the combination is too lightweight
b. the caravan is underloaded
c. the car is overloaded
d. the caravan hasn't been loaded properly

22 You give an indicator signal when driving and notice the repeater light
on the dashboard flashing faster than usual. What does this mean?
Choose one answer

a. you are taking corners too quickly
b. your car's battery is overcharged
c. one of your indicator bulbs may have blown
d. the fuse has blown on the indicator circuit

23 You notice oil leaking from your car and should:
Choose one answer

a.   keep adding more oil to the engine
b.   investigate and have the leak repaired
c.   mention it when you next have your car serviced
d.   not worry unless the oil warning light comes on when driving

24 You are in a slow-moving traffic queue on a motorway. You may:
Choose one answer

a.   move left to overtake
b.   not overtake
c.   pass on the left if your traffic queue is moving faster than traffic in the lane on your right
d.   use the hard shoulder to overtake

25 What is the purpose of this post at the side of a motorway?

Choose one answer

a.   it advises police of the direction to the nearest speed trap point
b.   it advises the direction to the nearest emergency telephone
c.   it advises the distance to the nearest service station
d.   it advises the direction to the next motorway exit

26 Whilst driving on a busy road, you realize that your car is losing power. You should:
Choose one answer

a.   drive to the nearest petrol station
b.   drive faster to complete your journey
c.   pull in as soon as you safely can
d.   slow down to a crawl and hope that your car will make it home

27 In what circumstance would you try to move a traffic accident casualty?
Choose one answer

a. only if the casualty was awake
b. only if the casualty was unconscious
c. only if the casualty was in further danger
d. only if you had a first aid qualification

28 At a T-junction your view to the right is partly blocked by pedestrians standing at the corner. You should:

Choose one answer

a. open the window and ask the pedestrians to move
b. just pull out and hope for the best
c. lean forward in your seat and edge out to get a better view
d. sound your horn before you emerge

29 What does this sign mean?

Choose one answer

a. minimum speed 30 mph
b. distance to next services
c. maximum speed 30 mph
d. waiting limited to 30 minutes

30 Where would you most expect to see this type of sign?

Choose one answer

a. on motorways
b. in a one-way street
c. in tourist areas
d. on minor roads

31 A driver behind you is very close and flashing his or her headlights.
You should: *Choose one answer*

 a.   keep to the speed limit
 b.   pull in and wave the driver through
 c.   slow down and allow the driver to overtake you
 d.   touch the brakes to show your stop lights as a warning

32 Driving too slowly for the road and traffic conditions is:
Choose two answers

 a.   not likely to cause a hazard
 b.   potentially dangerous
 c.   safe in wet conditions
 d.   likely to irritate other drivers
 e.   not likely to affect other road users

33 Any load carried on a roof rack on your car must be:
Choose one answer

 a.   as light as possible
 b.   covered with a tarpaulin
 c.   as heavy as possible
 d.   properly secured

34 You are going on holiday and wish to take the family pet.
You should only carry the pet in your car if: *Choose one answer*

 a.   it can't be secured on a roof rack
 b.   you can keep it tied up
 c.   it is in a box
 d.   you can keep it from roaming freely in the car
 e.   it is trained to sit quietly

35 Which of the following MUST be in good working order for your car
to be legally roadworthy? *Choose four answers*

 a.   speedometer
 b.   rev counter, if fitted
 c.   brakes
 d.   horn
 e.   temperature gauge
 f.   oil warning light
 g.   windscreen washers

36 How should you carry spare fuel in your vehicle?
Choose one answer

   a. in an old oil can
   b. in a plastic bottle
   c. in an approved container
   d. in a thick glass container

37 What could cause your tyre tread to wear excessively in the centre?
Choose one answer

   a. power steering
   b. driving for short distances in very cold conditions
   c. driving at high speed for long periods
   d. having too little pressure in the tyre
   e. having the tyre over-inflated

38 Why should you check the condition of your vehicle before
   a motorway journey?
Choose one answer

   a. you will be braking more often
   b. breakdowns are expensive
   c. you will be changing gear more often
   d. high speeds increase the risk of breakdowns

39 In an accident involving a tanker, what should you do before
   dialling 999?
Choose one answer

   a. get the tanker off the road
   b. plug up any leaks from the tanker
   c. wash away any liquid that has been spilled
   d. try to identify what the tanker was carrying by reading the hazard
       information plate

40 What is the correct thing to do if you injure someone when driving?
Choose one answer

   a. nothing
   b. leave it to the injured person to report the accident
   c. inform the police as soon as possible
   d. inform the police within 14 days

41 You see horse riders ahead riding side by side. You should:
Choose one answer

   a. ask yourself whether both riders are experienced
   b. sound your horn in annoyance
   c. accelerate promptly to pass safely
   d. shout at the riders as you pass

42 Which of the following should you show particular concern for?
Choose two answers

   a. elderly drivers
   b. learner drivers
   c. drivers of your own age
   d. more experienced drivers

43 What can help you to keep your concentration on a long journey?
Choose one answer

   a. driving only on long straight roads
   b. driving slowly
   c. fast driving
   d. regular rest stops
   e. listening to the radio

44 The good driver should always:
Choose three answers

   a. drive at the speed limit
   b. make effective use of the driving mirrors
   c. look well ahead
   d. anticipate the actions of other road users
   e. show off his or her skill

45 What can happen to a road surface in very hot weather?
Choose one answer

   a. nothing
   b. it will become firmer
   c. it could get softer
   d. it will become safer to drive on

46 Compared to a dry road, in wet conditions you should allow:
    Choose one answer

    a. twice your usual braking distance
    b. four times your usual braking distance
    c. 10 times your usual braking distance
    d. six times your usual braking distance

47 Why should you always check the label of any prescribed medicine
    you take before driving?
    Choose one answer

    a. in case the medicine is out of date
    b. to make sure the medicine is legal
    c. some medicines can cause drowsiness
    d. in case the medicine increases your level of concentration

48 Where should you not park?
    Choose four answers

    a. near the brow of a hill
    b. at a bus stop
    c. near a police station
    d. across a driveway
    e. opposite a traffic island
    f. in a recognized parking place

49 When overtaking at night you should:
    Choose one answer

    a. wait until you can see oncoming headlights
    b. take care because you can see less
    c. put your headlights on full beam
    d. sound your horn

50 What lights must you leave on if parked at night on a 40 mph road?
    Choose one answer

    a. none
    b. sidelights
    c. dipped headlights
    d. hazard warning lights

Paper 6
Theory test assessment

Case Study for questions 1–5

Harry has a busy morning ahead. He is going to deliver some unwanted pieces of furniture to a friend's house in the next town. Harry's friend has given him a roof rack for his estate car in exchange, helped him load the furniture and will be travelling with Harry to give him directions. On the way, Harry has to take the family pet cat to the vet for a small operation, and drop his children Tom aged 15 and Sarah aged 12 at school. He will pick the cat and the children up again later on return from his day's work.

1   Who is responsible for ensuring that the vehicle and roof rack are safely loaded?
    Choose one answer

    a. Harry
    b. Harry's friend
    c. the police
    d. the local authority

2   What effects will the loaded roof rack have on the vehicle?
    Choose two answers

    a. it will increase stability, especially in bends
    b. it will reduce stability
    c. it will cause the car to handle differently
    d. it will reduce fuel consumption

3   Who is responsible for ensuring that Sarah wears her seatbelt?
Choose one answer

   a.   Sarah
   b.   Harry's friend
   c.   Tom
   d.   Harry

4   How should the cat be carried in the car? *Choose one answer*

   a.   in a cardboard box
   b.   one of the children should hold it
   c.   in a suitable pet carrier
   d.   tied to the rear seat

5   With the furniture unloaded at his friend's house, Harry sets off for
     work. What will he notice about carrying the empty roof rack on his car?
     Choose one answer

   a.   it will make the car unstable
   b.   it will reduce noise levels
   c.   it will cause increased fuel consumption
   d.   it will be noisy and increase fuel economy

6   On a single carriageway the speed limit for goods vehicles under
     7.5 tonnes is: *Choose one answer*

   a.   60 mph
   b.   70 mph
   c.   50 mph
   d.   55 mph

7   You are driving on a multi-lane road and see these overhead gantry
     signs. What do they mean?

Choose one answer

   a.   traffic in the right lanes should stop
   b.   the two right lanes are open
   c.   the two left lanes are open
   d.   traffic in the middle lane should leave the road

8 You are driving in daylight when it is raining.
   Which lights should you use?
   Choose one answer

   a. full headlights
   b. dipped headlights
   c. sidelights only
   d. hazard warning lights

9 How can you dry your brakes after driving through a flood?
   Choose one answer

   a. with tissue paper
   b. by practising emergency stops
   c. by driving slowly with your left foot gently on the brake pedal
   d. by driving with one foot on the brake and one foot on the clutch

10 When driving, you press the accelerator pedal on your car and notice
   the engine speed increase but the car doesn't accelerate very well.
   This means that:
   Choose one answer

   a. the accelerator cable has snapped
   b. the clutch is worn
   c. the brakes have seized
   d. your exhaust system needs replacing

11 Which shape of sign is used to indicate a 'Give way' junction?
   Choose one answer

   a.

   b.

   c.

   d.

12 Your car has a five-speed gear box. When would you use fifth gear?
    Choose one answer

    a. only at low speed
    b. for greatest acceleration
    c. when cruising at high speed
    d. in slow-moving traffic

13 When parked at the left kerb, facing uphill, you should leave your car:
    Choose three answers

    a. in top gear
    b. with the parking brake firmly applied
    c. with the front wheels turned to the right
    d. in first gear
    e. with the front wheels turned to the left

14 What is the best way to control your speed when driving down
    a steep hill? *Choose one answer*

    a. constant use of the footbrake
    b. using the parking brake
    c. using a low gear to avoid constant pressure on the footbrake
    d. switching off the engine and coasting

15 Your car pulls sharply to the right when braking. What is likely to be
    wrong? *Choose one answer*

    a. your steering mechanism has seized
    b. you are not braking hard enough
    c. your brakes need adjusting
    d. your brakes have faded

16 What does this sign mean?

    Choose one answer

    a. be ready for a surprise
    b. warning of danger ahead
    c. overhead cables
    d. hospital ahead

17 Approaching a junction you should:
Choose one answer

a. look out for pedestrians only as you begin to turn
b. look out for pedestrians well before and during the turn
c. only be concerned with pedestrians in the road
d. always sound your horn to warn any pedestrians who are out of sight

18 Where would you see a sign like this?

Choose one answer

a. at a junction
b. on a long vehicle
c. on a vehicle with an overhanging load
d. at a level crossing

19 The purpose of the compulsory MOT test is to ensure that:
Choose one answer

a. drivers are competent
b. vehicles reach a minimum safety standard
c. vehicles are mechanically sound
d. vehicles are unlikely to break down

20 What are the three most important things to think about when deciding on a safe speed at which to drive?
Choose three answers

a. the engine size of your car
b. the weather conditions
c. the road surface conditions
d. the national speed limit
e. how far you can see ahead
f. your level of high-speed driving skill

21 A fire engine showing flashing blue lights is following your car in
    a very narrow residential road with a lot of parked cars. You should:

Choose one answer

a. stop immediately
b. concentrate on looking for the fire
c. pull in at a suitable passing place when you can do so safely
d. speed up if there is no suitable place for the fire engine to pass

22 You need to park and see a space marked with these red lines.
    You should:

Choose one answer

a. assume that parking is never permitted
b. park and use your hazard warning lights
c. check for information signs to find out if parking restrictions are
    in force
d. park but leave your engine running

23 Driving on a motorway, you see a large package fall from a lorry head.
    The lorry driver doesn't appear to notice, so you should:
    Choose one answer

a. stop on the carriageway and retrieve the package
b. swerve to avoid the package and then drive on
c. stop on the hard shoulder and contact the police on an emergency
    phone
d. pull in on the hard shoulder and pick up the package when safe

24 You switch on your lights as night falls and notice this symbol light up on your instrument panel. This means:

Choose one answer

a. your front fog lights are on
b. your headlights are on main beam
c. you need to put on full headlights
d. it isn't dark enough for headlights yet

25 Your car has an anti-lock braking system (ABS). This is designed to:
Choose one answer

a. make it is impossible to skid
b. prevent your car being broken into
c. help you with car control
d. stop you having to use the footbrake early

26 If your car has a catalytic converter, you should remember that:
Choose one answer

a. unleaded petrol can damage it
b. it is most efficient on short journeys
c. it is only for use with diesel fuel
d. it could cause more pollution than ordinary exhaust systems on short journeys

27 When may you overtake on the left?
Choose two answers

a. in a one-way system
b. at any time
c. if a vehicle ahead is signalling to turn right and positioned to do so
d. in fast-moving traffic when the right lane is blocked

28 After a motorway breakdown you have stopped on the hard shoulder and should: *Choose two answers*

a. get out of your car on the left side and leave it unlocked
b. get out of your car and lock it
c. put on your hazard warning lights
d. wait in your car for assistance

29 Towing a trailer on a three-lane motorway, you are not permitted to:
Choose two answers

a. use the left-hand lane
b. exceed 60 mph
c. use the middle or third lanes
d. use the right-hand lane
e. exceed 50 mph

30 In an emergency, you have to stop the car suddenly and should:
Choose two answers

a. grip the steering wheel firmly
b. not brake before checking the mirrors
c. brake firmly
d. use the parking brake to help stop the car

31 After a frosty morning, the sun has begun to thaw ice on the road.
Where in particular would you expect the road to remain slippery?
Choose one answer

a. where there has been a steady flow of early morning traffic
b. where the road has had plenty of sunlight but little traffic
c. where the road surface is in the shade
d. where the road has been treated with salt and grit

32 You want to overtake the van and should be aware that:

Choose one answer

a. it will be easier since the van will be slowing down
b. you will be safer because you can pick up speed more quickly
on the hill
c. you will not be able to accelerate so well on the hill
d. it could take longer than you expect

33 Your car needs a new battery. How should you dispose of the old one?
Choose one answer

a. take it to a local authority recycling site
b. break it up and bury it in your garden
c. leave it at the roadside
d. burn it

34 In areas where there are 'traffic calming' measures you should:
Choose one answer

a. travel at a reduced speed
b. always travel at the speed limit
c. position in the centre of the road
d. only slow down if pedestrians are near

35 Which four of these must not use motorways?
Choose four answers

a. learner car drivers
b. motorcycles over 50 cc
c. double-deck buses
d. farm tractors
e. horse riders
f. cyclists

36 Why would this temporary speed limit sign be shown?

Choose one answer

a. to warn of the end of the motorway
b. to warn you of a low bridge
c. to warn you of a junction ahead
d. to warn of road works ahead

37 What do these yellow markings on the kerb indicate?

Choose one answer

a. no parking except for loading
b. passenger set-down prohibited
c. loading restrictions in force
d. loading bay, no waiting permitted

38 You have third-party-only insurance. What does this cover?
Choose three answers

a. collision damage to your own vehicle
b. theft of your vehicle
c. injury to another road user
d. damage you cause to someone's property
e. damage you cause to other vehicles
f. any injury you suffer in an accident that you cause

39 Signals to other road users should normally be given by direction
indicators and: *Choose one answer*

a. fog lights
b. the horn
c. brake lights
d. flashing headlights

40 You are on a road that has street lights. Unless traffic signs tell you
otherwise, the speed limit is: *Choose one answer*

a. 20 mph
b. 30 mph
c. 40 mph
d. 60 mph

41 What is meant by 'tailgating'? *Choose one answer*

a. a way to keep pets in the rear of an estate car
b. reversing into a driveway
c. following another vehicle too closely
d. reversing out of a driveway

42 By taking a Pass Plus course after passing your driving test you will:
Choose one answer

   a.   get a discount on your MOT
   b.   learn how to tune your engine
   c.   gain more experience and improve your driving skills
   d.   be exempt from the 'new driver' regulations

43 What does this sign mean?

Choose one answer

   a.   dual carriageway ahead
   b.   no entry
   c.   vehicles may pass either side to reach the same destination
   d.   go back

44 You wish to turn right at a crossroads where an oncoming driver is also turning right. It will normally be safer to:
Choose one answer

   a.   keep the other vehicle to your right and turn behind it (offside to offside)
   b.   keep the other vehicle to your left and turn in front of it (nearside to nearside)
   c.   hold back so the oncoming driver can turn ahead of you
   d.   turn left and find another route to your destination

45 At an accident scene you are dealing with a casualty who is bleeding from a cut on his or her arm. The wound seems clean so you should:
Choose two answers

   a.   apply firm pressure over the wound
   b.   lower the arm to keep the circulation stable
   c.   give the casualty plenty of fluids
   d.   raise the arm to reduce blood flow
   e.   keep the casualty moving to prevent a faint

46 Powered wheelchairs driven by the disabled have a maximum speed of:
Choose one answer

a. 8 mph
b. 12 mph
c. 22 mph
d. 30 mph

47 When might it be useful to look at the reflections of vehicles in shop windows? *Choose one answer*

a. to pass the time when waiting in a traffic queue
b. when emerging at a junction and your view of approaching traffic is restricted
c. when trying to avoid eye contact with others after you have made a mistake
d. when deciding whether it is time to switch on your headlights

48 Snow is falling heavily and the weather forecast suggests it will continue for some time. You had planned a long journey and should:
Choose one answer

a. follow a snow plough or road gritter
b. not drive unless the journey is essential
c. make sure your fuel tank is full because you won't have time to stop
d. only drive in a low gear

49 When driving a car with automatic transmission, what would you use 'kick-down' for? *Choose one answer*

a. an emergency stop
b. quick acceleration
c. to control speed going downhill
d. to reduce fuel consumption

50 The left-hand lane of a motorway should be used for:
Choose one answer

a. rest breaks
b. normal driving
c. overtaking
d. emergencies only

Paper 7
Theory test assessment

Case Study for questions 1–5

You work in the city centre and are driving in from your village home. You notice there is a side wind as you drive along a section of dual carriageway. After overtaking some large vehicles you see ahead a motorcyclist riding quite slowly as you near the end of the dual carriageway. Later, as you enter town your view ahead is restricted by a delivery truck. The truck turns off your route but traffic seems to be very slow and heavy making you anxious about being late for work.

1   What should you anticipate as you overtake the large vehicles? *Choose one answer*

    a.   that your car may pull sharply to one side as you pass
    b.   that your speed will increase suddenly as you pass
    c.   that the large vehicles will be pushed to one side as you pass
    d.   that the large vehicle drivers will slow down for you as you pass

2   What should you do as you approach the end of the dual carriageway? *Choose one answer*

    a.   speed up to get past the motorcyclist before the road narrows
    b.   check your speed
    c.   sound your horn to warn the motorcyclist of your presence
    d.   pull in close behind the motorcyclist

3   How can you improve your view ahead when you are behind the delivery truck? *Choose one answer*

    a.   by straddling the centre line of the carriageway
    b.   by keeping well back
    c.   by signalling the delivery truck driver to pull over
    d.   by driving well to the left of your lane

4   The truck driver gives a left signal but moves towards the centre of the road. You should: *Choose two answers*

   a.   assume the driver will turn right and pass on the left
   b.   assume the driver wants to turn into a narrow road on the left
   c.   sound your horn and pass on the right
   d.   keep back until the truck driver has turned off your route

5   You see a bus stop ahead and the bus driver gives a right signal as you get near. You should: *Choose one answer*

   a.   accelerate to get past the bus quickly
   b.   sound your horn as a warning of your presence
   c.   expect the bus driver to wait for you to pass
   d.   give way and let the bus pull out if you can do so safely

6   On approach to a speed hump you should:

   Choose one answer

   a.   try to avoid it
   b.   accelerate in readiness
   c.   slow down
   d.   coast over it with the clutch down

7   When you are turning left on a slippery road, the back of your car slides to the right. What should you do? *Choose one answer*

   a.   brake firmly
   b.   steer more to the left
   c.   accelerate for stability
   d.   steer gently to the right

8   When you are not using the clutch pedal, your left foot should be: *Choose one answer*

   a.   resting on the clutch pedal
   b.   tucked under your seat
   c.   over the footbrake
   d.   within easy reach of the clutch pedal

9 You see this sign on a busy road. What hazard should you expect?

Choose one answer

  a. the road will narrow ahead
  b. merging traffic ahead
  c. traffic joining from your left
  d. a difficult Y-junction

10 Whilst driving on a motorway you feel tired. What should you do?
Choose one answer

  a. keep to 50 mph
  b. drive more quickly to shorten your journey
  c. stop on the hard shoulder for a rest
  d. leave the motorway at the next exit or service station

11 What does this sign mean?

Choose one answer

  a. no sharp bends ahead
  b. you must not turn left at the next junction
  c. you are in a one-way street
  d. you must drive on the right

12 What is the first thing you should do when you see a hazard in
    the road ahead?
Choose one answer

  a. show your brake lights
  b. change gear
  c. check your mirrors
  d. ease off the accelerator pedal

13 Why must you not enter a box junction if your exit isn't clear?

Choose one answer

a. traffic lights could force you to reverse
b. you could block the junction
c. you are never permitted to wait in a box junction
d. to give cyclists a chance in heavy traffic conditions

14 Why do you need to try your brakes after passing through a flood?
Choose one answer

a. your brakes may be wet and not work
b. to shake any water from the brake linings
c. to dry out the brake linings
d. because the road may be wet

15 Why should you check your lights before driving in thick daytime fog?
Choose one answer

a. to avoid dazzling other drivers
b. to make sure you can be seen
c. you will need your main beam
d. it will probably be very dark on the road

16 What should you avoid doing when driving in a bend?
Choose two answers

a. using full headlights
b. braking sharply
c. making sudden steering movements
d. keeping light pressure on the accelerator pedal
e. checking your mirrors

17 What does the road marking along the centre of the road tell drivers?

Choose one answer

a. give way to oncoming traffic
b. end of dual carriageway
c. not to cross the lines
d. parking permitted

18 What does this sign mean?

Choose one answer

a. holiday route
b. hot spot for accidents and emergencies
c. hospital with accident and emergency unit
d. high vehicles use A and E roads

19 What does this sign mean?

Choose one answer

a. motorways merging
b. no hard shoulder ahead
c. motorway widening
d. motorway contraflow

20 Who must ensure that a vehicle has a valid MOT certificate if needed?
Choose one answer

a. the owner of the vehicle
b. the person who intends to drive it
c. the police
d. the registered keeper of the vehicle

21 You want to overtake the lorry in front. Another car has just
    overtaken it. You:

Choose one answer

a. can overtake safely if you follow the other car through
b. shouldn't rely on the other car to protect you
c. must wait until the lorry driver moves left
d. should get much closer to the lorry first

22 At a puffin crossing, red and amber lights mean that you should:

Choose one answer

a. drive on
b. wave on pedestrians who are waiting to cross
c. not stop if following traffic is too close
d. stop

23 Which statement is true about lane discipline on a motorway?
    Choose one answer

a. it isn't important because all the lanes are very wide
b. you should keep to the middle lane for a long journey
c. you should keep to the centre of your lane
d. you should be safest keeping to the left of your lane

24 Why should you not keep loose items on the shelf behind your car's rear seats:

Choose two answers

a. they will be difficult to reach when you are driving
b. they could fly forward and cause injury if the car stopped suddenly
c. they will interfere with your rear view
d. they will distract following drivers

25 You are loading a caravan ready for a holiday trip. Heavier items should be placed:

Choose one answer

a. higher off the floor than lighter items
b. closer to the back of the caravan than lighter items
c. nearer to the floor than lighter items
d. as high off the floor as possible
e. on the offside of the caravan and lighter items on the nearside

26 Which of the following should you never do at a petrol station forecourt?

Choose two answers

a. put diesel in your car
b. light a match or smoke
c. use a catalytic converter
d. clean your windscreen and lights
e. top up your washer bottle
f. use a mobile phone

27 On a motorway, a sign like this advises you:

Choose one answer

a. that road works are complete
b. to move to the opposite carriageway
c. to drive at 70 mph
d. that the lane layout changes ahead

28 Which of these may not use motorways?
Choose one answer

a. disabled drivers
b. riders of mopeds under 50 cc
c. buses
d. learner lorry drivers

29 In thick motorway fog you see reflective red studs on your right.
This means:
Choose one answer

a. you are in the right-hand lane
b. you are on a slip road
c. there is a service area ahead
d. you are on the hard shoulder

30 If involved in a traffic accident you:
Choose one answer

a. must stop, even if the accident is slight
b. need only stop if a person is injured
c. need not stop if the accident is slight
d. must show your insurance details at the scene

31 What may happen if you don't replace your car's air filter at the
interval recommended by the manufacturer?
Choose one answer

a. You will use less fuel
b. You will get fewer miles to the gallon
c. Your engine will run too cold
d. Your car's demister will fail

32 How should you find out if a liquid spill from a tanker involved in
an accident was dangerous?
Choose one answer

a. test the liquid with a lighted match and touch it gingerly
b. by asking the tanker driver
c. by waiting for the fire brigade
d. by looking for a plate on the tanker that displays information
    about the liquid

33 You are towing a trailer when it begins to swerve or snake.
    What should you do?
    Choose one answer

    a. steer with the snaking motion
    b. brake sharply to regain control
    c. ease off the accelerator until the trailer stabilizes
    d. gently apply the parking brake

34 If the wheels on your car aren't properly balanced:
    Choose one answer

    a. the steering may pull to one side
    b. the steering may shudder
    c. the brakes could fail
    d. the tyres could deflate

35 Which of these signs means that no motor vehicles are allowed?
    Choose one answer

    a.   b.   c.   d.

36 You are travelling on a motorway. Unless signs show a lower speed
    limit you must not exceed:
    Choose one answer

    a. 55 mph
    b. 60 mph
    c. 70 mph
    d. 77 mph

37 Your car insurance policy has an excess of £250. What does this mean?
    Choose one answer

    a. the insurance company will pay the first £250 of any claim
    b. you will be paid a £250 bonus if you don't make a claim
    c. your policy will pay a maximum of £250 in a claim
    d. you will have to pay the first £250 of the cost of any claim

38 You are approaching traffic lights. They have been on green for some
time. You should:
Choose one answer

   a. speed up in case they change
   b. slow down to a crawl
   c. be ready to stop
   d. pull in and wait for following traffic to deal with the problem

39 You are parking on a two-way road at night. There is a 40 mph speed
limit on the road. You should park:
Choose one answer

   a. on the left with parking lights on
   b. on the right with parking lights on
   c. on the left without lights
   d. on the right without lights

40 Which of the following are most likely to waste fuel?
Choose four answers

   a. driving defensively
   b. carrying unnecessary weight in the car
   c. harsh braking
   d. under-inflated tyres
   e. gentle acceleration
   f. carrying a roof rack with no load

41 What does this motorway sign mean?

Choose one answer

   a. minimum speed 50 mph
   b. maintain a gap of 50 metres between vehicles
   c. 50 miles to the next services
   d. temporary maximum speed 50 mph

42 Your car has broken down on an automatic railway level crossing. What should you do first?
Choose one answer

   a. get everyone out of the car and clear of the crossing
   b. phone the signal operator
   c. try to repair the car but keep a lookout for trains
   d. ask your passengers to push the car clear of the crossing

43 You are taking medicines that are likely to affect your driving. What should you do?
Choose one answer

   a. seek medical advice before driving
   b. only drive for essential journeys
   c. only drive for short distances
   d. ask a friend to accompany you when driving

44 You intend to turn left into a minor road. On the approach you should:
Choose one answer

   a. keep just left of the centre of the road
   b. keep to the middle of the road before turning
   c. keep left and swing out before turning
   d. keep to the left of the road

45 You are driving on a motorway and need to use your mobile phone. You should:
Choose one answer

   a. find a safe place to stop on the hard shoulder
   b. leave the motorway and stop in a safe place to make your call
   c. leave at the next exit and park on the slip road to make the call
   d. drive in the slow lane whilst making your call

46 You should use the right-hand lane of a motorway to:
Choose one answer

   a. keep clear of goods vehicles
   b. turn right
   c. overtake slower vehicles
   d. avoid safety cameras

47 You are turning right on to a dual carriageway. Before pulling out you should:
Choose two answers

a. assess the speed of the traffic
b. position your car to the left of the side road
c. check the width of the central reservation
d. sound your horn to warn of the danger

48 Driving up a steep hill you need to be aware that:
Choose two answers

a. higher gears will give better acceleration
b. you will slow down sooner if you ease off the accelerator
c. overtaking will be much easier
d. there will be more work for the engine to do
e. lower gears should be avoided

49 You have just passed your driving test and will need to drive on motorways for your job. To reduce your risk of having an accident you should:
Choose one answer

a. take further training
b. use L plates on your car
c. keep to a maximum of 50 mph for the first few weeks
d. only drive in the left-hand lane

50 Diamond-shaped signs give instructions to:

Choose one answer

a. bus drivers
b. cyclists
c. tram drivers
d. taxi drivers

Paper 8
Theory test assessment

Case Study for questions 1–5

Jeff has just got a new job and will be driving to work the following morning. He hasn't driven his car for a few weeks and knows it is overdue for a service. He gives it a quick check over and notices one of the tyres has a bit of a cut in the wall. He decides to change the wheel and finds the spare seems a bit flat. He drives to the nearest garage to check the tyre pressures. On the way home he notices the steering seems to be pulling to one side when he presses the footbrake.

1 What should Jeff do about the tyre with the cut in the wall?
   Choose one answer
   a. check the tyre pressure and keep it as the spare
   b. deal with it when the car is next serviced
   c. have it replaced with a new tyre as soon as possible
   d. let some of the pressure out and keep it as a spare

2 What could be badly affected by under-inflated tyres?
   Choose two answers
   a. braking
   b. steering
   c. gear changing
   d. manoeuvring at low speed

3 Why would Jeff be better to keep his car serviced at the correct intervals?
   Choose two answers
   a. it will reduce the cost of his tax disc
   b. it will help to lower pollution
   c. it help improve fuel economy
   d. it will guarantee the car passes its next MOT test

4 What is the most likely cause of the car pulling to one side?
Choose one answer

a.   the tyres being correctly inflated
b.   the tyres being over-inflated
c.   a fault with the brakes
d.   a fault with the steering

5 What should Jeff do about the problem he experiences when braking?
Choose one answer

a.   seek qualified help from a garage as soon as possible
b.   not worry about it until he takes the car for a service
c.   try changing the wheels round to see if it makes a difference
d.   top up the brake fluid and avoid heavy braking

6 You are driving the red car (arrowed) and intend to go ahead at the crossroads. You should:

Choose one answer

a.   be ready to give way to the other driver
b.   assume the other driver has seen you
c.   assume the other driver will give way because you are on his or her right
d.   flash your headlights and drive through

7 You buy a non-prescription medicine from your pharmacist. How can you tell if the medicine will affect your driving?
Choose two answers

a.   check the label on the medicine
b.   try a short journey after taking it
c.   ask the pharmacist
d.   ask another driver to try it

8 Which type of sign tells you that parking is always forbidden:
Choose one answer

a.

b.

c.

d.

9 Where are you not allowed to park?
Choose two answers

a. at a bus stop
b. on a pedestrian crossing
c. near a police station
d. in a one-way street

10 Where are you permitted to overtake on a one-way street?
Choose one answer

a. on the right only
b. on the left only
c. on the right or left
d. you are not permitted to overtake on a one-way street

11 When should you signal to leave a roundabout?
Choose one answer

a. there is no need to signal
b. you should signal left throughout the roundabout
c. you should signal left after passing the exit before the one you want
d. you should only give a signal if there is traffic behind you

12 To overtake a long vehicle you should make sure that you:
Choose one answer

a. are far enough back to get a clear view of the road ahead
b. get as close to the vehicle as possible
c. flash your headlights before signalling
d. change to a high gear before moving out to look ahead

13 Where are traffic accidents most likely to happen?
Choose one answer

a. on motorways
b. near junctions
c. in car parks
d. on busy dual carriageways

14 A driver who sees a bus parked on the opposite side of the road needs to be particularly aware of what dangers?

Choose two answers

a. the bus pulling out without warning
b. pedestrians stepping out from behind the bus
c. people running for the bus
d. sudden gusts of diesel fumes

 15 You should only use rear fog lights in falling snow if:
Choose one answer

a. your brake lights are not working
b. visibility is less than 100 metres
c. the driver ahead uses his or her fog lights
d. your minimum braking distance is more than the distance you can see to be clear ahead

 16 What does this sign mean?

Choose one answer

a. narrow right lanes ahead
b. end of dual carriageway
c. no overtaking
d. right lanes closed ahead

17 Where would you see a sign like this?

Choose one answer

a.   at a junction
b.   on a long vehicle
c.   on a vehicle that has an overhanging load
d.   on approach to a level crossing

18 What is a 'cover note'? *Choose one answer*

a.   a temporary insurance certificate
b.   a letter from your GP excusing you from using a seat belt
c.   a temporary parking permit
d.   the note you should display on your windscreen if you've forgotten to renew your tax disc

19 Which of these types of insurance would cover damage to your own vehicle if you caused an accident? *Choose one answer*

a.   third-party-only insurance
b.   third-party, fire and theft insurance
c.   fully comprehensive insurance
d.   public liability insurance
e.   term insurance

20 When driving past parked cars or other stationary obstructions you should allow enough room. This means that: *Choose one answer*

a.   you should always allow 1 metre (3 feet) of clearance
b.   you should never leave more than 1 metre (3 feet) of clearance
c.   the faster you are going, the bigger the gap should be
d.   you must never get closer than an open car door's width from the obstruction

21 A flashing amber light on a vehicle means that: *Choose one answer*

a.   the vehicle belongs to the emergency services
b.   the vehicle is slow moving
c.   the vehicle is dangerously overloaded
d.   the vehicle is carrying a wide load

22 If you can't see properly to reverse, you should: *Choose one answer*

   a. open your car door to see behind you as you reverse
   b. ask someone to guide you
   c. reverse so slowly that you are not likely to injure anyone
   d. rely on your door mirrors
   e. use hazard warning lights and look out of your side windows

23 The only time you may use hazard warning lights on a moving vehicle is: *Choose one answer*

   a. when being towed
   b. briefly, when on a motorway or unrestricted dual carriageway and you need to warn following traffic of a problem ahead
   c. when towing another vehicle
   d. when driving slowly because your vehicle has a mechanical fault

24 When should you use the left-hand lane of a motorway? *Choose one answer*

   a. only when driving at less than 60 mph
   b. whenever it is clear
   c. only to leave the motorway
   d. to undertake another vehicle

25 You may ONLY stop on the hard shoulder of a motorway: *Choose one answer*

   a. when too tired to drive
   b. in an emergency
   c. to drop off a passenger
   d. to answer a call on your mobile phone

26 What does this motorway sign mean?

Choose one answer

   a. end of speed limit
   b. end of motorway
   c. end of restriction
   d. the road ahead is clear

27 How should you dispose of waste engine oil? *Choose one answer*

    a.   burn it

    b.   pour into the ground or a drain

    c.   wash it into a drain with plenty of hot water and detergent

    d.   take it to a local authority site or garage for recycling

28 You have a breakdown on a motorway and have stopped on the hard shoulder. You have a hazard warning triangle in your car. You should: *Choose one answer*

    a.   place it at least 100 metres behind your vehicle

    b.   not use it on the motorway

    c.   put it on top of your vehicle

    d.   place it at least 45 metres behind your vehicle

29 The best advice when leaving your vehicle is to: *Choose one answer*

    a.   hide any valuables under the seats

    b.   take all valuables with you

    c.   cover up any valuables with a coat

    d.   put any valuables in the boot

30 Which of these signs means turn left ahead? *Choose one answer*

a.

b.

c.

d.

31 Which of these are likely to make you lose concentration when driving? *Choose three answers*

    a.   looking at a map

    b.   changing a CD in your car audio system

    c.   using cruise control

    d.   looking in your mirrors

    e.   using a mobile phone

    f.   using the air conditioning system

32 Which of these would help you stay alert during a long journey?
Choose two answers

a. driving as fast as you can
b. taking regular rest stops
c. making sure that there is plenty of fresh air in the car
d. playing loud music

33 You notice that an ambulance is following you. It is showing its flashing blue lights. You should:

Choose one answer

a. pull over as soon as it is safely possible to let it pass
b. speed up to get out of its path
c. maintain your speed and let the ambulance driver take the risks
d. brake to an immediate stop

34 What does this sign mean?

Choose one answer

a. direction to park-and-ride car park
b. parking and service area for buses or coaches
c. direction to coach park
d. combined parking for cars and coaches

35 You are following a cyclist on approach to a roundabout. The cyclist is in the left-hand lane. Which direction should you expect the cyclist to go?
Choose one answer

a. left
b. right
c. ahead
d. any direction

36 At an accident a casualty is unconscious. As a matter of urgency you should check the victim's:
Choose three answers

   a. circulation
   b. airway
   c. limbs for sign of fracture
   d. breathing
   e. address
   f. identity

37 What is the main benefit of having four-wheel drive?
Choose one answer

   a. to impress your friends
   b. to reduce fuel consumption
   c. to improve road holding
   d. to lower your carbon emissions

38 Which of these will help lessen the environmental damage caused by driving?
Choose three answers

   a. keeping your vehicle properly serviced and maintained
   b. inappropriate use of the gears
   c. removing any roof rack when it is not in use
   d. using public transport when possible
   e. keeping the tyres at less than the recommended pressure

39 You intend to reverse into a side road. When would you present the greatest hazard to passing traffic?
Choose one answer

   a. before you start the manoeuvre
   b. just as you begin to move
   c. when the front of your vehicle swings out from the kerb
   d. when you've entered the side road and continue back in a straight line

40 What does this sign mean?

Choose one answer

a. route for trams only
b. buses only
c. pedestrian route to tram station
d. tram manoeuvring area only

41 Anti-lock brakes are of most benefit when you are: *Choose one answer*

a. driving on ice
b. braking hard in an emergency
c. skidding
d. aquaplaning

42 You are on a motorway and see lights flashing from side to side above every lane. You must: *Choose one answer*

a. pull on to the hard shoulder and report the fault
b. slow down to 30 mph or less and proceed cautiously
c. stop in lane and wait before the signs
d. leave the motorway at the next exit

43 What does this sign mean?

Choose one answer

a. queuing traffic ahead
b. no overtaking
c. priority to oncoming vehicles
d. keep to the left-hand lane

44 When is it permitted to reverse from a side road into a main road?
Choose one answer

   a. at any time
   b. not at any time
   c. only if the side road is clear of traffic
   d. only if the main road is wide enough

45 You are driving at night with your headlights on full beam. There is no approaching traffic, but a following driver begins to overtake. You should:
Choose one answer

   a. switch your lights off until the driver has passed you
   b. dip your headlights when the driver is ahead of you
   c. dip your headlights as the driver gets alongside you
   d. switch on rear fog lights to assist the other driver

46 You are testing the suspension on your car and notice that it keeps bouncing when you press down on the front wing.
What is this likely to mean?
Choose one answer

   a. Your tyres are over-inflated
   b. You are parked on soft tarmac
   c. Your shock absorbers are worn
   d. There is a fault with the braking system

47 Where should drivers be particularly careful to look out for motorcyclists?
Choose one answer

   a. on motorways
   b. in traffic-calmed areas
   c. when emerging at junctions
   d. when parking

48 Unless it is essential, why should you usually not attempt to remove the helmet of a motorcyclist who is an accident casualty?
Choose one answer

a. it could take you a long time if you are unfamiliar with the straps
b. you could cause more serious injury
c. it will protect the rider's head in the ambulance
d. the rider could forget to take the helmet with him or her when he or she leaves

49 Whilst driving you notice an instrument panel warning light come on. You should:
Choose one answer

a. have the problem checked out at the next service
b. ignore the light if the engine sounds fine
c. stop and investigate as soon as you safely can
d. consult the vehicle owner's handbook whilst you drive to the nearest garage

50 What might indicate that you were driving on black ice?
Choose one answer

a. there would be skid marks on the road surface
b. road noise would seem to increase
c. the steering would feel very light
d. the road surface would appear very dry

Answers to theory test assessment papers

Assessment paper 1

1. d	11. b	21. a	31. d	41. c
2. c	12. a	22. b	32. b	42. a, b, d
3. a, d	13. c	23. b	33. b	43. b, d, e
4. b	14. b	24. b	34. d	44. d
5. c	15. b	25. d	35. d	45. c
6. b	16. c	26. c	36. b	46. b
7. b	17. b	27. b	37. c	47. c
8. a	18. c	28. c	38. b, c	48. b
9. d	19. d	29. b	39. b	49. b
10. c	20. c	30. d	40. c, e	50. d

Assessment paper 2

1. d	11. b, d	21. b	31. b	41. a
2. a	12. c	22. c	32. c, d	42. d
3. d	13. a, c	23. c, e	33. c	43. a
4. b, c	14. b	24. c	34. d	44. c
5. b, d	15. b	25. c	35. a	45. b
6. c	16. c	26. b	36. c	46. c
7. d	17. b	27. b	37. b	47. b
8. b	18. c	28. d	38. b, d	48. b
9. b	19. b	29. b	39. d	49. b
10. c	20. c	30. c	40. b	50. a, d

Assessment paper 3

1. b	11. d	21. a	31. a	41. c
2. c	12. c	22. c	32. b, e	42. c
3. b	13. b	23. a	33. b	43. a, c
4. c	14. a	24. b	34. c	44. b, c, d
5. b	15. d	25. a, d	35. d	45. d
6. d	16. a	26. a, b, e, f	36. b	46. b
7. b	17. b	27. b	37. c	47. b, e
8. b, c	18. c	28. b, d	38. b	48. b
9. a, c	19. c	29. a	39. b	49. c
10. b	20. a	30. d	40. b	50. d

Assessment paper 4

1. c	11. d	21. d	31. b	41. a
2. b	12. a, d	22. b	32. d	42. b, c
3. c	13. b	23. b	33. b, c	43. d, e
4. d	14. b	24. b	34. c	44. c
5. d	15. c, d	25. c	35. a	45. c
6. a	16. b, d, e	26. b	36. a, d	46. b, d
7. b, d	17. b	27. a	37. b	47. b
8. c	18. c	28. e	38. c	48. d
9. c	19. c	29. b	39. d	49. b
10. b	20. b	30. b	40. b	50. c

Assessment paper 5

1. c	11. b	21. d	31. c	41. a
2. b, c	12. c	22. c	32. b, d	42. a, b
3. a	13. a	23. b	33. d	43. d
4. c	14. d	24. c	34. d	44. b, c, d
5. c	15. d	25. b	35. a, c, d, g	45. c
6. c	16. b	26. c	36. c	46. a
7. a, b, d	17. b	27. c	37. e	47. c
8. c	18. a, c	28. c	38. d	48. a, b, d, e
9. a	19. b	29. a	39. d	49. b
10. b, d	20. b, d	30. c	40. c	50. b

Assessment paper 6

1. a	11. b	21. c	31. c	41. c
2. b, c	12. c	22. a	32. d	42. c
3. d	13. b, c, d	23. c	33. a	43. c
4. c	14. c	24. b	34. a	44. a
5. c	15. c	25. c	35. a, d, e, f	45. a, d
6. c	16. b	26. d	36. d	46. a
7. c	17. b	27. a, c	37. c	47. b
8. b	18. d	28. a, c	38. c, d, e	48. b
9. c	19. b	29. b, d	39. c	49. b
10. b	20. b, c, e	30. a, c	40. b	50. b

Assessment paper 7

1. a	11. b	21. b	31. b	41. d
2. b	12. c	22. d	32. d	42. a
3. b	13. b	23. c	33. c	43. a
4. b, d	14. a	24. b, c	34. b	44. d
5. d	15. b	25. c	35. d	45. b
6. c	16. b, c	26. b, f	36. c	46. c
7. d	17. c	27. d	37. d	47. a, c
8. d	18. c	28. b	38. c	48. b, d
9. b	19. a	29. d	39. a	49. a
10. d	20. b	30. a	40. b, c, d, f	50. c

Assessment paper 8

1. c	11. c	21. b	31. a, b, e	41. b
2. a, b	12. a	22. b	32. b, c	42. c
3. b, c	13. b	23. b	33. a	43. b
4. c	14. b, c	24. b	34. a	44. b
5. a	15. b	25. b	35. d	45. c
6. a	16. d	26. c	36. a, b, d	46. c
7. a, c	17. c	27. d	37. c	47. c
8. d	18. a	28. b	38. a, c, d	48. b
9. a, b	19. c	29. b	39. c	49. c
10. c	20. c	30. c	40. a	50. c

PART THREE
THE HIGHWAY CODE

Rules and appendices

The Highway Code
Rules for car drivers

To assist users of *Learn to Drive*, this section contains extracts from *The Highway Code* directly relevant to drivers. Please note:

The content of this section including text and graphics has been sourced from the 2007 edition of *The Official Highway Code*. This material is Crown Copyright supplied by the Driving Standards Agency, the Department for Transport and the Controller of HMSO and is reproduced under the terms of the Click-Use Licence from HMSO. All rights reserved.

The Official Highway Code by the Department for Transport is published by the Stationery Office. Further information can also be accessed at www.direct.gov.uk/highwaycode.

Contents

Annexes

Introduction

The Highway Code is essential reading for everyone. The most vulnerable road users are pedestrians, particularly children, older or disabled people, cyclists, motorcyclists and horse riders. It is important that all road users are aware of the Code and are considerate towards each other. This applies to pedestrians as much as to drivers and riders.

Many of the rules in the Code are legal requirements, and if you disobey these rules you are committing a criminal offence. You may be fined, given penalty points on your licence or be disqualified from driving. In the most serious cases you may be sent to prison. Such rules are identified by the use of the words '**MUST/MUST NOT**'.

Although failure to comply with the other rules of the Code will not, in itself, cause a person to be prosecuted, *The Highway Code* may be used in evidence in any court proceedings under the Traffic Acts to establish liability. This includes rules which use advisory wording such as 'should/should not' or 'do/do not'.

Knowing and applying the rules contained in *The Highway Code* could significantly reduce road casualties. Cutting the number of deaths and injuries that occur on our roads every day is a responsibility we all share. *The Highway Code* can help us discharge that responsibility. Further information on driving/ riding techniques can be found in *The Official DSA Guide to Driving: The essential skills* and *The Official DSA Guide to Riding: The essential skills*.

Rules about animals

Rule 57   When in a vehicle make sure dogs or other animals are suitably restrained so they cannot distract you while you are driving or injure you, or themselves, if you stop quickly. A seat belt harness, pet carrier, dog cage or dog guard are ways of restraining animals in cars.

Rules for drivers and motorcyclists

Rule 89 Vehicle condition. You **MUST** ensure your vehicle and trailer comply with the full requirements of the Road Vehicles (Construction and Use) Regulations and Road Vehicles Lighting Regulations.

Fitness to drive

Rule 90 Make sure that you are fit to drive. You **MUST** report to the Driver and Vehicle Licensing Agency (DVLA) any health condition likely to affect your driving.

Rule 91 Driving when you are tired greatly increases your risk of collision. To minimise this risk:

- make sure you are fit to drive. Do not begin a journey if you are tired. Get a good night's sleep before embarking on a long journey;
- avoid undertaking long journeys between midnight and 6 am, when natural alertness is at a minimum;
- plan your journey to take sufficient breaks. A minimum break of at least 15 minutes after every two hours of driving is recommended;
- if you feel at all sleepy, stop in a safe place. Do not stop on the hard shoulder of a motorway;
- the most effective ways to counter sleepiness are to drink, for example, two cups of caffeinated coffee and to take a short nap (at least 15 minutes).

Rule 92 Vision. You **MUST** be able to read a vehicle number plate, in good daylight, from a distance of 20 metres (or 20.5 metres where the old style number plate is used). If you need to wear glasses (or contact lenses) to do this, you **MUST** wear them at all times while driving. The police have the power to require a driver to undertake an eyesight test.

Rule 93 Slow down, and if necessary stop, if you are dazzled by bright sunlight.

Rule 94 At night or in poor visibility, do not use tinted glasses, lenses or visors if they restrict your vision.

Alcohol and drugs

Rule 95 Do not drink and drive as it will seriously affect your judgement and abilities. You **MUST NOT** drive with a breath alcohol level higher than 35 microgrammes/100 millilitres of breath or a blood alcohol level of more than 80 milligrammes/100 millilitres of blood. Alcohol will:

- give a false sense of confidence;
- reduce co-ordination and slow down reactions;
- affect judgement of speed, distance and risk;
- reduce your driving ability, even if you're below the legal limit;
- take time to leave your body; you may be unfit to drive in the evening after drinking at lunchtime, or in the morning after drinking the previous evening.

The best solution is not to drink at all when planning to drive because any amount of alcohol affects your ability to drive safely. If you are going to drink, arrange another means of transport.

Rule 96 You **MUST NOT** drive under the influence of drugs or medicine. Check the instructions or ask your doctor or pharmacist. Using illegal drugs is highly dangerous. Never take them if you intend to drive; the effects are unpredictable, but can be even more severe than alcohol and may result in fatal or serious road crashes.

Rule 97 Before setting off. You should ensure that:

- you have planned your route and allowed sufficient time;
- clothing and footwear do not prevent you using the controls in the correct manner;
- you know where all the controls are and how to use them before you need them. Not all vehicles are the same; do not wait until it is too late to find out;
- your mirrors and seat are adjusted correctly to ensure comfort, full control and maximum vision;
- head restraints are properly adjusted to reduce the risk of neck and spine injuries in the event of a collision;
- you have sufficient fuel before commencing your journey, especially if it includes motorway driving. It can be dangerous to lose power when driving in traffic;

Rule 97 – Make sure head
restraints are properly adjusted

- ensure your vehicle is legal and roadworthy;
- switch off your mobile phone.

Rule 98   Vehicle towing and loading. As a driver:

- you **MUST NOT** tow more than your licence permits. If you passed a car test after 1 Jan 1997 you are restricted on the weight of trailer you can tow;
- you **MUST NOT** overload your vehicle or trailer. You should not tow a weight greater than that recommended by the manufacturer of your vehicle;
- you **MUST** secure your load and it **MUST NOT** stick out dangerously. Make sure any heavy or sharp objects and any animals are secured safely. If there is a collision, they might hit someone inside the vehicle and cause serious injury;
- you should properly distribute the weight in your caravan or trailer with heavy items mainly over the axle(s) and ensure a downward load on the tow ball. Manufacturer's recommended weight and tow ball load should not be exceeded. This should avoid the possibility of swerving or snaking and going out of control. If this does happen, ease off the accelerator and reduce speed gently to regain control;
- carrying a load or pulling a trailer may require you to adjust the headlights.

In the event of a breakdown, be aware that towing a vehicle on a tow rope is potentially dangerous. You should consider professional recovery.

Seat belts and child restraints

Rule 99   You **MUST** wear a seat belt in cars, vans and other goods vehicles if one is fitted (see table below). Adults, and children aged 14 years and over, **MUST** use a seat belt or child restraint, where fitted, when seated in minibuses, buses and coaches. Exemptions are allowed for the holders of medical exemption certificates and those making deliveries or collections in goods vehicles when travelling less than 50 metres (approx 162 feet).

Seat belt requirements. This table summarises the main legal requirements for wearing seat belts in cars, vans and other goods vehicles.

	Front seat	Rear seat	Who is responsible?
Driver	Seat belt **MUST** be worn if fitted	–	Driver
Child under 3 years of age	Correct child restraint **MUST** be used	Correct child restraint **MUST** be used. If one is not available in a taxi, may travel unrestrained	Driver
Child from 3rd birthday up to 1.35 metres in height (or 12th birthday, whichever they reach first)	Correct child restraint **MUST** be used	Correct child restraint **MUST** be used where seat belts fitted. **MUST** use adult belt if correct child restraint is not available in a licensed taxi or private hire vehicle, or for reasons of unexpected necessity over a short distance, or if two occupied restraints prevent fitment of a third	Driver
Child over 1.35 metres (approx 4ft 5 ins) in height or 12 or 13 years	Seat belt **MUST** be worn if available	Seat belt **MUST** be worn if available	Driver
Adult passengers aged 14 and over	Seat belt **MUST** be worn if available	Seat belt **MUST** be worn if available	Passenger

Rule 100   The driver **MUST** ensure that all children under 14 years of age in cars, vans and other goods vehicles wear seat belts or sit in an approved child restraint where required (see table above). If a child is under 1.35 metres (approx 4 feet 5 inches) tall, a baby seat, child seat, booster seat or booster cushion **MUST** be used suitable for the child's weight and fitted to the manufacturer's instructions.

Rule 100 – Make sure that a child uses a suitable restraint which is correctly adjusted

Rule 101   A rear-facing baby seat **MUST NOT** be fitted into a seat protected by an active frontal airbag, as in a crash it can cause serious injury or death to the child.

Rule 102   Children in cars, vans and other goods vehicles. Drivers who are carrying children in cars, vans and other goods vehicles should also ensure that:

- children should get into the vehicle through the door nearest the kerb;
- child restraints are properly fitted to manufacturer's instructions;
- children do not sit behind the rear seats in an estate car or hatchback, unless a special child seat has been fitted;
- the child safety door locks, where fitted, are used when children are in the vehicle;
- children are kept under control.

General rules, techniques and advice for all drivers and riders

This section should be read by all drivers, motorcyclists, cyclists and horse riders. The rules in *The Highway Code* do not give you the right of way in any circumstance, but they advise you when you should give way to others. Always give way if it can help to avoid an incident.

Signals

Rule 103   Signals warn and inform other road users, including pedestrians (see page 382), of your intended actions. You should always:

- give clear signals in plenty of time, having checked it is not misleading to signal at that time;
- use them to advise other road users before changing course or direction, stopping or moving off;
- cancel them after use;
- make sure your signals will not confuse others. If, for instance, you want to stop after a side road, do not signal until you are passing the road. If you signal earlier it may give the impression that you intend to turn into the road. Your brake lights will warn traffic behind you that you are slowing down;
- use an arm signal to emphasise or reinforce your signal if necessary. Remember that signalling does not give you priority.

Rule 104   You should also:

- watch out for signals given by other road users and proceed only when you are satisfied that it is safe;
- be aware that an indicator on another vehicle may not have been cancelled.

Rule 105   You **MUST** obey signals given by police officers, traffic officers, traffic wardens (see pages 383–85) and signs used by school crossing patrols.

Rule 106   Police stopping procedures. If the police want to stop your vehicle they will, where possible, attract your attention by:

- flashing blue lights, headlights or sounding their siren or horn, usually from behind;
- directing you to pull over to the side by pointing and/or using the left indicator.

You **MUST** then pull over and stop as soon as it is safe to do so. Then switch off your engine.

Other stopping procedures

Rule 107   Vehicle & Operator Services Agency Officers have powers to stop vehicles on all roads, including motorways and trunk roads, in England and Wales. They will attract your attention by flashing amber lights:

- either from the front requesting you to follow them to a safe place to stop;
- or from behind directing you to pull over to the side by pointing and/or using the left indicator.

It is an offence not to comply with their directions. You **MUST** obey any signals given (see page 384).

Rule 108   Highways Agency Traffic Officers have powers to stop vehicles on most motorways and some 'A' class roads, in England only. If HA traffic officers in uniform want to stop your vehicle on safety grounds (eg an insecure load) they will, where possible, attract your attention by:

- flashing amber lights, usually from behind;
- directing you to pull over to the side by pointing and/or using the left indicator.

You **MUST** then pull over and stop as soon as it is safe to do so. Then switch off your engine. It is an offence not to comply with their directions (see page 384).

Rule 109   Traffic light signals and traffic signs. You **MUST** obey all traffic light signals (see page 381) and traffic signs giving orders, including temporary signals and signs (see pages 381–82). Make sure you know, understand and act on all other traffic and information signs and road markings (see pages 385–98).

Rule 110   Flashing headlights. Only flash your headlights to let other road users know that you are there. Do not flash your headlights to convey any other message or intimidate other road users.

Rule 111   Never assume that flashing headlights is a signal inviting you to proceed. Use your own judgement and proceed carefully.

Rule 112 The horn. Use only while your vehicle is moving and you need to warn other road users of your presence. Never sound your horn aggressively. You **MUST NOT** use your horn:

- while stationary on the road;
- when driving in a built-up area between the hours of 11.30 pm and 7.00 am;
- *except* when another road user poses a danger.

Lighting requirements

Rule 113 You **MUST**:

- ensure all sidelights and rear registration plate lights are lit between sunset and sunrise;
- use headlights at night, except on a road which has lit street lighting. These roads are generally restricted to a speed limit of 30 mph (48 km/h) unless otherwise specified;
- use headlights when visibility is seriously reduced (see Rule 226).

Night (the hours of darkness) is defined as the period between half an hour after sunset and half an hour before sunrise.

Rule 114 You **MUST NOT**:

- use any lights in a way which would dazzle or cause discomfort to other road users, including pedestrians, cyclists and horse riders;
- use front or rear fog lights unless visibility is seriously reduced. You **MUST** switch them off when visibility improves to avoid dazzling other road users (see Rule 226).

In stationary queues of traffic, drivers should apply the parking brake and, once the following traffic has stopped, take their foot off the footbrake to deactivate the vehicle brake lights. This will minimise glare to road users behind until the traffic moves again.

Rule 115   You should also:

- use dipped headlights, or dim-dip if fitted, at night in built-up areas and in dull daytime weather, to ensure that you can be seen;

- keep your headlights dipped when overtaking until you are level with the other vehicle and then change to main beam if necessary, unless this would dazzle oncoming road users;

- slow down, and if necessary stop, if you are dazzled by oncoming headlights.

Rule 116   Hazard warning lights. These may be used when your vehicle is stationary, to warn that it is temporarily obstructing traffic. Never use them as an excuse for dangerous or illegal parking. You **MUST NOT** use hazard warning lights while driving or being towed unless you are on a motorway or unrestricted dual carriageway and you need to warn drivers behind you of a hazard or obstruction ahead. Only use them for long enough to ensure that your warning has been observed.

Control of the vehicle

Braking

Rule 117   In normal circumstances. The safest way to brake is to do so early and lightly. Brake more firmly as you begin to stop. Ease the pressure off just before the vehicle comes to rest to avoid a jerky stop.

Rule 118   In an emergency. Brake immediately. Try to avoid braking so harshly that you lock your wheels. Locked wheels can lead to loss of control.

Rule 119   Skids. Skidding is usually caused by the driver braking, accelerating or steering too harshly or driving too fast for the road conditions. If skidding occurs, remove the cause by releasing the brake pedal fully or easing off the accelerator. Turn the steering wheel in the direction of the skid. For example, if the rear of the vehicle skids to the right, steer immediately to the right to recover.

Rule 119 – Rear of the car skids to the right. Driver steers to the right

Rule 120 ABS. If your vehicle is fitted with anti-lock brakes, you should follow the advice given in the vehicle handbook. However, in the case of an emergency, apply the footbrake firmly; do not release the pressure until the vehicle has slowed to the desired speed. The ABS should ensure that steering control will be retained, but do not assume that a vehicle with ABS will stop in a shorter distance.

Rule 121 Brakes affected by water. If you have driven through deep water your brakes may be less effective. Test them at the first safe opportunity by pushing gently on the brake pedal to make sure that they work. If they are not fully effective, gently apply light pressure while driving slowly. This will help to dry them out.

Rule 122 Coasting. This term describes a vehicle travelling in neutral or with the clutch pressed down. It can reduce driver control because:

- engine braking is eliminated;
- vehicle speed downhill will increase quickly;
- increased use of the footbrake can reduce its effectiveness;
- steering response will be affected, particularly on bends and corners;
- it may be more difficult to select the appropriate gear when needed.

Rule 123 The driver and the environment. You **MUST NOT** leave a parked vehicle unattended with the engine running or leave a vehicle engine running unnecessarily while that vehicle is stationary on a public road. Generally, if the vehicle is stationary and is likely to remain so for more than a couple of minutes, you should apply the parking brake and switch off the engine to reduce emissions and noise pollution. However it is permissible to leave the engine running if the vehicle is stationary in traffic or for diagnosing faults.

Speed limits	Built-up areas*	Single carriageways	Dual carriageways	Motorways
Type of vehicle	Mph (km/h)	Mph (km/h)	Mph (km/h)	Mph (km/h)
Cars & motorcycles (including car-derived vans up to 2 tonnes maximum laden weight)	30 (48)	60 (96)	70 (112)	70 (112)
Cars towing caravans or trailers (including car-derived vans and motorcycles)	30 (48)	50 (80)	60 (96)	60 (96)
Buses, coaches and minibuses (not exceeding 12 metres in overall length)	30 (48)	50 (80)	60 (96)	70 (112)
Goods vehicles (not exceeding 7.5 tonnes maximum laden weight)	30 (48)	50 (80)	60 (96)	70** (112)
Goods vehicles (exceeding 7.5 tonnes maximum laden weight)	30 (48)	40 (64)	50 (80)	60 (96)

*   The 30 mph limit usually applies to all traffic on all roads with street lighting unless signs show otherwise

** 60 mph (96 km/h) if articulated or towing a trailer

Speed limits

Rule 124   You **MUST NOT** exceed the maximum speed limits for the road and for your vehicle (see the table above). The presence of street lights generally means that there is a 30 mph (48 km/h) speed limit unless otherwise specified.

Rule 125   The speed limit is the absolute maximum and does not mean it is safe to drive at that speed irrespective of conditions. Driving at speeds too fast for the road and traffic conditions is dangerous. You should always reduce your speed when:

- the road layout or condition presents hazards, such as bends;
- sharing the road with pedestrians, cyclists and horse riders, particularly children, and motorcyclists;
- weather conditions make it safer to do so;
- driving at night as it is more difficult to see other road users.

Rule 126   Stopping distances. Drive at a speed that will allow you to stop well within the distance you can see to be clear. You should:

- leave enough space between you and the vehicle in front so that you can pull up safely if it suddenly slows down or stops. The safe rule is never to get closer than the overall stopping distance (see Typical Stopping Distances diagram below);
- allow at least a two-second gap between you and the vehicle in front on roads carrying faster-moving traffic and in tunnels where visibility is reduced. The gap should be at least doubled on wet roads and increased still further on icy roads;
- remember, large vehicles and motorcycles need a greater distance to stop. If driving a large vehicle in a tunnel, you should allow a four-second gap between you and the vehicle in front.

Rule 126 – Use a fixed point to help measure a two-second gap

If you have to stop in a tunnel, leave at least a 5-metre gap between you and the vehicle in front.

20 mph (32 km/h)	6m 6m	= 12 metres (40 feet) or three car lengths
30 mph (48 km/h)	9m 14m	= 23 metres (75 feet) or six car lengths
40 mph (64 km/h)	12m 24m	= 36 metres (118 feet) or nine car lengths
50 mph (80 km/h)	15m 38m	= 53 metres (175 feet) or thirteen car lengths
60 mph (96 km/h)	18m 55m	= 73 metres (240 feet) or eighteen car lengths
70 mph (112 km/h)	21m 75m	= 96 metres (315 feet) or twenty-four car lengths

The distances shown are a general guide. The distance will depend on your attention (thinking distance), the road surface, the weather conditions and the condition of your vehicle at the time.

Thinking distance | Braking distance

Average car length = 4 metres (13 feet)

Lines and lane markings on the road

Diagrams of all lines are shown on page 398.

Rule 127   A broken white line. This marks the centre of the road. When this line lengthens and the gaps shorten, it means that there is a hazard ahead. Do not cross it unless you can see the road is clear and wish to overtake or turn off.

Rule 128   Double white lines where the line nearest to you is broken. This means you may cross the lines to overtake if it is safe, provided you can complete the manoeuvre before reaching a solid white line on your side. White direction arrows on the road indicate that you need to get back onto your side of the road.

Rule 129   Double white lines where the line nearest you is solid. This means you **MUST NOT** cross or straddle it unless it is safe and you need to enter adjoining premises or a side road. You may cross the line if necessary, provided the road is clear, to pass a stationary vehicle, or overtake a pedal cycle, horse or road maintenance vehicle, if they are travelling at 10 mph (16 km/h) or less.

Rule 130   Areas of white diagonal stripes or chevrons painted on the road. These are to separate traffic lanes or to protect traffic turning right.

- If the area is bordered by a broken white line, you should not enter the area unless it is necessary and you can see that it is safe to do so.

- If the area is marked with chevrons and bordered by solid white lines you **MUST NOT** enter it except in an emergency.

Rule 131 Lane dividers. These are short, broken white lines which are used on wide carriageways to divide them into lanes. You should keep between them.

Rule 132 Reflective road studs may be used with white lines.

- White studs mark the lanes or the middle of the road.
- Red studs mark the left edge of the road.
- Amber studs mark the central reservation of a dual carriageway or motorway.
- Green studs mark the edge of the main carriageway at lay-bys and slip roads.
- Green/yellow studs indicate temporary adjustments to lane layouts, eg where road works are taking place.

Rule 132 – Reflective road studs mark the lanes and edges of the carriageway

Multi-lane carriageways

Lane discipline

Rule 133 If you need to change lane, first use your mirrors and if necessary take a quick sideways glance to make sure you will not force another road user to change course or speed. When it is safe to do so, signal to indicate your intentions to other road users and when clear, move over.

Rule 134 You should follow the signs and road markings and get into the lane as directed. In congested road conditions do not change lanes unnecessarily. Merging in turn is recommended but only if safe and appropriate when vehicles are travelling at a very low speed, eg when approaching road works or a road traffic incident. It is not recommended at high speed.

Single carriageway

Rule 135   Where a single carriageway has three lanes and the road markings or signs do not give priority to traffic in either direction:

- use the middle lane only for overtaking or turning right. Remember, you have no more right to use the middle lane than a driver coming from the opposite direction;
- do not use the right-hand lane.

Rule 136   Where a single carriageway has four or more lanes, use only the lanes that signs or markings indicate.

Dual carriageways

A dual carriageway is a road which has a central reservation to separate the carriageways.

Rule 137   On a two-lane dual carriageway you should stay in the left-hand lane. Use the right-hand lane for overtaking or turning right. After overtaking, move back to the left-hand lane when it is safe to do so.

Rule 138   On a three-lane dual carriageway, you may use the middle lane or the right-hand lane to overtake but return to the middle and then the left-hand lane when it is safe.

Rule 139   Climbing and crawler lanes. These are provided on some hills. Use this lane if you are driving a slow-moving vehicle or if there are vehicles behind you wishing to overtake. Be aware of the signs and road markings which indicate the lane is about to end.

Rule 140   Cycle lanes. These are shown by road markings and signs. You **MUST NOT** drive or park in a cycle lane marked by a solid white line during its times of operation. Do not drive or park in a cycle lane marked by a broken white line unless it is unavoidable. You **MUST NOT** park in any cycle lane while waiting restrictions apply.

Rule 141   Bus lanes. These are shown by road markings and signs that indicate which (if any) other vehicles are permitted to use the bus lane. Unless otherwise indicated, you should not drive in a bus lane during its period of operation. You may enter a bus lane to stop, to load or unload where this is not prohibited.

Rule 142 High-occupancy vehicle lanes and other designated vehicle lanes. Lanes may be restricted for use by particular types of vehicle; these restrictions may apply some or all of the time. The operating times and vehicle types will be indicated on the accompanying traffic signs. You **MUST NOT** drive in such lanes during their times of operation unless signs indicate that your vehicle is permitted (see page 394).

Vehicles permitted to use designated lanes may or may not include cycles, buses, taxis, licensed private hire vehicles, motorcycles, heavy goods vehicles (HGVs) and high occupancy vehicles (HOVs).

Where HOV lanes are in operation, they **MUST ONLY** be used by:

- vehicles containing at least the minimum number of people indicated on the traffic signs;
- any other vehicles, such as buses and motorcycles, as indicated on signs prior to the start of the lane, irrespective of the number of occupants.

Rule 143 One-way streets. Traffic **MUST** travel in the direction indicated by signs. Buses and/or cycles may have a contraflow lane. Choose the correct lane for your exit as soon as you can. Do not change lanes suddenly. Unless road signs or markings indicate otherwise, you should use:

- the left-hand lane when going left;
- the right-hand lane when going right;
- the most appropriate lane when going straight ahead.
  Remember – traffic could be passing on both sides.

General advice

Rule 144 You **MUST NOT**:

- drive dangerously;
- drive without due care and attention;
- drive without reasonable consideration for other road users.

Rule 145 You **MUST NOT** drive on or over a pavement, footpath or bridleway except to gain lawful access to property, or in the case of an emergency.

Rule 146 Adapt your driving to the appropriate type and condition of road you are on. In particular:

- do not treat speed limits as a target. It is often not appropriate or safe to drive at the maximum speed limit;
- take the road and traffic conditions into account. Be prepared for unexpected or difficult situations, for example, the road being blocked beyond a blind bend. Be prepared to adjust your speed as a precaution;
- where there are junctions, be prepared for road users emerging;
- in side roads and country lanes look out for unmarked junctions where nobody has priority;
- be prepared to stop at traffic control systems, road works, pedestrian crossings or traffic lights as necessary;
- try to anticipate what pedestrians and cyclists might do. If pedestrians, particularly children, are looking the other way, they may step out into the road without seeing you.

Rule 147 Be considerate. Be careful of and considerate towards all types of road users, especially those requiring extra care (see Rule 204). You should:

- try to be understanding if other road users cause problems; they may be inexperienced or not know the area well;
- be patient; remember that anyone can make a mistake;
- not allow yourself to become agitated or involved if someone is behaving badly on the road. This will only make the situation worse. Pull over, calm down and, when you feel relaxed, continue your journey;
- slow down and hold back if a road user pulls out into your path at a junction. Allow them to get clear. Do not overreact by driving too close behind to intimidate them;
- not throw anything out of a vehicle, for example, cigarette ends, cans, paper or carrier bags. This can endanger other road users, particularly motorcyclists and cyclists.

Rule 148 Safe driving and riding needs concentration. Avoid distractions when driving or riding such as:

- loud music (this may mask other sounds);
- trying to read maps;
- inserting a cassette or CD or tuning a radio;

- arguing with your passengers or other road users;
- eating and drinking;
- smoking.

You **MUST NOT** smoke in public transport vehicles or in vehicles used for work purposes in certain prescribed circumstances. Separate regulations apply to England, Wales and Scotland.

Mobile phones and in-vehicle technology

Rule 149   You **MUST** exercise proper control of your vehicle at all times. You **MUST NOT** use a hand-held mobile phone, or similar device, when driving or when supervising a learner driver, except to call 999 or 112 in a genuine emergency when it is unsafe or impractical to stop. Never use a hand-held microphone when driving. Using hands-free equipment is also likely to distract your attention from the road. It is far safer not to use any telephone while you are driving or riding – find a safe place to stop first or use the voicemail facility and listen to messages later.

Rule 150   There is a danger of driver distraction being caused by in-vehicle systems such as satellite navigation systems, congestion warning systems, PCs, multi-media, etc. You **MUST** exercise proper control of your vehicle at all times. Do not rely on driver assistance systems such as cruise control or lane departure warnings. They are available to assist but you should not reduce your concentration levels. Do not be distracted by maps or screen-based information (such as navigation or vehicle management systems) while driving or riding. If necessary find a safe place to stop.

Rule 151   In slow-moving traffic. You should:

- reduce the distance between you and the vehicle ahead to maintain traffic flow;
- never get so close to the vehicle in front that you cannot stop safely;

Rule 151 – Do not block access to a side road

- leave enough space to be able to manoeuvre if the vehicle in front breaks down or an emergency vehicle needs to get past;
- not change lanes to the left to overtake;
- allow access into and from side roads, as blocking these will add to congestion;
- be aware of cyclists and motorcyclists who may be passing on either side.

Driving in built-up areas

Rule 152　Residential streets. You should drive slowly and carefully on streets where there are likely to be pedestrians, cyclists and parked cars. In some areas a 20 mph (32 km/h) maximum speed limit may be in force. Look out for:

- vehicles emerging from junctions or driveways;
- vehicles moving off;
- car doors opening;
- pedestrians;
- children running out from between parked cars;
- cyclists and motorcyclists.

Rule 153　Traffic-calming measures. On some roads there are features such as road humps, chicanes and narrowings which are intended to slow you down. When you approach these features reduce your speed. Allow cyclists and motorcyclists room to pass through them. Maintain a reduced speed along the whole of the stretch of road within the calming measures. Give way to oncoming road users if directed to do so by signs. You should not overtake other moving road users while in these areas.

Rule 153 – Chicanes may be used to slow traffic down

Country roads

Rule 154   Take extra care on country roads and reduce your speed at approaches to bends, which can be sharper than they appear, and at junctions and turnings, which may be partially hidden. Be prepared for pedestrians, horse riders, cyclists, slow-moving farm vehicles or mud on the road surface. Make sure you can stop within the distance you can see to be clear. You should also reduce your speed where country roads enter villages.

Rule 155   Single-track roads. These are only wide enough for one vehicle. They may have special passing places. If you see a vehicle coming towards you, or the driver behind wants to overtake, pull into a passing place on your left, or wait opposite a passing place on your right. Give way to road users coming uphill whenever you can. If necessary, reverse until you reach a passing place to let the other vehicle pass. Slow down when passing pedestrians, cyclists and horse riders.

Rule 156   Do not park in passing places.

Vehicles prohibited from using roads and pavements

Rule 157   Certain motorised vehicles do not meet the construction and technical requirements for road vehicles and are generally not intended, not suitable and not legal for road, pavement, footpath, cycle path or bridleway use. These include most types of miniature motorcycles, also called mini motos, and motorised scooters, also called go peds, which are powered by electric or internal combustion engines. These types of vehicle **MUST NOT** be used on roads, pavements, footpaths or bridleways.

Rule 158   Certain models of motorcycles, motor tricycles and quadricycles, also called quad bikes, are suitable only for off-road use and do not meet legal standards for use on roads. Vehicles that do not meet these standards **MUST NOT** be used on roads. They **MUST NOT** be used on pavements, footpaths, cycle paths or bridleways either. You **MUST** make sure that any motorcycle, motor tricycle, quadricycle or any other motor vehicle meets legal standards and is properly registered, taxed and insured before using it on the roads. Even when registered, taxed and insured for the road, vehicles **MUST NOT** be used on pavements.

Using the road

General rules

Rule 159 Before moving off you should:

- use all mirrors to check the road is clear;
- look round to check the blind spots (the areas you are unable to see in the mirrors);
- signal if necessary before moving out;
- look round for a final check.

Move off only when it is safe to do so.

Rule 159 – Check the blind spot before moving off

Rule 160 Once moving you should:

- keep to the left, unless road signs or markings indicate otherwise. The exceptions are when you want to overtake, turn right or pass parked vehicles or pedestrians in the road;
- keep well to the left on right-hand bends. This will improve your view of the road and help avoid the risk of colliding with traffic approaching from the opposite direction;
- drive with both hands on the wheel where possible. This will help you to remain in full control of the vehicle at all times;
- be aware of other road users, especially cycles and motorcycles who may be filtering through the traffic. These are more difficult to see than larger vehicles and their riders are particularly vulnerable. Give them plenty of room, especially if you are driving a long vehicle or towing a trailer;
- select a lower gear before you reach a long downhill slope. This will help to control your speed;

- when towing, remember the extra length will affect overtaking and manoeuvring. The extra weight will also affect the braking and acceleration.

Rule 161   Mirrors. All mirrors should be used effectively throughout your journey. You should:

- use your mirrors frequently so that you always know what is behind and to each side of you;
- use them in good time before you signal or change direction or speed;
- be aware that mirrors do not cover all areas and there will be blind spots. You will need to look round and check.

Remember: Mirrors – Signal – Manoeuvre

Overtaking

Rule 162   Before overtaking you should make sure:

- the road is sufficiently clear ahead;
- road users are not beginning to overtake you;
- there is a suitable gap in front of the road user you plan to overtake.

Rule 163   Overtake only when it is safe and legal to do so. You should:

- not get too close to the vehicle you intend to overtake;
- use your mirrors, signal when it is safe to do so, take a quick sideways glance if necessary into the blind spot area and then start to move out;
- not assume that you can simply follow a vehicle ahead which is overtaking; there may only be enough room for one vehicle;
- move quickly past the vehicle you are overtaking, once you have started to overtake. Allow plenty of room. Move back to the left as soon as you can but do not cut in;
- take extra care at night and in poor visibility when it is harder to judge speed and distance;
- give way to oncoming vehicles before passing parked vehicles or other obstructions on your side of the road;

- only overtake on the left if the vehicle in front is signalling to turn right, and there is room to do so;

- stay in your lane if traffic is moving slowly in queues. If the queue on your right is moving more slowly than you are, you may pass on the left;

- give motorcyclists, cyclists and horse riders at least as much room as you would when overtaking a car (see Rules 211–215).

Remember: Mirrors – Signal – Manoeuvre

Rule 163 – Give vulnerable road users at least as much space as you would a car

Rule 164   Large vehicles. Overtaking these is more difficult. You should:

- drop back. This will increase your ability to see ahead and should allow the driver of the large vehicle to see you in their mirrors. Getting too close to large vehicles, including agricultural vehicles such as a tractor with a trailer or other fixed equipment, will obscure your view of the road ahead and there may be another slow-moving vehicle in front;

- make sure that you have enough room to complete your overtaking manoeuvre before committing yourself. It takes longer to pass a large vehicle. If in doubt do not overtake;

- not assume you can follow a vehicle ahead which is overtaking a long vehicle. If a problem develops, they may abort overtaking and pull back in.

Rule 164 – Do not cut in too quickly

Rule 165   You **MUST NOT** overtake:

- if you would have to cross or straddle double white lines with a solid line nearest to you (but see Rule 129);
- if you would have to enter an area designed to divide traffic, if it is surrounded by a solid white line;
- the nearest vehicle to a pedestrian crossing, especially when it has stopped to let pedestrians cross;
- if you would have to enter a lane reserved for buses, trams or cycles during its hours of operation;
- after a 'No Overtaking' sign and until you pass a sign cancelling the restriction.

Rule 166   DO NOT overtake if there is any doubt, or where you cannot see far enough ahead to be sure it is safe. For example, when you are approaching:

- a corner or bend;
- a hump bridge;
- the brow of a hill.

Rule 167   DO NOT overtake where you might come into conflict with other road users. For example:

- approaching or at a road junction on either side of the road;
- where the road narrows;
- when approaching a school crossing patrol;
- between the kerb and a bus or tram when it is at a stop;
- where traffic is queuing at junctions or road works;
- when you would force another road user to swerve or slow down;
- at a level crossing;
- when a road user is indicating right, even if you believe the signal should have been cancelled. Do not take a risk; wait for the signal to be cancelled;
- stay behind if you are following a cyclist approaching a roundabout or junction, and you intend to turn left;
- when a tram is standing at a kerbside tram stop and there is no clearly marked passing lane for other traffic.

Rule 168 Being overtaken. If a driver is trying to overtake you, maintain a steady course and speed, slowing down if necessary to let the vehicle pass. Never obstruct drivers who wish to pass. Speeding up or driving unpredictably while someone is overtaking you is dangerous. Drop back to maintain a two-second gap if someone overtakes and pulls into the gap in front of you.

Rule 169 Do not hold up a long queue of traffic, especially if you are driving a large or slow-moving vehicle. Check your mirrors frequently, and if necessary, pull in where it is safe and let traffic pass.

Road junctions

Rule 170 Take extra care at junctions. You should:

- watch out for cyclists, motorcyclists, powered wheelchairs/mobility scooters and pedestrians as they are not always easy to see. Be aware that they may not have seen or heard you if you are approaching from behind;
- watch out for pedestrians crossing a road into which you are turning. If they have started to cross they have priority, so give way;
- watch out for long vehicles which may be turning at a junction ahead; they may have to use the whole width of the road to make the turn (see Rule 221);
- watch out for horse riders who may take a different line on the road from that which you would expect;
- not assume, when waiting at a junction, that a vehicle coming from the right and signalling left will actually turn. Wait and make sure;
- look all around before emerging. Do not cross or join a road until there is a gap large enough for you to do so safely.

Rule 170 – Give way to pedestrians who have started to cross

Rule 171   You **MUST** stop behind the line at a junction with a 'Stop' sign and a solid white line across the road. Wait for a safe gap in the traffic before you move off.

Rule 172   The approach to a junction may have a 'Give Way' sign or a triangle marked on the road. You **MUST** give way to traffic on the main road when emerging from a junction with broken white lines across the road.

Rule 173   Dual carriageways. When crossing or turning right, first assess whether the central reservation is deep enough to protect the full length of your vehicle.

- If it is, then you should treat each half of the carriageway as a separate road. Wait in the central reservation until there is a safe gap in the traffic on the second half of the road.

- If the central reservation is too shallow for the length of your vehicle, wait until you can cross both carriageways in one go.

Rule 173 – Assess your vehicle's length and do not obstruct traffic

Rule 174   Box junctions. These have criss-cross yellow lines painted on the road (see page 401). You **MUST NOT** enter the box until your exit road or lane is clear. However, you may enter the box and wait when you want to turn right, and are only stopped from doing so by oncoming traffic, or by other vehicles waiting to turn right. At signalled roundabouts you **MUST NOT** enter the box unless you can cross over it completely without stopping.

Rule 174 – Enter a box junction only if your exit road is clear

Junctions controlled by traffic lights

Rule 175   You **MUST** stop behind the white 'Stop' line across your side of the road unless the light is green. If the amber light appears you may go on only if you have already crossed the stop line or are so close to it that to stop might cause a collision.

Rule 176   You **MUST NOT** move forward over the white line when the red light is showing. Only go forward when the traffic lights are green if there is room for you to clear the junction safely or you are taking up a position to turn right. If the traffic lights are not working, treat the situation as you would an unmarked junction and proceed with great care.

Rule 177   Green filter arrow. This indicates a filter lane only. Do not enter that lane unless you want to go in the direction of the arrow. You may proceed in the direction of the green arrow when it, or the full green light shows. Give other traffic, especially cyclists, time and room to move into the correct lane.

Rule 178   Advanced stop lines. Some signal-controlled junctions have advanced stop lines to allow cycles to be positioned ahead of other traffic. Motorists, including motorcyclists, **MUST** stop at the first white line reached if the lights are amber or red and should avoid blocking the way or encroaching on the marked area at other times, eg if the junction ahead is blocked. If your vehicle has proceeded over the first white line at the time that the signal goes red, you **MUST** stop at the second white line, even if your vehicle is in the marked area. Allow cyclists time and space to move off when the green signal shows.

Rule 178 – Do not unnecessarily encroach on a cyclist's waiting area

Turning right

Rule 179   Well before you turn right you should:

- use your mirrors to make sure you know the position and movement of traffic behind you;
- give a right-turn signal;
- take up a position just left of the middle of the road or in the space marked for traffic turning right;
- leave room for other vehicles to pass on the left, if possible.

Rule 180   Wait until there is a safe gap between you and any oncoming vehicle. Watch out for cyclists, motorcyclists, pedestrians and other road users. Check your mirrors and blind spot again to make sure you are not being overtaken, then make the turn. Do not cut the corner. Take great care when turning into a main road; you will need to watch for traffic in both directions and wait for a safe gap.

Remember: Mirrors – Signal – Manoeuvre

Rule 180 – Position your vehicle correctly to avoid obstructing traffic

Rule 181   When turning right at crossroads where an oncoming vehicle is also turning right, there is a choice of two methods:

- turn right side to right side; keep the other vehicle on your right and turn behind it. This is generally the safer method as you have a clear view of any approaching traffic when completing your turn;

Rule 181 – Turning right side to right side   **Turning left side to left side**

- left side to left side, turning in front of each other. This can block your view of oncoming vehicles, so take extra care. Cyclists and motorcyclists in particular may be hidden from your view. Road layout, markings or how the other vehicle is positioned can determine which course should be taken.

Turning left

Rule 182   Use your mirrors and give a left-turn signal well before you turn left. Do not overtake just before you turn left and watch out for traffic coming up on your left before you make the turn, especially if driving a large vehicle. Cyclists, motorcyclists and other road users in particular may be hidden from your view.

Rule 182 – Do not cut in on a cyclist

Rule 183   When turning:

- keep as close to the left as is safe and practicable;
- give way to any vehicles using a bus lane, cycle lane or tramway from either direction.

Roundabouts

Rule 184   On approaching a roundabout take notice and act on all the information available to you, including traffic signs, traffic lights and lane markings which direct you into the correct lane. You should:

- use Mirrors – Signal – Manoeuvre at all stages;
- decide as early as possible which exit you need to take;
- give an appropriate signal (see Rule 186). Time your signals so as not to confuse other road users;
- get into the correct lane;
- adjust your speed and position to fit in with traffic conditions;
- be aware of the speed and position of all the road users around you.

Rule 185 When reaching the roundabout you should:

- give priority to traffic approaching from your right, unless directed otherwise by signs, road markings or traffic lights;
- check whether road markings allow you to enter the roundabout without giving way. If so, proceed, but still look to the right before joining;
- watch out for all other road users already on the roundabout; be aware they may not be signalling correctly or at all;
- look forward before moving off to make sure traffic in front has moved off.

Rule 185 – Follow the correct procedures at roundabouts

Rule 186 Signals and position.
When taking the first exit to the left, unless signs or markings indicate otherwise:

- signal left and approach in the left-hand lane;
- keep to the left on the roundabout and continue signalling left to leave.

When taking an exit to the right or going full circle, unless signs or markings indicate otherwise:

- signal right and approach in the right-hand lane;
- keep to the right on the roundabout until you need to change lanes to exit the roundabout;
- signal left after you have passed the exit before the one you want.

When taking any intermediate exit, unless signs or markings indicate otherwise:

- select the appropriate lane on approach to the roundabout;
- you should not normally need to signal on approach;

- stay in this lane until you need to alter course to exit the roundabout;
- signal left after you have passed the exit before the one you want.

When there are more than three lanes at the entrance to a roundabout, use the most appropriate lane on approach and through it.

Rule 187   In all cases watch out for and give plenty of room to:

- pedestrians who may be crossing the approach and exit roads;
- traffic crossing in front of you on the roundabout, especially vehicles intending to leave by the next exit;
- traffic which may be straddling lanes or positioned incorrectly;
- motorcyclists;
- cyclists and horse riders who may stay in the left-hand lane and signal right if they intend to continue round the roundabout. Allow them to do so;
- long vehicles (including those towing trailers). These might have to take a different course or straddle lanes either approaching or on the roundabout because of their length. Watch out for their signals.

Rule 188   Mini-roundabouts. Approach these in the same way as normal roundabouts. All vehicles **MUST** pass round the central markings except large vehicles which are physically incapable of doing so. Remember, there is less space to manoeuvre and less time to signal. Avoid making U-turns at mini-roundabouts. Beware of others doing this.

Rule 189   At double mini-roundabouts treat each roundabout separately and give way to traffic from the right.

Rule 190   Multiple roundabouts. At some complex junctions, there may be a series of mini-roundabouts at each intersection. Treat each mini-roundabout separately and follow the normal rules.

Rule 190 – Treat each roundabout separately

Pedestrian crossings

Rule 191   You **MUST NOT** park on a crossing or in the area covered by the zig-zag lines. You **MUST NOT** overtake the moving vehicle nearest the crossing or the vehicle nearest the crossing which has stopped to give way to pedestrians.

Rule 192   In queuing traffic, you should keep the crossing clear.

Rule 192 – Keep the crossing clear

Rule 193   You should take extra care where the view of either side of the crossing is blocked by queuing traffic or incorrectly parked vehicles. Pedestrians may be crossing between stationary vehicles.

Rule 194   Allow pedestrians plenty of time to cross and do not harass them by revving your engine or edging forward.

Rule 195   Zebra crossings. As you approach a zebra crossing:

- look out for pedestrians waiting to cross and be ready to slow down or stop to let them cross;
- you **MUST** give way when a pedestrian has moved onto a crossing;
- allow more time for stopping on wet or icy roads;
- do not wave or use your horn to invite pedestrians across; this could be dangerous if another vehicle is approaching;
- be aware of pedestrians approaching from the side of the crossing.

A zebra crossing with a central island is two separate crossings.

Signal-controlled crossings

Rule 196   Pelican crossings. These are signal-controlled crossings where flashing amber follows the red 'Stop' light. You **MUST** stop when the red light shows. When the amber light is flashing, you **MUST** give way to any pedestrians on the crossing. If the amber light is flashing and there are no pedestrians on the crossing, you may proceed with caution.

Rule 196 – Allow pedestrians to cross when the amber light is flashing

Rule 197   Pelican crossings which go straight across the road are one crossing, even when there is a central island. You **MUST** wait for pedestrians who are crossing from the other side of the island.

Rule 198   Give way to anyone still crossing after the signal for vehicles has changed to green. This advice applies to all crossings.

Rule 199   Toucan, puffin and equestrian crossings. These are similar to pelican crossings, but there is no flashing amber phase; the light sequence for traffic at these three crossings is the same as at traffic lights. If the signal-controlled crossing is not working, proceed with extreme caution.

Reversing

Rule 200   Choose an appropriate place to manoeuvre. If you need to turn your vehicle around, wait until you find a safe place. Try not to reverse or turn round in a busy road; find a quiet side road or drive round a block of side streets.

Rule 201   Do not reverse from a side road into a main road. When using a driveway, reverse in and drive out if you can.

Rule 202   Look carefully before you start reversing. You should:

- use all your mirrors;
- check the 'blind spot' behind you (the part of the road you cannot see easily in the mirrors);
- check there are no pedestrians (particularly children), cyclists, other road users or obstructions in the road behind you.

Reverse slowly while:

- checking all around;
- looking mainly through the rear window;
- being aware that the front of your vehicle will swing out as you turn.

Get someone to guide you if you cannot see clearly.

Rule 202 – Check all round when reversing

Rule 203   You **MUST NOT** reverse your vehicle further than necessary.

Road users requiring extra care

Rule 204   The most vulnerable road users are pedestrians, cyclists, motorcyclists and horse riders. It is particularly important to be aware of children, older and disabled people, and learner and inexperienced drivers and riders.

Pedestrians

Rule 205   There is a risk of pedestrians, especially children, stepping unexpectedly into the road. You should drive with the safety of children in mind at a speed suitable for the conditions.

Rule 206   Drive carefully and slowly when:

- in crowded shopping streets, Home Zones and Quiet Lanes (see Rule 218) or residential areas;
- driving past bus and tram stops; pedestrians may emerge suddenly into the road;

- passing parked vehicles, especially ice cream vans; children are more interested in ice cream than traffic and may run into the road unexpectedly;

- needing to cross a pavement or cycle track; for example, to reach or leave a driveway. Give way to pedestrians and cyclists on the pavement;

- reversing into a side road; look all around the vehicle and give way to any pedestrians who may be crossing the road;

- turning at road junctions; give way to pedestrians who are already crossing the road into which you are turning;

- the pavement is closed due to street repairs and pedestrians are directed to use the road;

- approaching pedestrians on narrow rural roads without a footway or footpath. Always slow down and be prepared to stop if necessary, giving them plenty of room as you drive past.

Rule 206 – Watch out for children in busy areas

Rule 207   Particularly vulnerable pedestrians. These include:

- children and older pedestrians who may not be able to judge your speed and could step into the road in front of you. At 40 mph (64 km/h) your vehicle will probably kill any pedestrians it hits. At 20 mph (32 km/h) there is only a 1 in 20 chance of the pedestrian being killed. So kill your speed;

- older pedestrians who may need more time to cross the road. Be patient and allow them to cross in their own time. Do not hurry them by revving your engine or edging forward;

- people with disabilities. People with hearing impairments may not be aware of your vehicle approaching. Those with walking difficulties require more time;

- blind or partially sighted people, who may be carrying a white cane or using a guide dog. They may not be able to see you approaching;

- deaf blind people who may be carrying a white cane with a red band or using a dog with a red and white harness. They may not see or hear instructions or signals.

Rule 208   Near schools. Drive slowly and be particularly aware of young cyclists and pedestrians. In some places, there may be a flashing amber signal below the 'School' warning sign which tells you that there may be children crossing the road ahead. Drive very slowly until you are clear of the area.

Rule 209   Drive carefully and slowly when passing a stationary bus showing a 'School Bus' sign (see page 403) as children may be getting on or off.

Rule 210   You **MUST** stop when a school crossing patrol shows a 'Stop for children' sign (see page 385).

Motorcyclists and cyclists

Rule 211   It is often difficult to see motorcyclists and cyclists, especially when they are coming up from behind, coming out of junctions, at roundabouts, overtaking you or filtering through traffic. Always look out for them before you emerge from a junction; they could be approaching faster than you think. When turning right across a line of slow-moving or stationary traffic, look out for cyclists or motorcyclists on the inside of the traffic you are crossing. Be especially careful when turning, and when changing direction or lane. Be sure to check mirrors and blind spots carefully.

Rule 211 – Look out for motorcyclists and cyclists at juntions

Rule 212   When passing motorcyclists and cyclists, give them plenty of room (see Rules 162–167). If they look over their shoulder it could mean that they intend to pull out, turn right or change direction. Give them time and space to do so.

Rule 213   Motorcyclists and cyclists may suddenly need to avoid uneven road surfaces and obstacles such as drain covers or oily, wet or icy patches on the road. Give them plenty of room and pay particular attention to any sudden change of direction they may have to make.

Other road users

Rule 214   Animals. When passing animals, drive slowly. Give them plenty of room and be ready to stop. Do not scare animals by sounding your horn, revving your engine or accelerating rapidly once you have passed them. Look out for animals being led, driven or ridden on the road and take extra care. Keep your speed down at bends and on narrow country roads. If a road is blocked by a herd of animals, stop and switch off your engine until they have left the road. Watch out for animals on unfenced roads.

Rule 215   Horse riders and horse-drawn vehicles. Be particularly careful of horse riders and horse-drawn vehicles especially when overtaking. Always pass wide and slowly. Horse riders are often children, so take extra care and remember riders may ride in double file when escorting a young or inexperienced horse or rider. Look out for horse riders' and horse drivers' signals and heed a request to slow down or stop. Take great care and treat all horses as a potential hazard; they can be unpredictable, despite the efforts of their rider/driver.

Rule 216   Older drivers. Their reactions may be slower than other drivers. Make allowance for this.

Rule 217   Learners and inexperienced drivers. They may not be so skilful at anticipating and responding to events. Be particularly patient with learner drivers and young drivers. Drivers who have recently passed their test may display a 'New driver' plate or sticker (see Annex 8 – Safety code for new drivers).

Rule 218   Home Zones and Quiet Lanes. These are places where people could be using the whole of the road for a range of activities such as children playing or for a community event. You should drive slowly and carefully   and be prepared to stop to allow people extra time to make space for you to pass them in safety.

Other vehicles

Rule 219 Emergency and Incident Support vehicles. You should look and listen for ambulances, fire engines, police, doctors or other emergency vehicles using flashing blue, red or green lights and sirens or flashing head-lights, or Highways Agency Traffic Officer and Incident Support vehicles using flashing amber lights. When one approaches do not panic. Consider the route of such a vehicle and take appropriate action to let it pass, while complying with all traffic signs. If necessary, pull to the side of the road and stop, but try to avoid stopping before the brow of a hill, a bend or narrow section of road. Do not endanger yourself, other road users or pedestrians and avoid mounting the kerb. Do not brake harshly on approach to a junction or roundabout, as a following vehicle may not have the same view as you.

Rule 220 Powered vehicles used by disabled people. These small vehicles travel at a maximum speed of 8 mph (12 km/h). On a dual carriageway where the speed limit exceeds 50 mph (80 km/h) they **MUST** have a flashing amber beacon, but on other roads you may not have that advance warning.

Rule 221 Large vehicles. These may need extra road space to turn or to deal with a hazard that you are not able to see. If you are following a large vehicle, such as a bus or articulated lorry, be aware that the driver may not be able to see you in the mirrors. Be prepared to stop and wait if it needs room or time to turn.

Rule 221 – Large vehicles need extra room

Rule 222 Large vehicles can block your view. Your ability to see and to plan ahead will be improved if you pull back to increase your separation distance. Be patient, as larger vehicles are subject to lower speed limits than cars and motorcycles. Many large vehicles may be fitted with speed limiting devices which will restrict speed to 56 mph (90 km/h) even on a motorway.

Rule 223   Buses, coaches and trams. Give priority to these vehicles when you can do so safely, especially when they signal to pull away from stops. Look out for people getting off a bus or tram and crossing the road.

Rule 224   Electric vehicles. Be careful of electric vehicles such as milk floats and trams. Trams move quickly but silently and cannot steer to avoid you.

Rule 225   Vehicles with flashing amber beacons. These warn of a slow-moving or stationary vehicle (such as a Traffic Officer vehicle, salt spreader, snow plough or recovery vehicle) or abnormal loads, so approach with caution. On unrestricted dual carriageways, motor vehicles first used on or after 1 January 1947 with a maximum speed of 25 mph (40 km/h) or less (such as tractors) **MUST** use a flashing amber beacon (also see Rule 220).

Driving in adverse weather conditions

Rule 226   You **MUST** use headlights when visibility is seriously reduced, generally when you cannot see for more than 100 metres (328 feet). You may also use front or rear fog lights but you **MUST** switch them off when visibility improves (see Rule 236).

Rule 227   Wet weather. In wet weather, stopping distances will be at least double those required for stopping on dry roads (see page 333). This is because your tyres have less grip on the road. In wet weather:

- you should keep well back from the vehicle in front. This will increase your ability to see and plan ahead;
- if the steering becomes unresponsive, it probably means that water is preventing the tyres from gripping the road. Ease off the accelerator and slow down gradually;
- the rain and spray from vehicles may make it difficult to see and be seen;
- be aware of the dangers of spilt diesel that will make the surface very slippery (see Annex 6);
- take extra care around pedestrians, cyclists, motorcyclists and horse riders.

Icy and snowy weather

Rule 228   In winter check the local weather forecast for warnings of icy or snowy weather. DO NOT drive in these conditions unless your journey is essential. If it is, take great care and allow more time for your journey. Take an emergency kit of de-icer and ice scraper, torch, warm clothing and boots, first aid kit, jump leads and a shovel, together with a warm drink and emergency food in case you get stuck or your vehicle breaks down.

Rule 229   Before you set off:

- you **MUST** be able to see, so clear all snow and ice from all your windows;
- you **MUST** ensure that lights are clean and number plates are clearly visible and legible;
- make sure the mirrors are clear and the windows are demisted thoroughly;
- remove all snow that might fall off into the path of other road users;
- check your planned route is clear of delays and that no further snowfalls or severe weather are predicted.

Rule 229 – Make sure your car windscreen is completely clear

Rule 230   When driving in icy or snowy weather:

- drive with care, even if the roads have been treated;
- keep well back from the road user in front as stopping distances can be ten times greater than on dry roads;
- take care when overtaking vehicles spreading salt or other de-icer, particularly if you are riding a motorcycle or cycle;

- watch out for snowploughs which may throw out snow on either side. Do not overtake them unless the lane you intend to use has been cleared;

- be prepared for the road conditions to change over relatively short distances;

- listen to travel bulletins and take note of variable message signs that may provide information about weather, road and traffic conditions ahead.

Rule 231 Drive extremely carefully when the roads are icy. Avoid sudden actions as these could cause loss of control. You should:

- drive at a slow speed in as high a gear as possible; accelerate and brake very gently;

- drive particularly slowly on bends where loss of control is more likely. Brake progressively on the straight before you reach a bend. Having slowed down, steer smoothly round the bend, avoiding sudden actions;

- check your grip on the road surface when there is snow or ice by choosing a safe place to brake gently. If the steering feels unresponsive this may indicate ice and your vehicle losing its grip on the road. When travelling on ice, tyres make virtually no noise.

Windy weather

Rule 232 High-sided vehicles are most affected by windy weather, but strong gusts can also blow a car, cyclist, motorcyclist or horse rider off course. This can happen on open stretches of road exposed to strong cross-winds, or when passing bridges or gaps in hedges.

Rule 233 In very windy weather your vehicle may be affected by turbulence created by large vehicles. Motorcyclists are particularly affected, so keep well back from them when they are overtaking a high-sided vehicle.

Fog

Rule 234 Before entering fog check your mirrors then slow down. If the word 'Fog' is shown on a roadside signal but the road is clear, be prepared for a bank of fog or drifting patchy fog ahead. Even if it seems to be clearing, you can suddenly find yourself in thick fog.

Rule 235   When driving in fog you should:

- use your lights as required (see Rule 226);

- keep a safe distance behind the vehicle in front. Rear lights can give a false sense of security;

- be able to pull up well within the distance you can see clearly. This is particularly important on motorways and dual carriageways, as vehicles are travelling faster;

- use your windscreen wipers and demisters;

- beware of other drivers not using headlights;

- not accelerate to get away from a vehicle which is too close behind you;

- check your mirrors before you slow down. Then use your brakes so that your brake lights warn drivers behind you that you are slowing down;

- stop in the correct position at a junction with limited visibility and listen for traffic. When you are sure it is safe to emerge, do so positively and do not hesitate in a position that puts you directly in the path of approaching vehicles.

Rule 236   You **MUST NOT** use front or rear fog lights unless visibility is seriously reduced (see Rule 226) as they dazzle other road users and can obscure your brake lights. You **MUST** switch them off when visibility improves.

Rule 237   Hot weather. Keep your vehicle well ventilated to avoid drowsiness. Be aware that the road surface may become soft or if it rains after a dry spell it may become slippery. These conditions could affect your steering and braking. If you are dazzled by bright sunlight, slow down and if necessary, stop.

Waiting and parking

Rule 238   You **MUST NOT** wait or park on yellow lines during the times of operation shown on nearby time plates (or zone entry signs if in a Controlled Parking Zone) – see pages 399–400. Double yellow lines indicate a prohibition of waiting at any time even if there are no upright signs. You

MUST NOT wait or park, or stop to set down and pick up passengers, on school entrance markings (see page 401) when upright signs indicate a prohibition of stopping.

Parking

Rule 239 Use off-street parking areas, or bays marked out with white lines on the road as parking places, wherever possible. If you have to stop on the roadside:

- do not park facing against the traffic flow;
- stop as close as you can to the side;
- do not stop too close to a vehicle displaying a Blue Badge: remember, the occupant may need more room to get in or out;
- you **MUST** switch off the engine, headlights and fog lights;
- you **MUST** apply the handbrake before leaving the vehicle;
- you **MUST** ensure you do not hit anyone when you open your door. Check for cyclists or other traffic;
- it is safer for your passengers (especially children) to get out of the vehicle on the side next to the kerb;
- put all valuables out of sight and make sure your vehicle is secure;
- lock your vehicle.

Rule 239 – Check before opening your door

Rule 240 You **MUST NOT** stop or park on:

- the carriageway or the hard shoulder of a motorway except in an emergency (see Rule 270);
- a pedestrian crossing, including the area marked by the zig-zag lines (see Rule 191);
- a clearway (see page 387);

- taxi bays as indicated by upright signs and markings;

- an urban clearway within its hours of operation, even when a broken white line is on your side of the road, except to pick up or set down passengers (see page 387);

- a road marked with double white lines, except to pick up or set down passengers;

- a tram or cycle lane during its period of operation;

- a cycle track;

- red lines, in the case of specially designated 'red routes', unless otherwise indicated by signs.

Any vehicle may enter a bus lane to stop, load or unload where this is not prohibited (see Rule 141).

Rule 241   You **MUST NOT** park in parking spaces reserved for specific users, such as Blue Badge holders, residents or motorcycles, unless entitled to do so.

Rule 242   You **MUST NOT** leave your vehicle or trailer in a dangerous position or where it causes any unnecessary obstruction of the road.

Rule 243   DO NOT stop or park:

- near a school entrance;

- anywhere you would prevent access for Emergency Services;

- at or near a bus or tram stop or taxi rank;

- on the approach to a level crossing/tramway crossing;

- opposite or within 10 metres (32 feet) of a junction, except in an authorised parking space;

- near the brow of a hill or hump bridge;

- opposite a traffic island or (if this would cause an obstruction) another parked vehicle;

- where you would force other traffic to enter a tram lane;

- where the kerb has been lowered to help wheelchair users and powered mobility vehicles;

- in front of an entrance to a property;

- on a bend;

- where you would obstruct cyclists' use of cycle facilities;
- *except* when forced to do so by stationary traffic.

Rule 244 You **MUST NOT** park partially or wholly on the pavement in London, and should not do so elsewhere unless signs permit it. Parking on the pavement can obstruct and seriously inconvenience pedestrians, people in wheelchairs or with visual impairments and people with prams or pushchairs.

Rule 245 Controlled Parking Zones. The zone entry signs indicate the times when the waiting restrictions within the zone are in force. Parking may be allowed in some places at other times. Otherwise parking will be within separately signed and marked bays.

Rule 246 Goods vehicles. Vehicles with a maximum laden weight of over 7.5 tonnes (including any trailer) **MUST NOT** be parked on a verge, pavement or any land situated between carriageways, without police permission. The only exception is when parking is essential for loading and unloading, in which case the vehicle **MUST NOT** be left unattended.

Rule 247 Loading and unloading. Do not load or unload where there are yellow markings on the kerb and upright signs advise restrictions are in place (see pages 400–01). This may be permitted where parking is otherwise restricted. On red routes, specially marked and signed bays indicate where and when loading and unloading is permitted.

Parking at night

Rule 248 You **MUST NOT** park on a road at night facing against the direction of the traffic flow unless in a recognized parking space.

Rule 249 All vehicles **MUST** display parking lights when parked on a road or a lay-by on a road with a speed limit greater than 30 mph (48 km/h).

Rule 250 Cars, goods vehicles not exceeding 1,525 kg unladen weight, invalid carriages, motorcycles and pedal cycles may be parked without lights on a road (or lay-by) with a speed limit of 30 mph (48 km/h) or less if they are:

- at least 10 metres (32 feet) away from any junction, close to the kerb and facing in the direction of the traffic flow;
- in a recognised parking place or lay-by.

Other vehicles and trailers, and all vehicles with projecting loads, **MUST NOT** be left on a road at night without lights.

Rule 251   Parking in fog. It is especially dangerous to park on the road in fog. If it is unavoidable, leave your parking lights or sidelights on.

Rule 252   Parking on hills. If you park on a hill you should:

- park close to the kerb and apply the handbrake firmly;
- select a forward gear and turn your steering wheel away from the kerb when facing uphill;
- select reverse gear and turn your steering wheel towards the kerb when facing downhill;
- use 'park' if your car has an automatic gearbox.

Rule 252 – Turn your wheels away from the curb when parking facing uphill. Turn them towards the curb when parking facing downhill

Decriminalised Parking Enforcement (DPE)

DPE is becoming increasingly common as more authorities take on this role. The local traffic authority assumes responsibility for enforcing many parking contraventions in place of the police. Further details on DPE may be found at the following websites:

www.trafficpenaltytribunal.gov.uk (outside London)

www.parkingandtrafficappeals.gov.uk (inside London)

Motorways

Many other Rules apply to motorway driving, either wholly or in part: Rules 46, 57, 83–126, 130–134, 139, 144, 146–151, 160, 161, 219, 221–222, 225, 226–237, 274–278, 280, and 281–290.

General

Rule 253   Prohibited vehicles. Motorways **MUST NOT** be used by pedestrians, holders of provisional motorcycle or car licences, riders of motorcycles under 50 cc, cyclists, horse riders, certain slow-moving vehicles and those carrying oversized loads (except by special permission), agricultural vehicles, and powered wheelchairs/powered mobility scooters.

Rule 254   Traffic on motorways usually travels faster than on other roads, so you have less time to react. It is especially important to use your mirrors earlier and look much further ahead than you would on other roads.

Motorway signals

Rule 255   Motorway signals (see page 381) are used to warn you of a danger ahead. For example, there may be an incident, fog, a spillage or road workers on the carriageway which you may not immediately be able to see.

Rule 256   Signals situated on the central reservation apply to all lanes. On very busy stretches, signals may be overhead with a separate signal for each lane.

Rule 257   Amber flashing lights. These warn of a hazard ahead. The signal may show a temporary maximum speed limit, lanes that are closed or a message such as 'Fog'. Adjust your speed and look out for the danger until you pass a signal which is not flashing or one that gives the 'All clear' sign and you are sure it is safe to increase your speed.

Rule 258   Red flashing lights. If red lights on the overhead signals flash above your lane and a red 'X' is showing, you **MUST NOT** go beyond the signal in that lane. If red lights flash on a signal in the central reservation or at the side of the road, you **MUST NOT** go beyond the signal in any lane.

Driving on the motorway

Rule 259 Joining the motorway. When you join the motorway you will normally approach it from a road on the left (a slip road) or from an adjoining motorway. You should:

- give priority to traffic already on the motorway;
- check the traffic on the motorway and match your speed to fit safely into the traffic flow in the left-hand lane;
- not cross solid white lines that separate lanes or use the hard shoulder;
- stay on the slip road if it continues as an extra lane on the motorway;
- remain in the left-hand lane long enough to adjust to the speed of traffic before considering overtaking.

On the motorway

Rule 260 When you can see well ahead and the road conditions are good, you should:

- drive at a steady cruising speed which you and your vehicle can handle safely and is within the speed limit (see table on page 331);
- keep a safe distance from the vehicle in front and increase the gap on wet or icy roads, or in fog (see Rules 126 and 235).

Rule 261 You **MUST NOT** exceed 70 mph (112 km/h), or the maximum speed limit permitted for your vehicle (see page 331). If a lower speed limit is in force, either permanently or temporarily, at road works for example, you **MUST NOT** exceed the lower limit. On some motorways, mandatory motorway signals (which display the speed within a red ring) are used to vary the maximum speed limit to improve traffic flow. You **MUST NOT** exceed this speed limit.

Rule 262 The monotony of driving on a motorway can make you feel sleepy. To minimise the risk, follow the advice in Rule 91.

Rule 263 You **MUST NOT** reverse, cross the central reservation, or drive against the traffic flow. If you have missed your exit, or have taken the wrong route, carry on to the next exit.

Lane discipline

Rule 264   You should always drive in the left-hand lane when the road ahead is clear. If you are overtaking a number of slower-moving vehicles, you should return to the left-hand lane as soon as you are safely past. Slow-moving or speed-restricted vehicles should always remain in the left-hand lane of the carriageway unless overtaking. You **MUST NOT** drive on the hard shoulder except in an emergency or if directed to do so by the police, HA traffic officers in uniform or by signs.

Rule 265   The right-hand lane of a motorway with three or more lanes **MUST NOT** be used (except in prescribed circumstances) if you are driving:

- any vehicle drawing a trailer;
- a goods vehicle with a maximum laden weight exceeding 3.5 tonnes but not exceeding 7.5 tonnes, which is required to be fitted with a speed limiter;
- a goods vehicle with a maximum laden weight exceeding 7.5 tonnes;
- a passenger vehicle with a maximum laden weight exceeding 7.5 tonnes constructed or adapted to carry more than eight seated passengers in addition to the driver;
- a passenger vehicle with a maximum laden weight not exceeding 7.5 tonnes which is constructed or adapted to carry more than eight seated passengers in addition to the driver, which is required to be fitted with a speed limiter.

Rule 266   Approaching a junction. Look well ahead for signals or signs. Direction signs may be placed over the road. If you need to change lanes, do so in good time. At some junctions a lane may lead directly off the motorway. Only get in that lane if you wish to go in the direction indicated on the overhead signs.

Overtaking

Rule 267   Do not overtake unless you are sure it is safe and legal to do so. Overtake only on the right. You should:

- check your mirrors;
- take time to judge the speeds correctly;

- make sure that the lane you will be joining is sufficiently clear ahead and behind;

- take a quick sideways glance into the blind spot area to verify the position of a vehicle that may have disappeared from your view in the mirror;

- remember that traffic may be coming up behind you very quickly. Check all your mirrors carefully. Look out for motorcyclists. When it is safe to do so, signal in plenty of time, then move out;

- ensure you do not cut in on the vehicle you have overtaken;

- be especially careful at night and in poor visibility when it is harder to judge speed and distance.

Rule 268   Do not overtake on the left or move to a lane on your left to overtake. In congested conditions, where adjacent lanes of traffic are moving at similar speeds, traffic in left-hand lanes may sometimes be moving faster than traffic to the right. In these conditions you may keep up with the traffic in your lane even if this means passing traffic in the lane to your right. Do not weave in and out of lanes to overtake.

Rule 269   Hard shoulder. You **MUST NOT** use the hard shoulder for overtaking. In areas where an Active Traffic Management (ATM) Scheme is in force, the hard shoulder may be used as a running lane. You will know when you can use this because a speed limit sign will be shown above all open lanes, including the hard shoulder. A red cross or blank sign above the hard shoulder means that you **MUST NOT** drive on the hard shoulder except in an emergency or breakdown. Emergency refuge areas have also been built into these areas for use in cases of emergency or breakdown.

Rule 269 – Overhead gantry showing red cross over hard shoulder

Stopping

Rule 270 You **MUST NOT** stop on the carriageway, hard shoulder, slip road, central reservation or verge except in an emergency, or when told to do so by the police, HA traffic officers in uniform, an emergency sign or by flashing red light signals. Do not stop on the hard shoulder to either make or receive mobile phone calls.

Rule 271 You **MUST NOT** pick up or set down anyone, or walk on a motorway, except in an emergency.

Leaving the motorway

Rule 272 Unless signs indicate that a lane leads directly off the motorway, you will normally leave the motorway by a slip road on your left. You should:

- watch for the signs letting you know you are getting near your exit;
- move into the left-hand lane well before reaching your exit;
- signal left in good time and reduce your speed on the slip road as necessary.

Rule 273 On leaving the motorway or using a link road between motorways, your speed may be higher than you realise – 50 mph may feel like 30 mph. Check your speedometer and adjust your speed accordingly. Some slip roads and link roads have sharp bends, so you will need to slow down.

Breakdowns and incidents

Breakdowns

Rule 274 If your vehicle breaks down, think first of all other road users and:

- get your vehicle off the road if possible;
- warn other traffic by using your hazard warning lights if your vehicle is causing an obstruction;
- help other road users see you by wearing light-coloured or fluorescent clothing in daylight and reflective clothing at night or in poor visibility;

- put a warning triangle on the road at least 45 metres (147 feet) behind your broken-down vehicle on the same side of the road, or use other permitted warning devices if you have them. Always take great care when placing or retrieving them, but never use them on motorways;
- if possible, keep your sidelights on if it is dark or visibility is poor;
- do not stand (or let anybody else stand) between your vehicle and oncoming traffic;
- at night or in poor visibility do not stand where you will prevent other road users seeing your lights.

Additional rules for the motorway

Rule 275   If your vehicle develops a problem, leave the motorway at the next exit or pull into a service area. If you cannot do so, you should:

- pull on to the hard shoulder and stop as far to the left as possible, with your wheels turned to the left;
- try to stop near an emergency telephone (situated at approximately one-mile intervals along the hard shoulder);
- leave the vehicle by the left-hand door and ensure your passengers do the same. You **MUST** leave any animals in the vehicle or, in an emergency, keep them under proper control on the verge. Never attempt to place a warning triangle on a motorway;
- do not put yourself in danger by attempting even simple repairs;
- ensure that passengers keep away from the carriageway and hard shoulder, and that children are kept under control;
- walk to an emergency telephone on your side of the carriageway (follow the arrows on the posts at the back of the hard shoulder) – the telephone is free of charge and connects directly to the Highways Agency or the police. Use these in preference to a mobile phone (see Rule 283). Always face the traffic when you speak on the phone;
- give full details to the Highways Agency or the police; also inform them if you are a vulnerable motorist such as disabled, older or travelling alone;
- return and wait near your vehicle (well away from the carriageway and hard shoulder);

- if you feel at risk from another person, return to your vehicle by a left-hand door and lock all doors. Leave your vehicle again as soon as you feel this danger has passed.

Rule 275 – Keep well back from the hard shoulder

Rule 276   Before you rejoin the carriageway after a breakdown, build up speed on the hard shoulder and watch for a safe gap in the traffic. Be aware that other vehicles may be stationary on the hard shoulder.

Rule 277   If you cannot get your vehicle onto the hard shoulder:

- do not attempt to place any warning device on the carriageway;
- switch on your hazard warning lights;
- leave your vehicle only when you can safely get clear of the carriageway.

Rule 278   Disabled drivers. If you have a disability which prevents you from following the above advice you should:

- stay in your vehicle;
- switch on your hazard warning lights;
- display a 'Help' pennant or, if you have a car or mobile telephone, contact the emergency services and be prepared to advise them of your location.

Obstructions

Rule 279   If anything falls from your vehicle (or any other vehicle) on to the road, stop and retrieve it only if it is safe to do so.

Rule 280   Motorways. On a motorway do not try to remove the obstruction yourself. Stop at the next emergency telephone and call the Highways Agency or the police.

Incidents

Rule 281 Warning signs or flashing lights. If you see or hear emergency or incident support vehicles in the distance, be aware there may be an incident ahead (see Rule 219). Police officers and Highways Agency Traffic Officers may be required to work in the carriageway, for example dealing with debris, collisions or conducting rolling road blocks. Police officers will use rear-facing flashing red and blue lights and HA Traffic Officers will use rear-facing flashing red and amber lights in these situations. Watch out for such signals, slow down and be prepared to stop. You **MUST** follow any directions given by police officers or traffic officers as to whether you can safely pass the incident or blockage.

Rule 282 When passing the scene of an incident or crash do not be distracted or slow down unnecessarily (for example if an incident is on the other side of a dual carriageway). This may cause a collision or traffic congestion, but see Rule 283.

Rule 283 If you are involved in a crash or stop to give assistance:

- use your hazard warning lights to warn other traffic;
- ask drivers to switch off their engines and stop smoking;
- arrange for the emergency services to be called immediately with full details of the incident location and any casualties (on a motorway, use the emergency telephone which allows easy location by the emergency services. If you use a mobile phone, first make sure you have identified your location from the marker posts on the side of the hard shoulder);
- move uninjured people away from the vehicles to safety; on a motorway this should, if possible, be well away from the traffic, the hard shoulder and the central reservation;
- do not move injured people from their vehicles unless they are in immediate danger from fire or explosion;
- do not remove a motorcyclist's helmet unless it is essential to do so;
- be prepared to give first aid as shown on pages 412–14;
- stay at the scene until emergency services arrive.

If you are involved in any other medical emergency on the motorway you should contact the emergency services in the same way.

Incidents involving dangerous goods

Rule 284   Vehicles carrying dangerous goods in packages will be marked with plain orange reflective plates. Road tankers and vehicles carrying tank containers of dangerous goods will have hazard warning plates (see pages 402–03).

Rule 285   If an incident involves a vehicle containing dangerous goods, follow the advice in Rule 283 and, in particular:

- switch off engines and DO NOT SMOKE;
- keep well away from the vehicle and do not be tempted to try to rescue casualties as you yourself could become one;
- call the emergency services and give as much information as possible about the labels and markings on the vehicle. DO NOT use a mobile phone close to a vehicle carrying flammable loads.

Documentation

Rule 286   If you are involved in a collision which causes damage or injury to any other person, vehicle, animal or property, you **MUST**:

- stop;
- give your own and the vehicle owner's name and address, and the registration number of the vehicle, to anyone having reasonable grounds for requiring them;
- if you do not give your name and address at the time of the collision, report it to the police as soon as reasonably practicable, and in any case within 24 hours.

Rule 287   If another person is injured and you do not produce your insurance certificate at the time of the crash to a police officer or to anyone having reasonable grounds to request it, you **MUST**:

- report it to the police as soon as possible and in any case within 24 hours;
- produce your insurance certificate for the police within seven days.

Road works

Rule 288   When the 'Road Works Ahead' sign is displayed, you will need to be more watchful and look for additional signs providing more specific instructions. Observe all signs – they are there for your safety and the safety of road workers.

- You **MUST NOT** exceed any temporary maximum speed limit.
- Use your mirrors and get into the correct lane for your vehicle in good time and as signs direct.
- Do not switch lanes to overtake queuing traffic.
- Take extra care near cyclists and motorcyclists as they are vulnerable to skidding on grit, mud or other debris at road works.
- Where lanes are restricted due to road works, merge in turn (see Rule 134).
- Do not drive through an area marked off by traffic cones.
- Watch out for traffic entering or leaving the works area, but do not be distracted by what is going on there. Concentrate on the road ahead, not the road works.
- Bear in mind that the road ahead may be obstructed by the works or by slow-moving or stationary traffic.
- Keep a safe distance – there could be queues in front.

To obtain further information about road works see pages 397.

Additional rules for high-speed roads

Rule 289   Take special care on motorways and other high-speed dual carriageways.

- One or more lanes may be closed to traffic and a lower speed limit may apply.
- Works vehicles that are slow-moving or stationary with a large 'Keep Left' or 'Keep Right' sign on the back are sometimes used to close lanes for repairs, and a flashing light arrow may also be used to make the works vehicle more conspicuous from a distance and give earlier warning to drivers that they need to move over to the next lane.

- Check mirrors, slow down and change lanes if necessary.
- Keep a safe distance from the vehicle in front (see Rule 126).

Rule 290 Contraflow systems mean that you may be travelling in a narrower lane than normal and with no permanent barrier between you and oncoming traffic. The hard shoulder may be used for traffic, but be aware that there may be broken-down vehicles ahead of you. Keep a good distance from the vehicle ahead and observe any temporary speed limits.

Level crossings

Rule 291 A level crossing is where a road crosses a railway or tramway line. Approach and cross it with care. Never drive onto a crossing until the road is clear on the other side and do not get too close to the car in front. Never stop or park on, or near, a crossing.

Rule 292 Overhead electric lines. It is dangerous to touch overhead electric lines. You **MUST** obey the safe height warning road signs and you should not continue forward onto the railway if your vehicle touches any height barrier or bells. The clearance available is usually 5 metres (16 feet 6 inches) but may be lower.

Rule 293 Controlled crossings. Most crossings have traffic light signals with a steady amber light, twin flashing red stop lights (see page 381) and an audible alarm for pedestrians. They may have full, half or no barriers.

- You **MUST** always obey the flashing red stop lights.
- You **MUST** stop behind the white line across the road.
- Keep going if you have already crossed the white line when the amber light comes on.
- Do not reverse onto or over a controlled crossing.
- You **MUST** wait if a train goes by and the red lights continue to flash. This means another train will be passing soon.
- Only cross when the lights go off and barriers open.
- Never zig-zag around half-barriers; they lower automatically because a train is approaching.

- At crossings where there are no barriers, a train is approaching when the lights show.

Rule 293 – Stop when the traffic lights show

Rule 294   Railway telephones. If you are driving a large or slow-moving vehicle, a long, low vehicle with a risk of grounding, or herding animals, a train could arrive before you are clear of the crossing. You **MUST** obey any sign instructing you to use the railway telephone to obtain permission to cross. You **MUST** also telephone when clear of the crossing if requested to do so.

Rule 295   Crossings without traffic lights. Vehicles should stop and wait at the barrier or gate when it begins to close and not cross until the barrier or gate opens.

Rule 296   User-operated gates or barriers. Some crossings have 'Stop' signs and small red and green lights. You **MUST NOT** cross when the red light is showing, only cross if the green light is on. If crossing with a vehicle, you should:

- open the gates or barriers on both sides of the crossing;
- check that the green light is still on and cross quickly;
- close the gates or barriers when you are clear of the crossing.

Rule 297   If there are no lights, follow the procedure in Rule 296. Stop, look both ways and listen before you cross. If there is a railway telephone, always use it to contact the signal operator to make sure it is safe to cross. Inform the signal operator again when you are clear of the crossing.

Rule 298   Open crossings. These have no gates, barriers, attendant or traffic lights but will have a 'Give Way' sign. You should look both ways, listen and make sure there is no train coming before you cross.

Rule 299 Incidents and breakdowns. If your vehicle breaks down, or if you have an incident on a crossing you should:

- get everyone out of the vehicle and clear of the crossing immediately;
- use a railway telephone if available to tell the signal operator. Follow the instructions you are given;
- move the vehicle clear of the crossing if there is time before a train arrives. If the alarm sounds, or the amber light comes on, leave the vehicle and get clear of the crossing immediately.

Tramways

Rule 300 You **MUST NOT** enter a road, lane or other route reserved for trams. Take extra care where trams run along the road. You should avoid driving directly on top of the rails and should take care where trams leave the main carriageway to enter the reserved route, to ensure you do not follow them. The width taken up by trams is often shown by tram lanes marked by white lines, yellow dots or by a different type of road surface. Diamond-shaped signs and white light signals give instructions to tram drivers only.

Rule 301 Take extra care where the track crosses from one side of the road to the other and where the road narrows and the tracks come close to the kerb. Tram drivers usually have their own traffic signals and may be permitted to move when you are not. Always give way to trams. Do not try to race or overtake them or pass them on the inside, unless they are at tram stops or stopped by tram signals and there is a designated tram lane for you to pass.

Rule 302 You **MUST NOT** park your vehicle where it would get in the way of trams or where it would force other drivers to do so. Do not stop on any part of a tram track, except in a designated bay where this has been provided alongside and clear of the track. When doing so, ensure that all parts of your vehicle are outside the delineated tram path. Remember that a tram cannot steer round an obstruction.

Rule 303   Tram stops. Where the tram stops at a platform, either in the middle or at the side of the road, you **MUST** follow the route shown by the road signs and markings. At stops without platforms you **MUST NOT** drive between a tram and the left-hand kerb when a tram has stopped to pick up passengers. If there is no alternative route signed, do not overtake the tram – wait until it moves off.

Rule 304   Look out for pedestrians, especially children, running to catch a tram approaching a stop.

Rule 305   Always give priority to trams, especially when they signal to pull away from stops, unless it would be unsafe to do so. Remember that they may be carrying large numbers of standing passengers who could be injured if the tram had to make an emergency stop. Look out for people getting off a bus or tram and crossing the road.

Rule 306   All road users, but particularly cyclists and motorcyclists, should take extra care when driving or riding close to or crossing the tracks, especially if the rails are wet. You should take particular care when crossing the rails at shallow angles, on bends and at junctions. It is safest to cross the tracks directly at right angles. Other road users should be aware that cyclists and motorcyclists may need more space to cross the tracks safely.

Rule 307   Overhead electric lines. Tramway overhead wires are normally 5.8 metres above any carriageway, but can be lower. You should ensure that you have sufficient clearance between the wire and your vehicle (including any load you are carrying) before driving under an overhead wire. Drivers of vehicles with extending cranes, booms, tipping apparatus or other types of variable height equipment should ensure that the equipment is fully lowered. Where overhead wires are set lower than 5.8 metres, these will be indicated by height clearance markings – similar to 'low bridge' signs. The height clearances on these plates should be carefully noted and observed. If you are in any doubt as to whether your vehicle will pass safely under the wires, you should always contact the local police or the tramway operator. Never take a chance as this can be extremely hazardous.

Light signals controlling traffic

Traffic light signals

RED means 'Stop'. Wait behind the stop line on the carriageway.

RED AND AMBER also means 'Stop'. Do not pass through or start until GREEN shows.

GREEN means you may go on if the way is clear. Take special care if you intend to turn left or right and give way to pedestrians who are crossing.

AMBER means 'Stop' at the line. You may go on only if the AMBER appears after you have crossed the stop line or are so close to it that to pull up might cause an accident.

A GREEN ARROW may be provided in addition to the full green signal if movement in a certain direction is allowed before or after the full green phase. If the way is clear you may go but only in the direction shown by the arrow. You may do this whatever other lights may be showing. White light signals may be provided for trams.

Flashing red lights

Alternately flashing red lights mean YOU **MUST** STOP

At level crossings, lifting bridges, airfields, fire stations, etc

Motorway signals

You MUST NOT proceed further in this lane

Leave motorway at next exit

Change lane

Temporary maximum speed advised

Reduced visibility ahead

Lane ahead closed

End of restriction

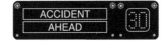

Temporary maximum speed advised and information message

Lane control signals

Green arrow – lane available to
   traffic facing the sign

Red crosses – lane closed to traffic facing
   the sign
White diagonal arrow – change lanes
   in direction shown

Signals to other road users

Direction indicator signals

I intend to move out to
the right or turn right

I intend to move into
the left or turn left or
stop on the left

Brake light signals

I am applying the brakes

Reversing light signals

I intend to reverse

These signals should not be used except for the purposes described.

Arm signals

For use when direction indicator signals are not used, or when necessary to reinforce direction indicator signals and stop lights. *Also for use by pedal cyclists and those in charge of horses.*

I intend to move in to the left or turn left

I intend to move out to the right or turn right

I intend to slow down or stop

Signals by authorised persons

Police officers

Stop

Traffic approaching from the front

Traffic approaching from both front and behind

Traffic approaching from behind

To beckon traffic on

| From the side | From the front | From behind |

Arm signals to persons controlling traffic

I want to go straight on | I want to turn left; use either hand | I want to turn right

Vehicle and Operator Services Agency and Highways Agency Traffic Officers

Highways Agency Traffic Officer | VOSA Traffic Officer

These officers now have new powers to stop/direct vehicles and will be using hand signals and light signals similar to those used by police. You MUST obey any signals given (see Rules 107 and 108)

School crossing patrols

Not ready to cross pedestrians   **Barrier to stop pedestrians crossing**   **Ready to cross pedestrians, vehicles must be prepared to stop**   **All vehicles must stop**

Traffic signs

Signs giving orders

Signs with red circles are mostly prohibitive. Plates below signs qualify their message

Entry to 20mph zone   **End of 20mph zone**   **Maximum speed**   **National speed limit applies**   **School crossing patrol**

Stop and give way   **Give way to traffic on major road**   **Manually operated temporary STOP sign**   **Manually operated temporary GO sign**   **No entry for vehicular traffic**

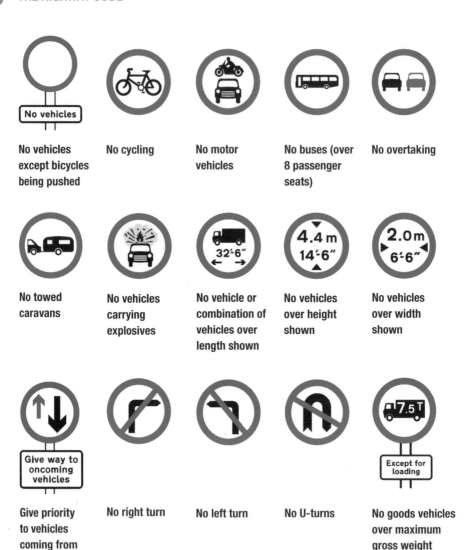

No vehicles except bicycles being pushed

No cycling

No motor vehicles

No buses (over 8 passenger seats)

No overtaking

No towed caravans

No vehicles carrying explosives

No vehicle or combination of vehicles over length shown

No vehicles over height shown

No vehicles over width shown

Give priority to vehicles coming from the other direction

No right turn

No left turn

No U-turns

No goods vehicles over maximum gross weight (in tonnes except for loading and unloading)

Note: Although *The Highway Code* shows many of the signs commonly in use, a comprehensive explanation of our signing system is given in the Department's booklet *Know Your Traffic Signs*, which is on sale at booksellers. The booklet also illustrates and explains the vast majority of signs the road user is likely to encounter. The signs illustrated in *The Highway Code* are not all drawn to the same scale. In Wales, bilingual versions of some signs are used including Welsh and English versions of place names. Some older designs of signs may still be seen on the roads.

No vehicles over maximum gross weight shown (in tonnes)

Parking restricted to permit holders

No stopping during period indicated except for buses

No stopping during times shown except for as long as necessary to set down or pick up passengers

No waiting

No stopping (Clearway)

Signs with blue circles but no red border mostly give positive instruction

Ahead only

Turn left ahead (right if symbol reversed)

Turn left (right if symbol reversed)

Keep left (right if symbol reversed)

Vehicles may pass either side to reach same destination

Mini-roundabout (roundabout circulation – give way to vehicles from the immediate right

Route to be used by pedal cycles only

Segregated pedal cycle lane and pedestrian route

Minimum speed

End of minimum speed

Buses and cycles only

Trams only

Pedestrian crossing point over tramway

One-way traffic (note – compare circular 'Ahead Only' sign)

With-flow bus and cycle lane

Contra-flow bus lane

With-flow pedal cycle lane

Warning signs

Mostly triangular

Distance to 'STOP' line ahead

Dual carriageway ends

Road narrows on right (left if symbol reversed)

Road narrows both sides

Distance to 'Give Way' line ahead

Crossroads

Junction on bend ahead

T-junction with priority over vehicles from the right

Staggered junction

Traffic merging from left ahead

The priority through route is indicated by the broader line.

Double bend first to left (symbol may be reversed)

Bend to right (or left if symbol reversed)

Roundabout

Uneven road

Plate below some signs

Two-way traffic crosses one-way road

Two-way traffic ahead

Opening or swing bridge ahead

Low-flying aircraft or sudden aircraft noise

Falling or fallen rocks

Traffic signals not in use

Traffic signals

Slippery road

Steep hill downwards

Steep hill upwards

Gradients may be shown as ratio ie 20% = 1:5

Tunnel ahead

Trams crossing ahead

Level crossing with barrier or gate ahead

Level crossing without barrier or gate ahead

Level crossing without barrier

School crossing patrol ahead (some signs have amber lights which flash when crossings are in use)

Frail (or blind or disabled if shown) pedestrians likely to cross road ahead

Pedestrians in road ahead

Zebra crossing

Overhead electric cable; plate indicates maximum height of vehicles which can pass safely

Available width of headroom indicated

Sharp deviation of rout to left (or right if chevrons reversed)

Light signals ahead at level crossing, airfield or bridge

Miniature warning lights a level crossings

Cattle

Wild animals

Wild horses or ponies

Accompanied horses or ponies

Cycle route ahead

Risk of ice

Traffic queues likely ahead

Distance over which road humps extend

Other danger; plate indicates nature of danger

Soft verges

Side winds

Hump bridge

Worded warning sign

Quayside or river bank

Risk of grounding

Direction signs

Mostly rectangular

Signs on motorways – blue backgrounds

At a junction leading directly into a motorway (junction number may be show on black background)

On approach to junctions (junction number on black background)

Route confirmatory sign after junction

Downward pointing arrows mean 'Get in lane'. The left hand lane leads to a different destination from the other lanes

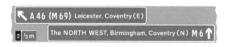

The panel with the inclined arrow indicates the destinations which can be reached by leaving the motorway at the next junction

Signs on primary routes – green backgrounds

On approaches to junctions

At the junction

On approaches to junctions

Route confirmatory sign after junction

On approaches to a junction in Wales (bilingual)

Blue panels indicate that the motorway starts at the junction ahead. Motorways shown in brackets can also be reached along the route indicated. White panels indicate local or non-primary routes leading from the junction ahead. Brown panels show the route to tourist attractions. The name of the junction may be shown at the top of the sign. The aircraft symbol indicates the route to an airport. A symbol may be included to warn of a hazard or restriction along that route.

Primary route forming part of a ring road

Signs on non-primary and local routes – black borders

On approaches to junctions

At the junction

Direction to toilets with
access for the disabled

Green panels indicate that the primary route starts at the junction ahead. Route numbers on a blue background show the direction to a motorway. Route numbers on a green background show the direction to a primary route.

Other direction signs

Picnic site

Ancient monument in the
care of English Heritage

Direction to car park

Tourist attraction

Direction to camping and
caravan site

Advisory route for lorries

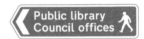

Route for pedal cycles forming part of a network

Recommended route for pedal cycles to place shown

Route for pedestrians

Symbols showing emergency diversion route for motorway and other main road traffic

Diversion route

Information signs

All rectangular

Entrance to controlled parking zone

Entrance to congestion charging zone

End of controlled parking zone

Advance warning of restriction or prohibition ahead

Parking place for solo motorcycles

With-flow bus lane ahead which pedal cycles and taxis may also use

Lane designated for use by high occupancy vehicles (HOV) – see Rule 142

Vehicles permitted to use an HOV lane ahead

End of motorway

Start of motorway and point from which motorway regulations apply

Appropriate traffic lanes at junction ahead

Traffic on the main carriageway coming from right has priority over joining traffic

Additional traffic joining from left ahead. Traffic on the main carriageway has priority over joining traffic from right hand lane of slip road

Traffic in right hand lane of slip road joining the main carriageway has priority over left hand lane

'Countdown' markers at exit from motorway
(each bar represents 100 yards to the exit).
Green-backed markers may be used on primary routes
and white-backed markers with black bars on other
routes. At approaches to concealed level crossings
white-backed markers with red bars may be used.
Although these will be erected at equal distances
the bars do not represent 100 yard intervals

Motorway service area sign
showing the operator's
name

Traffic has
priority over
oncoming
vehicles

Hospital ahead
with Accident
and Emergency
facilities

Tourist
information
point

No through
road for
vehicles

Recommended
route for pedal
cycles

Home Zone Entry

Area in which
cameras are used
to enforce traffic
regulations

Bus lane on road
at junction ahead

Road works signs

Road works

Loose chippings

Temporary hazard
at road works

Temporary lane closure
(the number and position
of the arrows and red bars
may be varied according
to lanes open and closed)

Slow-moving or
stationary works vehicle
blocking a traffic lane.
Pass in the direction
shown by the arrow

Mandatory speed
limit ahead

Road works
1 mile ahead

End of road works
and temporary
restrictions
including speed
limits

Signs used on the back of
slow-moving or stationary
vehicles warning of lane close
ahead by a works vehicle.
There are no cones in the road

Lane restrictions at
road works ahead

One lane crossover
at contraflow road
works

Road markings

Across the carriageway

Stop line at signals or police control

Stop line at 'Stop' sign

Stop line for pedestrians at level crossing

Give way to traffic on major roads (can also be used at mini-roundabouts)

Give way to traffic from the right at a roundabout

Give way to traffic from the right at a mini-roundabout

Along the carriageway

Edge line

Centre line. See Rule 127

Hazard warning line. See Rule 127

Double white lines. See Rules 128 and 129

See Rule 130

Lane line. See Rule 131

Along the edge of the carriageway

Waiting restrictions

Waiting restrictions indicated by yellow lines apply to the carriageway, pavement and verge. You may stop to load or unload (unless there are also loading restrictions as described below) or while passengers board or alight. Double yellow lines mean no waiting at any time, unless there are signs that specifically indicate seasonal restrictions. The times at which the restrictions apply for other road markings are shown on nearby plates or on entry signs to controlled parking zones. If no days are shown on the signs, the restrictions are in force every day including Sundays and Bank Holidays. White bay markings and upright signs (see below) indicate where parking is allowed.

No waiting at any time	No waiting at times shown on sign	Waiting is limited to duration specified during the days and times shown

Red Route stopping controls

Red lines are used on some roads instead of yellow lines. In London the double and single red lines used on Red Routes indicate that stopping to park, load/unload or to board and alight from a vehicle (except for a licensed taxi or if you hold a Blue Badge) is prohibited. The red lines apply to the carriageway, pavement and verge. The times that the red line prohibitions apply are shown on nearby signs, but the double red line ALWAYS means no stopping at any time. On Red Routes you may stop to park, load/unload in specially marked boxes and adjacent signs specify the times and purposes and duration allowed. A box MARKED IN RED indicates that it may only be available for the purpose specified for part of the day (eg between busy peak periods). A box MARKED IN WHITE means that it is available throughout the day.

RED AND SINGLE YELLOW LINES CAN ONLY GIVE A GUIDE TO THE RESTRICTIONS AND CONTROLS IN FORCE AND SIGNS, NEARBY OR AT A ZONE ENTRY, **MUST** BE CONSULTED.

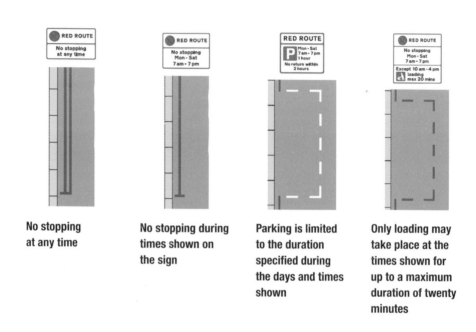

| No stopping at any time | No stopping during times shown on the sign | Parking is limited to the duration specified during the days and times shown | Only loading may take place at the times shown for up to a maximum duration of twenty minutes |

On the kerb or at the edge of the carriageway

Loading restrictions on roads other than Red Routes

Yellow marks on the kerb or at the edge of the carriageway indicate that loading or unloading is prohibited at the times shown on the nearby black and white plates. You may stop while passengers board or alight. If no days are indicated on the signs the restrictions are in force every day including Sundays and Bank Holidays.

ALWAYS CHECK THE TIMES SHOWN ON THE PLATES.

Lengths of road reserved for vehicles loading and unloading are indicated by a white 'bay' marking with the words 'Loading Only' and a sign with the white on blue 'trolley' symbol. This sign also shows whether loading and unloading is restricted to goods vehicles and the times at which the bay can be used. If no times or days are shown it may be used at any time. Vehicles may not park here if they are not loading or unloading.

No loading or unloading at any time

No loading or unloading at the times shown

Loading bay

Other road markings

Keep entrance clear of stationary vehicles, even if picking up or setting down children

Warning of 'Give Way' just ahead

Parking space reserved for vehicles named

See Rule 243

See Rule 141

Box junction – See Rule 174

Do not block that part of the carriageway indicated

Indication of traffic lanes

Vehicle markings

Large goods vehicle rear markings

Motor vehicles over 7,500 kilograms maximum gross weight and trailers over 3,500 kilograms maximum gross weight

The vertical markings are also required to be fitted to builders' skips placed in the road, commercial vehicles or combinations longer than 13 metres (optional on combinations between 11 and 13 metres)

Hazard warning plates

Certain tank vehicles carrying dangerous goods must display hazard information panels.

The panel illustrated is for flammable liquid

The above panel will be displayed by vehicles carrying certain dangerous goods in packages

Diamond symbols indicating other risks include:

Toxic
substance

Oxidising
substance

Non-flammable
compressed gas

Radioactive
substance

Spontaneously combustible substance

Corrosive substance

Projection markers

Side marker   **End marker**

Both required when load or equipment (eg crane jib) overhangs front or rear by more than two metres

Other

School bus (displayed in front or rear window of bus or coach)

Highway Code annexes

Annex 3: Motor vehicle documentation and learner driver requirements

Documents

Driving licence. You **MUST** have a valid driving licence for the category of motor vehicle you are driving. You **MUST** inform the Driver and Vehicle Licensing Agency (DVLA) if you change your name and/or address.

Holders of non-European Community licences who are now resident in the UK may only drive on that licence for a maximum of 12 months from the date they become resident in this country.

To ensure continuous driving entitlement:

- a British provisional licence should be obtained and a driving test(s) passed before the 12-month period elapses, or;
- in the case of a driver who holds a licence from a country which has been designated in law for licence exchange purposes, the driver should exchange the licence for a British one.

MOT. Cars and motorcycles **MUST** normally pass an MOT test three years from the date of the first registration and every year after that. You **MUST NOT** drive a motor vehicle without an MOT certificate when it should have one. Exceptionally, you may drive to a pre-arranged test appointment or to a garage for repairs required for the test. Driving an unroadworthy motor vehicle may invalidate your insurance.

Insurance. To use a motor vehicle on the road, you **MUST** have a valid insurance policy. This **MUST** at least cover you for injury or damage to a third party while using that motor vehicle. Before driving any motor vehicle, make sure that it has this cover for your use or that your own insurance provides adequate cover. You **MUST NOT** drive a motor vehicle without insurance. Also, be aware that even if a road traffic incident is not your fault, you may still be held liable by insurance companies.

Uninsured drivers can now be automatically detected by roadside cameras. Further to the penalties for uninsured driving listed on page 407, an offender's vehicle can now be seized by the police, taken away and crushed.

The types of cover available are indicated below:

- Third-party insurance – this is often the cheapest form of insurance, and is the minimum cover required by law. It covers anyone you might injure or whose property you might damage. It does not cover damage to your own motor vehicle or injury to yourself.

- Third-party, fire and theft insurance – similar to third-party, but also covers you against your motor vehicle being stolen, or damaged by fire.
- Comprehensive insurance – this is the most expensive but the best insurance. Apart from covering other persons and property against injury or damage, it also covers damage to your own motor vehicle, up to the market value of that vehicle, and personal injury to yourself.

Registration certificate. Registration certificates (also called harmonised registration certificates) are issued for all motor vehicles used on the road, describing them (make, model, etc) and giving details of the registered keeper. You **MUST** notify the Driver and Vehicle Licensing Agency in Swansea as soon as possible when you buy or sell a motor vehicle, or if you change your name or address. For registration certificates issued after 27 March 1997, the buyer and seller are responsible for completing the registration certificates. The seller is responsible for forwarding them to DVLA. The procedures are explained on the back of the registration certificates.

Vehicle Excise Duty (VED). All motor vehicles used or kept on public roads **MUST** display a valid Vehicle Excise Duty disc (tax disc) displayed at all times. Even motor vehicles exempt from duty **MUST** display a tax disc at all times.

Statutory Off-Road Notification (SORN). This is a notification to the DVLA that a motor vehicle is not being used on the road. If you are the vehicle keeper and want to keep a motor vehicle untaxed and off the public road you **MUST** declare SORN – it is an offence not to do so. You then won't have to pay any road tax for that vehicle for a period of 12 months. You need to send a further declaration after that period if the vehicle is still off the public road. The SORN will end if you sell the vehicle and the new owner will become immediately responsible.

Production of documents. You **MUST** be able to produce your driving licence and counterpart, a valid insurance certificate and (if appropriate) a valid MOT certificate, when requested by a police officer. If you cannot do this you may be asked to take them to a police station within seven days.

Learner drivers

Learners driving a car **MUST** hold a valid provisional licence. They **MUST** be supervised by someone at least 21 years old who holds a full EC/EEA licence for that type of car (automatic or manual) and has held one for at least three years.

Vehicles. Any vehicle driven by a learner **MUST** display red L plates. In Wales, either red D plates, red L plates, or both, can be used. Plates **MUST** conform to legal specifications and **MUST** be clearly visible to others from in front of the vehicle and from behind. Plates should be removed or covered when not being driven by a learner (except on driving school vehicles).

You **MUST** pass the theory test (if one is required) and then a practical driving test for the category of vehicle you wish to drive before driving unaccompanied.

Annex 5: Penalties

Parliament sets the maximum penalties for road traffic offences. The seriousness of the offence is reflected in the maximum penalty. It is for the courts to decide what sentence to impose according to circumstances.

The penalty table on pages 407–08 indicates some of the main offences, and the associated penalties. There is a wide range of other more specific offences which, for the sake of simplicity, are not shown here. The penalty points and disqualification system is described below.

Penalty points and disqualification

The penalty point system is intended to deter drivers and motorcyclists from following unsafe motoring practices. Certain non-motoring offences, eg failure to rectify vehicle defects, can also attract penalty points. The court **MUST** order points to be endorsed on the licence according to the fixed number or the range set by Parliament. The accumulation of penalty points acts as a warning to drivers and motorcyclists that they risk disqualification if further offences are committed.

A driver or motorcyclist who accumulates 12 or more penalty points within a three-year period **MUST** be disqualified. This will be for a minimum period of six months, or longer if the driver or motorcyclist has previously been disqualified.

For every offence which carries penalty points the court has a discretionary power to order the licence holder to be disqualified. This may be for any period the court thinks fit, but will usually be between a week and a few months.

In the case of serious offences, such as dangerous driving and drink-driving, the court **MUST** order disqualification. The minimum period is 12 months, but for repeat offenders or where the alcohol level is high, it may be longer. For example, a second drink-drive offence in the space of 10 years will result in a minimum of three years' disqualification.

Offence	Maximum penalties			
	Imprisonment	Fine	Disqualification	Penalty points
Causing death by dangerous driving	14 years	Unlimited	Obligatory – 2 years minimum	3–11 (if exceptionally not disqualified)
Dangerous driving	2 years	Unlimited	Obligatory	3–11 (if exceptionally not disqualified)
Causing death by careless driving under the influence of drink or drugs	14 years	Unlimited	Obligatory – 2 years minimum	3–11 (if exceptionally not disqualified)
Careless and inconsiderate driving	–	£5,000	Discretionary	3–9
Driving while unfit through drink or drugs or with excess alcohol; or failing to provide a specimen for analysis	6 months	£5,000	Obligatory	3–11 (if exceptionally not disqualified)
Failing to stop after an accident or failing to report an accident	6 months	£5,000	Discretionary	5–10
Driving when disqualified	6 months (12 months in Scotland)	£5,000	Discretionary	6
Driving after refusal or revocation of licence on medical grounds	6 months	£5,000	Discretionary	3–6
Driving without insurance	–	£5,000	Discretionary	6–8
Using a vehicle in dangerous condition	–	LGV £5,000 PCV £5,000 Other £2,500	Obligatory if offence committed within 3 years of a previous conviction for the same offence – 6 months min otherwise discretionary	3 in each case
Failure to have proper control of vehicle or full view of the road and traffic ahead, or using a hand-held mobile phone while driving	–	£1,000 (£2,500 for PCV or goods vehicle)	Discretionary	3

Offence	Maximum penalties			
	Imprisonment	Fine	Disqualification	Penalty points
Driving otherwise than in accordance with a licence	–	£1,000	Discretionary	3–6
Speeding	–	£1,000 (£2,500 for motorway offences)	Discretionary	3–6 or 3 (fixed penalty)
Traffic light offences	–	£1,000	Discretionary	3
No MOT certificate	–	£1,000	–	–
Seat belt offences	–	£500	–	–
Dangerous cycling	–	£2,500	–	–
Careless cycling	–	£1,000	–	–
Cycling on pavement	–	£500	–	–
Failing to identify driver of a vehicle	–	£1,000	Discretionary	6

* Where a court disqualifies a person on conviction for one of these offences, it must order an extended retest. The courts also have discretion to order a retest for any other offence which carries penalty points, an extended retest where disqualification is obligatory, and an ordinary test where disqualification is not obligatory.

Furthermore, in some serious cases, the court **MUST** (in addition to imposing a fixed period of disqualification) order the offender to be disqualified until they pass a driving test. In other cases the court has a discretionary power to order such disqualification. The test may be an ordinary length test or an extended test according to the nature of the offence.

New drivers. Special rules as set out below apply for a period of two years from the date of passing their first driving test, to drivers and motorcyclists from:

- the UK, EU/EEA, the Isle of Man, the Channel Islands or Gibraltar who passed their first driving test in any of those countries;

- other foreign countries who have to pass a UK driving test to gain a UK licence, in which case the UK driving test is treated as their first driving test and;

- other foreign countries who (without needing a test) exchanged their licence for a UK licence and subsequently passed a UK driving test to drive another type of vehicle, in which case the UK driving test is treated as their first driving test. For example a driver who exchanges a foreign licence (car) for a UK licence (car) and who later passes a test to drive another type of vehicle (eg an HGV) will be subject to the special rules.

Where a person subject to the special rules accumulates six or more penalty points before the end of the two-year period (including any points acquired before passing the test), their licence will be revoked automatically. To regain the licence they must reapply for a provisional licence and may drive only as a learner until they pass a further driving test (also see Annex 8 – Safety code for new drivers).

Note. This applies even if they pay for offences by fixed penalty. Drivers in the first group (UK, EU/EEA, etc) who already have a full licence for one type of vehicle are not affected by the special rules if they later pass a test to drive another type of vehicle.

Other consequences of offending

Where an offence is punishable by imprisonment then the vehicle used to commit the offence may be confiscated.

In addition to the penalties a court may decide to impose, the cost of insurance is likely to rise considerably following conviction for a serious driving offence. This is because insurance companies consider such drivers are more likely to be involved in a collision. Drivers disqualified for drinking and driving twice within 10 years, or once if they are over two and a half times the legal limit, or those who refused to give a specimen, also have to satisfy the Driver and Vehicle Licensing Agency's Medical Branch that they do not have an alcohol problem and are otherwise fit to drive before their licence is returned at the end of their period of disqualification.

Persistent misuse of drugs or alcohol may lead to the withdrawal of a driving licence.

Annex 6: Vehicle maintenance, safety and security

Vehicle maintenance

Take special care that lights, brakes, steering, exhaust system, seat belts, demisters, wipers and washers are all working. Also:

- lights, indicators, reflectors, and number plates **MUST** be kept clean and clear;
- windscreens and windows **MUST** be kept clean and free from obstructions to vision;
- lights **MUST** be properly adjusted to prevent dazzling other road users. Extra attention needs to be paid to this if the vehicle is heavily loaded;
- exhaust emissions **MUST NOT** exceed prescribed levels;
- ensure your seat, seat belt, head restraint and mirrors are adjusted correctly before you drive;
- ensure that items of luggage are securely stowed.

Warning displays. Make sure that you understand the meaning of all warning displays on the vehicle instrument panel. Do not ignore warning signs; they could indicate a dangerous fault developing.

- When you turn the ignition key, warning lights will be illuminated but will go out when the engine starts (except the handbrake warning light). If they do not, or if they come on while you are driving, stop and investigate the problem, as you could have a serious fault.
- If the charge warning light comes on while you are driving, it may mean that the battery isn't charging. This should also be checked as soon as possible to avoid loss of power to lights and other electrical systems.

Window tints. You **MUST NOT** use a vehicle with excessively dark tinting applied to the windscreen, or to the glass in any front window to either side of the driver. Window tinting applied during manufacture complies with the Visual Light Transmittance (VLT) standards. There are no VLT limits for rear windscreens or rear passenger windows.

Tyres. Tyres **MUST** be correctly inflated to the vehicle manufacturer's specification for the load being carried. Always refer to the vehicle's handbook or data. Tyres should also be free from certain cuts and other defects.

Cars, light vans and light trailers **MUST** have a tread depth of at least 1.6 mm across the central three-quarters of the breadth of the tread and around the entire circumference.

Motorcycles, large vehicles and passenger-carrying vehicles **MUST** have a tread depth of at least 1 mm across three-quarters of the breadth of the tread and in a continuous band around the entire circumference.

Mopeds should have visible tread.

Be aware that some vehicle defects can attract penalty points.

If a tyre bursts while you are driving, try to keep control of your vehicle. Grip the steering wheel firmly and allow the vehicle to roll to a stop at the side of the road.

If you have a flat tyre, stop as soon as it is safe to do so. Only change the tyre if you can do so without putting yourself or others at risk – otherwise call a breakdown service.

Tyre pressures. Check weekly. Do this before your journey, when tyres are cold. Warm or hot tyres may give a misleading reading.

Your brakes and steering will be adversely affected by under-inflated or over-inflated tyres. Excessive or uneven tyre wear may be caused by faults in the braking or suspension systems, or wheels which are out of alignment. Have these faults corrected as soon as possible.

Fluid levels. Check the fluid levels in your vehicle at least weekly. Low brake fluid may result in brake failure and a crash. Make sure you recognise the low fluid warning lights if your vehicle has them fitted.

Before winter. Ensure that the battery is well maintained and that there are appropriate anti-freeze agents in your radiator and windscreen bottle.

Other problems. If your vehicle:

- pulls to one side when braking, it is most likely to be a brake fault or incorrectly inflated tyres. Consult a garage or mechanic immediately;
- continues to bounce after pushing down on the front or rear, its shock absorbers are worn. Worn shock absorbers can seriously affect the operation of a vehicle and should be replaced;
- smells of anything unusual such as burning rubber, petrol or an electrical fault; investigate immediately. Do not risk a fire.

Overheated engines or fire. Most engines are water-cooled. If your engine overheats you should wait until it has cooled naturally. Only then remove the coolant filler cap and add water or other coolant.

If your vehicle catches fire, get the occupants out of the vehicle quickly and to a safe place. Do not attempt to extinguish a fire in the engine compartment, as opening the bonnet will make the fire flare. Call the fire brigade.

Petrol stations/fuel tank/fuel leaks. Ensure that, when filling up your vehicle's tank or any fuel cans you are carrying, you do not spill fuel on the forecourt. Any spilled fuel should be immediately reported to the petrol station attendant. Diesel spillage is dangerous to other road users, particularly motorcyclists, as it will significantly reduce the level of grip between the tyres and road surface. Double-check for fuel leaks and make sure that:

- you do not overfill your fuel tank;
- the fuel cap is fastened securely;
- the seal in the cap is not torn, perished or missing;
- there is no visual damage to the cap or the fuel tank.

Emergency fuel caps, if fitted, should form a good seal.

Never smoke, or use a mobile phone, on the forecourt of petrol stations as these are major fire risks and could cause an explosion.

Vehicle security

When you leave your vehicle you should:

- remove the ignition key and engage the steering lock;
- lock the car, even if you only leave it for a few minutes;
- close the windows completely;
- never leave children or pets in an unventilated car;
- take all contents with you, or lock them in the boot. Remember, for all a thief knows a carrier bag may contain valuables;
- never leave vehicle documents in the car.

For extra security fit an anti-theft device such as an alarm or immobiliser. If you are buying a new car it is a good idea to check the level of built-in security features. Consider having your registration number etched on all your car windows. This is a cheap and effective deterrent to professional thieves.

Annex 7: First aid on the road

In the event of an incident, you can do a number of things to help, even if you have had no training.

1. Deal with danger

Further collisions and fire are the main dangers following a crash. Approach any vehicle involved with care. Switch off all engines and, if possible, warn other traffic. Stop anyone from smoking.

2. Get help

Try to get the assistance of bystanders. Get someone to call the appropriate emergency services as soon as possible. They will need to know the exact location of the incident and the number of vehicles involved.

3. Help those involved

DO NOT move casualties still in vehicles unless further danger is threatened. DO NOT remove a motorcyclist's helmet unless it is essential. Remember the casualty may be suffering from shock. DO NOT give them anything to eat or drink. DO try to make them warm and as comfortable as you can, but avoid unnecessary movement. DO give reassurance confidently and try not to leave them alone or let them wander into the path of other traffic.

4. Provide emergency care

Remember the letters D R A B C:

D   Danger – check that you are not in danger.

R   Response – try to get a response by asking questions and gently shaking their shoulders.

A   Airway – the airway should be clear and kept open. Place one hand on the forehead, two fingers under the chin and gently tilt the head back.

B   Breathing – normal breathing should be established. Once the airway is open check breathing for up to 10 seconds.

C   Compressions – if they are not breathing normally compressions should be administered to maintain circulation; place two hands in the centre of the chest and press down 4–5 cms at a rate of 100/minute. You may only need one hand for a child. Give 30 chest compressions. Then tilt the head back gently, pinch the casualty's nostrils together and place your mouth over theirs. Give two breaths, each lasting one second (use gentle breaths for a small child).

If the casualty is unconscious and breathing, place them in the recovery position until medical help arrives

Bleeding. First check for anything that may be in the wound, such as glass. If there is nothing embedded apply firm pressure over the wound. Take care not to press on the object – build up padding on either side of it. Fasten a pad to the wound with a bandage or length of cloth. Use the cleanest material available. If a limb is bleeding, but not broken, raise it above the level of the heart to reduce the flow of blood. Any restriction of blood circulation for more than a short time could cause long-term injuries.

Burns. Try to cool the burn by dousing it with clean, cold water or similar non-toxic liquid for at least 10 minutes. Do not try to remove anything sticking to the burn.

5. Be prepared

Always carry a first aid kit. You could save a life by learning emergency aid and first aid from a qualified organisation, such as the local ambulance services, the St John Ambulance Association and Brigade, St Andrew's Ambulance Association, the British Red Cross or any suitable qualified body (see page xxx for contact details).

Annex 8: Safety code for new drivers

Once you have passed the driving test you will be able to drive on your own. This will provide you with lots of opportunities but you need to remain safe. Even though you have shown you have the skills you need to drive safely, many newly qualified drivers lack experience. You need to continue to develop your skills, especially anticipating other road users' behaviour to avoid having a collision. As many as one new driver in five has some kind of collision in their first year of driving. This code provides advice to help you get through the first 12 months after passing the driving test, when you are most vulnerable, as safely as possible.

- Many of the worst collisions happen at night. Between midnight and 6 am is a time of high risk for new drivers. Avoid driving then unless it's really necessary.

- If you are driving with passengers, you are responsible for their safety. Don't let them distract you or encourage you to take risks. Tell your passengers that you need to concentrate if you are to get to your destination safely.

- Never show off or try to compete with other drivers, particularly if they are driving badly.

- Don't drive if you have consumed any alcohol or taken drugs. Even over-the-counter medicines can affect your ability to drive safely – read the label to see if they may affect your driving.

- Make sure everyone in the car is wearing a seat belt throughout the journey.

- Keep your speed down – many serious collisions happen because the driver loses control, particularly on bends.

- Most new drivers have no experience of driving high-powered or sporty cars. Unless you have learnt to drive in such a vehicle you need to get plenty of experience driving on your own before driving a more powerful car.

- Driving while uninsured is an offence. See Annex 3 for information on types of insurance cover.

REMEMBER that under the New Drivers Act you will have your licence revoked if you get six penalty points on your licence within two years of passing your first driving test. You will need to pass both the theory and practical tests again to get back your full licence.

You could consider taking further training such as Pass Plus, which could also save you money on your insurance, as well as helping you reduce your risk of being involved in a collision. There are three ways to find out more:

- internet – www.direct.gov.uk/passplus
- telephone – DSA head office on 0115 936 6504;
- email – passplus@dsa.gsi.gov.uk.

Other information

Useful websites

www.sja.org.uk (St John Ambulance Association and Brigade)
www.firstaid.org.uk (St Andrew's Ambulance Association)
www.redcross.org.uk (the British Red Cross)
www.dft.gov.uk
www.direct.gov.uk
www.businesslink.gov.uk/transport
www.direct.gov.uk/trafficinfo

www.trafficscotland.org
www.traffic-wales.com
www.direct.gov.uk/highwaycode
www.roadsafetygb.org.uk
www.askthe.police.uk
www.trafficpenaltytribunal.gov.uk (outside London)
www.parkingandtrafficappeals.gov.uk (inside London)
www.highways.gov.uk

Further reading

Best practice

Further information about good driving and riding practice can be found
in the Driving Standards Agency books *The Official DSA Guide to Driving:
The essential skills* and *The Official DSA Guide to Riding: The essential
skills*. Information specifically for drivers of large vehicles can be found in
The Official DSA Guide to Driving Goods Vehicles and *The Official DSA
Guide to Driving Buses and Coaches.*

The Blue Badge Scheme

Information on this scheme can be found on the Department for Transport
website – www.direct.gov.uk/bluebadge

Code of Practice for Horse-Drawn Vehicles

The Code of Practice is available from the Department for Transport,
Transport Technology and Standards Division 6, 2nd Floor, Great Minster
House, 76 Marsham Street, London SW1P 4DR. Tel 0207 944 2114.

Road works

A leaflet giving further information on driving through road works can
be obtained from the Highway Agency Website – www.highways.gov.uk/
knowledge/documents/safer_driving.pdf or from Highway Agency
Publications, tel 0870 1226 236, quoting reference number HA113/04.
For general Highways Agency information, tel 0300 123 5000 or e-mail
ha_info@highways.gsi.gov.uk.

Appendix 1
Show me, tell me questions for car drivers

Driving test candidates are required to answer two vehicle safety questions at the beginning of their practical driving test. Known as 'Show me, tell me', these questions cover basic maintenance and operation procedures for the vehicle being used in the driving test. These checks may require you to open the bonnet of the car and identify fluid reservoirs. You are not asked to touch a hot engine or physically check any fluid levels. There are 19 questions in all, and they are asked in set combinations (shown in the table at the end of this appendix). As a driver you should recognize the importance of basic vehicle maintenance and safety – do not simply learn the questions and answers by rote.

WARNING: It can be dangerous to perform these safety checks if you are unsure of what to do. Your instructor will advise you how to make these checks safely on your driving test vehicle. You are recommended to wear disposable vinyl gloves for under-bonnet checks and to wear a high-visibility vest when making safety checks outside the vehicle.

'Show me' questions

These questions require you to demonstrate how to perform basic safety checks. These are the questions you may be asked and the minimum required for a correct answer.

Question S1: Open the bonnet, identify where you would check the engine oil level and tell me how you would check that the engine has sufficient oil.

Answer: *Identify the dipstick/oil level indicator; describe check of oil level against the minimum and maximum markers.*

Supplementary: *The dipstick is usually brightly coloured for easy identification. The engine should have been off for several minutes and the car parked on a level surface before checking the oil.*

Question S2: Show me/explain how you would check that the power-assisted steering is working before starting a journey.

Answer: *If the steering becomes heavy the system may not be working properly. Before starting a journey two simple checks can be made. Gentle pressure on the steering wheel, maintained while the engine is started, should result in a slight but noticeable movement as the system begins to operate. Alternatively turning the steering wheel just after moving off will give an immediate indication that the power assistance is functioning.*

Supplementary: *A warning light on the instrument panel may indicate a fault with power-assisted steering.*

Question S3: Open the bonnet, identify where you would check the engine coolant level and tell me how you would check that the engine has the correct level.

Answer: *Identify high/low level markings on header tank where fitted or identify the radiator filler cap, and describe how to top up to the correct level.*

Supplementary: *The coolant system is pressurized and it can be dangerous to unscrew the filler cap when the engine is hot! It is safest to check the coolant level when the engine is cold.*

Question S4: Show me how you would check the parking brake (handbrake) for excessive wear; make sure you keep safe control of the vehicle.

Answer: *Apply the footbrake firmly. Demonstrate by applying parking brake so that when it is fully applied it secures itself, and is not at the end of the working travel.*

Question S6: Show me how you would check that the horn is working (off road only).

Answer: *Check is carried out by using the control (turn on ignition if necessary).*

Supplementary: *Take care not to alarm other road users when making this check.*

Question S7: Open the bonnet, identify where the brake fluid reservoir is and tell me how you would check that you have a safe level of hydraulic brake fluid.

Answer: Identify the reservoir and check fluid level against high/low markings.

Supplementary: When checking the brake fluid level, be careful not to contaminate the reservoir with dust, dirt or water.

Question S8: Show me how you would check that the direction indicators are working.

Answer: *Operate the indicators or hazard warning switch and check functioning of all indicator lights.*

Supplementary: *You may need to switch the ignition on to answer this question, but there is no need to start the engine.*

Question S9: Show me how you would check that the brake lights are working on this car.

Answer: *Operate the brake pedal, make use of reflections in windows, garage doors, etc, or ask someone to help (the examiner will offer to help).*

Supplementary: *You may need to switch the ignition on to answer this question, but there is no need to start the engine.*

Question S14: Show me how you would clean the windscreen using the windscreen washer and wipers.

Answer: *Operate the control to wash and wipe the windscreen.*

Supplementary: *You may need to switch the ignition on to answer this question, but there is no need to start the engine.*

Question S15: Show me how you would set the demister controls to clear all the windows effectively; this should include both front and rear screens.

Answer: *Set all relevant controls including: fan, temperature, air direction/ source and heated screen to clear the windscreen and windows.*

Supplementary: *You may need to switch the ignition on to answer this question, but there is no need to start the engine. Opening a window should help screens clear more quickly.*

Question S16: Show me how you would switch on the rear fog light(s) and explain when you would use it/them. (There is no need to exit the vehicle.)

Answer: *Operate the switch (turn on dipped headlights and ignition if necessary). Check that the warning light is on. Explain use.*

Supplementary: *Remember that these high-intensity lamps can dazzle following drivers. Fog lights should only be used when visibility is seriously reduced (less than 100 metres).*

Question S17: Show me how you switch your headlight from dipped to main beam and explain how you would know the main beam is on whilst inside the car.

Answer: *Operate switch (with ignition or engine on if necessary) and check with the main beam warning light.*

Supplementary: *Remember that you can dazzle approaching drivers and those you are following if you don't dip headlights in good time.*

'Tell me' questions

These may require you to open the bonnet. Usually you need to identify the relevant part of the car or engine and describe how you would make the safety check. These are the questions you may be asked and the minimum required for a correct answer.

Question T5: Identify where the windscreen washer reservoir is and tell me how you would check the windscreen washer level.

Answer: *Identify the reservoir and explain how to check the level.*

Supplementary: *You may need to open the bonnet to answer this question. The reservoir may display the windscreen wiper symbol. Check the reservoir regularly.*

Question T10: Tell me how you would check that the brakes are working before starting a journey.

Answer: *Explain that the brakes should not feel spongy or slack. Brakes should be tested as you set off. The vehicle should not pull to one side.*

Supplementary: *To test the brakes, drive forwards slowly as you set off and when safe (mirrors!) apply the footbrake.*

Question T11: Tell me how you would check that the headlights and tail lights are working.

Answer: *Explain that you would operate the switch (turning on the ignition if necessary for your vehicle) and then walk round the vehicle. (As this is a 'Tell me' question, you don't need to exit vehicle to physically check the lights.)*

Supplementary: *Drivers must check that lights and indicators are working before using the car. Some cars have sensors that tell you when a light has failed. It is a good idea to keep a spare bulb kit in the car.*

Question T12: Tell me where you would find the information for the recommended tyre pressures for this car and how tyre pressures should be checked.

Answer: *Explain that you would refer to the manufacturer's guide, use a reliable pressure gauge, and check and adjust pressures when tyres are cold. Don't forget the spare tyre, and remember to refit the valve caps.*

Supplementary: *Information on tyre pressures will be found in the vehicle handbook and is often prominently displayed on the vehicle, eg behind the fuel cap door.*

Question T13: Tell me how you would check the tyres to ensure that they have sufficient tread depth and that their general condition is safe to use on the road.

Answer: *There should be no cuts and bulges in the tyre. There must be 1.6 millimetres of tread depth across the central three-quarters of the breadth of the tyre and around the entire outer circumference.*

Supplementary: *Get into the habit of checking tyre condition and pressures at least once a week. Good tyres are essential for road holding and controlled braking. Replace badly worn or damaged tyres immediately.*

Question T18: Tell me how you make sure your head restraint is correctly adjusted so it provides the best protection in the event of a crash.

Answer: *The head restraint should be adjusted so the rigid part of the head restraint is at least as high as the eye or top of the ears, and as close to the back of the head as is comfortable.*

Supplementary: *NB: Some restraints might not be adjustable.*

Question T19: Tell me how you would know if there was a problem with your anti-lock braking system.

Answer: *A warning light should illuminate if there is a fault with the anti-lock braking system.*

Supplementary: *You should know the meaning of all warning lights on the instrument panel and the appropriate action to take if they come on. Refer to the vehicle owner's handbook.*

Combinations

To ensure fairness in the driving test, examiners are only permitted to ask the questions in the following combinations:

Combination no.	1	2	3	4	5	6	7	8	9	10	11	12	13
'Show me' question	S8	S9	S2	S4	S1	S3	S7	S6	S14	S15	S16	S9	S17
'Tell me' question	T10	T5	T12	T5	T12	T18	T13	T13	T10	T11	T19	T11	T19

The vehicle safety questions and answers shown in this appendix are valid from 1 July 2008 and sourced from the Driving Standards Agency. Check with your instructor for any recent changes, and make sure that you understand how the safety questions apply to the car used for your driving test.

Appendix 2
Checkpoint answers and progress record

Answers to checkpoints

Checkpoint 1

1. b	6. d	11. b	16. b, d
2. d	7. d	12. a, c	17. b, d, e
3. d	8. b	13. c	18. b
4. b	9. b, d	14. b, c, d	19. b
5. b, c	10. a	15. c, d, e	20. c

Checkpoint 2

1. a, b	6. b	11. d	16. b
2. b, c	7. a, d, e	12. a	17. b
3. b, c	8. b, c	13. a, c, d	18. a, b
4. a, d	9. a, c, e	14. c	19. b
5. c	10. c, d, e	15. c	20. b

Checkpoint 3

1. a, c	6. b, c	11. a, b, c	16. a, b, c
2. c	7. b, c	12. b	17. c
3. c	8. a	13. c	18. b
4. c	9. a	14. a, d	19. c
5. a, b, d	10. a	15. a, c	20. c

Checkpoint 4

1. a	6. b	11. a, d	16. b
2. d	7. b, d	12. a, c	17. c
3. d	8. a	13. b, c	18. a, d
4. c	9. c	14. a, b	19. d
5. c	10. c	15. b, c, d	20. b, c

Checkpoint 5

1. b	6. d	11. c	16. c
2. d	7. c	12. c	17. a
3. b	8. a, b	13. d	18. c
4. c	9. c, d	14. c, d	19. a, d
5. c	10. b	15. b, c	20. c

Checkpoint 6

1. b	6. b, d	11. a, b, d	16. b, c
2. b	7. c, d	12. c	17. b, d
3. b, d	8. d	13. c	18. b
4. a, d	9. b, c	14. b, c	19. d
5. a	10. a, d	15. a	20. a, c

Checkpoint 7

1. b, c	6. b	11. b	16. b, d
2. a, d	7. b	12. a, b	17. b
3. a	8. a, d	13. a, d	18. b, c
4. a	9. b	14. b	19. b, c
5. b	10. a	15. b	20. b, c

Checkpoint 8

1. b, d, e	6. a, b, d	11. a	16. b
2. a, d	7. a, d	12. b	17. d
3. b, d	8. b	13. c	18. a
4. c	9. a, c, d	14. b	19. c, d
5. b, c	10. b, c	15. a, e	20. a, c, d

Checkpoint 9

1. b	6. a	11. b, c	16. d
2. a, b	7. b	12. d	17. a, d
3. d	8. b	13. b	18. b, d
4. a, c	9. a, d	14. c, d	19. b, c, f
5. b	10. a, d	15. b, c, d	20. c

Checkpoint 10

1. b	11. b	21. b, c, d	31. b
2. b	12. a, d	22. d	32. c
3. a	13. b, d	23. b, c, d	33. b, c, d
4. d	14. a	24. a	34. c, d, f
5. b, d	15. b	25. b	35. c
6. c	16. c	26. a, c	36. a
7. a	17. c	27. b, e	37. a, b, c
8. a, b	18. b, d	28. a, b	38. b, c
9. a, c, e	19. b	29. b	39. a
10. b	20. a, d	30. b	40. b

Checkpoint scores

This section of *Learn to Drive* is designed to help you build up a picture of your progress. It should help you understand whether you are ready to apply for your driving test or highlight any areas that need further revision and practice.

It is in your own interest not to cheat. You should have answered the questions at the end of each stage honestly. This will show where there are any weaknesses in your knowledge.

Your instructor or supervisor should also have been frequently checking by asking you questions on the rules and regulations.

As you complete the checkpoint at the end of each stage, record your scores below. If you cannot answer all of the questions, revise those you are not sure about and try again.

Stage	1st try	2nd try	3rd try	
1				
2				
3				
4				
5				
6				
7				
8				
9				
10				

Progress record

The driving test is designed so candidates will be able to show they can drive competently and safely, making decisions that will ensure their own safety and that of other road users.

The 'Can do' statements in this section should help you understand and measure your learning achievements. Learning about the rules should help you to make sensible decisions. Your confidence and ability should grow with plenty of practice. There are three levels of ability that you can note in this progress record:

- Talk through. To begin with, your instructor will control your actions and tell you exactly what to do.

- Prompted. As you improve, your instructor should only need to give you prompts, sometimes just by asking a question.

- Unaided. Finally, your ability and confidence should have developed so much that all your instructor has to do is check on your performance and give any corrective advice necessary. This is the level you need to aim for – the responsibility for making decisions has been passed to you, and you should be ready for taking your driving test.

You might feel self-assessment is too much bother! However, to get the best value from your training, you will need to be aware of your successes and failures. This will show you where progress is being achieved. You may be surprised to discover that your own marking would not differ too greatly from your instructor's.

As you work your way through the text of this book, fill in the dates in the 'Can do' statements table below to chart your progress at each lesson or practice session.

Notes:
I've studied it

Notes:
I can do it with help from my instructor

Notes:
I can do it without help

Subject	Talk through	Prompted	Unaided
Starting precautions			
Make proper use of:			
accelerator			
clutch			
gears			
footbrake			
parking brake			
steering			
Move off safely			
Emergency stop			
Reverse left			
Reverse right			
Turn in the road			
Reverse park			
Bay parking			
Use of mirrors			
Use of signals			
Act on signs/signals			
Making progress			
Side roads and T-junctions:			
MSM			
speed on approach			
observations			
position/left			
position/right			

Subject	Talk through	Prompted	Unaided
Crossroads:			
MSM			
speed on approach			
observations			
position/right			
position/left			
position/ahead			
Roundabouts:			
MSM			
speed on approach			
observations			
position/right			
position/left			
position/ahead			
Meet others			
Safety clearances			
Crossing path of others			
Pedestrian crossings			
Overtaking			
Dual carriageways			
Railway crossings			
Parking			
Anticipating:			
pedestrians			
cyclists			
other drivers			

Tick the appropriate column and make a note of the dates until you improve to the point where you can carry out most of the skills without any help.

Index

Index of advertisers